WATTO

WATTO
SHANE WATSON
WITH JIMMY THOMSON

ALLEN&UNWIN

First published in 2011
Copyright © Shane Watson and Jimmy Thomson 2011

All rights reserved. No part of this book may be reproduced or transmitted in any form or by any means, electronic or mechanical, including photocopying, recording or by any information storage and retrieval system, without prior permission in writing from the publisher. The Australian *Copyright Act 1968* (the Act) allows a maximum of one chapter or 10 per cent of this book, whichever is the greater, to be photocopied by any educational institution for its educational purposes provided that the educational institution (or body that administers it) has given a remuneration notice to Copyright Agency Limited (CAL) under the Act.

Allen & Unwin
Sydney, Melbourne, Auckland, London

83 Alexander Street
Crows Nest NSW 2065
Australia
Phone: (61 2) 8425 0100
Fax: (61 2) 9906 2218
Email: info@allenandunwin.com
Web: www.allenandunwin.com

Cataloguing-in-Publication details are available
from the National Library of Australia
www.trove.nla.gov.au

ISBN 978 1 74237 498 7

Internal design by Phil Campbell
Set in 11.5/16 pt Janson Text by Post Pre-press Group, Australia
Printed and bound in Australia by Griffin Press

10 9 8 7 6 5 4 3 2 1

MIX
Paper from responsible sources
FSC® C009448
www.fsc.org

The paper in this book is FSC certified. FSC promotes environmentally responsible, socially beneficial and economically viable management of the world's forests.

CONTENTS

My last option — 1
Chapter 1 Growing pains — 4
DRINKS BREAK 1 The kids are all right... — 15
Chapter 2 Taking a chance — 18
Chapter 3 Stepping up — 32
DRINKS BREAK 2 That's me in the spotlight... — 42
Chapter 4 Back to basics — 45
Chapter 5 Crossroads — 51
DRINKS BREAK 3 Too strong for my body — 57
Chapter 6 Out of India — 61
DRINKS BREAK 4 County versus Shield — 66
Chapter 7 The call — 69
DRINKS BREAK 5 The (not very) green grass of home — 76
Chapter 8 Testing times — 79
DRINKS BREAK 6 Wickets of the world — 85
Chapter 9 Openings — 91
Chapter 10 Boot camp — 99
DRINKS BREAK 7 Bat and ball — 107
Chapter 11 Another opening — 109
DRINKS BREAK 8 The bowler's run-up — 116
Chapter 12 Missed chances — 118
DRINKS BREAK 9 Left, right and centre — 129
Chapter 13 Fans with bats — 135

Chapter 14 Turning point	142
DRINKS BREAK 10 Ready, steady, go . . .	153
Chapter 15 Indian summer	155
Chapter 16 Dreadlock holiday	162
DRINKS BREAK 11 In the nets	167
Chapter 17 Back home	168
Chapter 18 Going back	179
DRINKS BREAK 12 The media	190
Chapter 19 Bat out of hell	192
Chapter 20 Right said Freddie	200
Chapter 21 Last man standing	209
DRINKS BREAK 13 Rent-a-quotes	222
Chapter 22 Best of enemies	225
Chapter 23 Lee and me	233
Chapter 24 Wedding bell blues	236
DRINKS BREAK 14 The second 50	245
Chapter 25 All bets are off	247
DRINKS BREAK 15 The Allan Border medal	253
Chapter 26 Foot on throat	255
Chapter 27 Ashes to ashes	261
DRINKS BREAK 16 Run-outs	267
Chapter 28 Only a game	270
Chapter 29 A world of pain	275
Chapter 30 The captain's knock	282
Chapter 31 Healing Australian cricket	289
Chapter 32 Stumps	293
Acknowledgements	297

MY LAST OPTION

'There's nothing more we can do for you . . . Maybe it's time you gave up bowling.'

I can't remember exactly who said this—that sort of statement kind of knocks you sideways—but it was in September 2007 and I was talking to Cricket Australia's medical team after the latest in a long line of injuries. Give up bowling? I had worked so hard on my bowling—my technique, my strength and my fitness—and my place in the Australian team was as an all-rounder. 'Concentrate on your batting,' this guy said.

Great. Thanks. These guys were doing their best to help me but when it came down to it, they were giving up on me. Yeah, well, I wasn't giving up on myself. For a cricketing all-rounder, it doesn't get much worse than being told by your team's medical experts that maybe you might never bowl again.

Let's rewind a bit. In 2007 I should have been on an all-time high. In April that year the World Cup final in the West Indies had been like a schoolkid's dream. It would have been enough to have been part of the winning team but the fact that I had performed well in the tournament was icing on the cake. This was very much the end of an era. My hero and mentor, Glenn McGrath, was named Player of the Tournament and announced his retirement from international cricket. It wouldn't be long before Adam Gilchrist and Matt Hayden went too. It was sad to see them go, but it meant my time was coming.

We had about four months off after that, when there was no cricket at all, so I just relaxed and enjoyed myself for the first few weeks. I was playing for Queensland but living in Sydney, so I had eight weeks full-on intensive training with the New South Wales conditioning guy. And by the end of that I was the strongest in my upper body and legs that I had ever been.

The next tour was to be the Twenty20 World Cup in South Africa in September. We had a training camp in Brisbane leading up to it and I strained my hamstring. It was only a very minor strain that didn't really show up much on a scan, but I stayed back to use the Brisbane Lions AFL team's hyperbaric chamber at the Gabba, trying to do everything I could to get it to heal as quickly as possible.

That's where I first met Victor Popov. It was a lucky meeting that changed my life. Victor was head physio with the Lions and he was supervising the hyperbaric chamber. But he was about to stop working with them full-time—a couple of weeks later and I would have missed him. I had my session and then we started talking. He knew his sport—football and cycling mainly—but he didn't know much about the demands of cricket, so he was listening as much as he was talking. A couple of things he said about core strength got me thinking.

John Buchanan, then the Australian team coach, had once said I was getting so many injuries because I was too strong for my own body, but that didn't make any sense to me. How could you be too strong for your own body? Victor spoke about having powerful legs and a powerful upper body but nothing in between to stop them tearing each other apart.

Soon after that I followed the rest of the team over to South Africa. The first game of my return was against Sri Lanka and, in just my third over, I felt my hamstring go again and I was back on the treatment table. Our medical staff were worried about how often I was breaking down and how it always seemed to happen at the wrong time. They said they didn't know what was wrong with me; maybe I had a collagen deficiency, or maybe I was born with something that made me more susceptible to minor strains. I could see this was as frustrating for them as it was for me. They wanted to help, for my sake as well as the team's, but they had run out of ideas. There was nothing more they could do for me.

I told them I'd had enough; I was fed up with all this. The only decision they'd left open to me was to stop bowling, because that was when I was getting injured. So I flew home the next day, but I said the only person I'd work with when I got back was Victor. At least he had some answers. I just hoped he'd have enough time to spend with me to get me right.

When I got back I rang him straightaway. He'd finished full-time with the Lions and was working at his practice because his wife was about to have a baby. The situation could not have been better for me because he had all the time in the world to do what needed to be done—break me down as an athlete, then rebuild me from scratch.

It was going to take months and there was no guarantee it would be a success but it was the only hope I had left. A lot of what he said went against everything I had ever been told about strength, speed and fitness. But there was one thing that made me want to give Victor a try: he was my last option.

CHAPTER 1 **GROWING PAINS**

I suppose you could say I was born lucky. My family was very keen on sport and while I got my love of cricket from my dad, Bob, I got my athletic genes and drive from my mum, Barbara. She was a really good swimmer—she swam 100-metres freestyle and 100-metres backstroke—and just missed out on selection for the Montreal Olympics. The same dedication it takes to swim up and down that black line for hour after hour is, I guess, what helped me to spend days on end in the nets developing my batting and bowling. Her experience of working so hard, and then just missing out on a dream, helped me to realise—eventually—I needed something else in my life too.

I was born in Ipswich, Queensland, in 1981. Dad was in the RAAF—a radio technician for F-111 jet fighter-bombers—and when I was four he got posted to Edinburgh, on the outskirts of Adelaide. We lived there for four years, but then he decided to get out of the air force. His own father had been in the RAAF when he was growing up so they moved around a lot and he didn't want that for his family. He didn't want us going through different state education systems, constantly changing schools and leaving friends behind.

He took a job with the RAAF as a civilian technician, looking after the flight simulator out at Amberley air base, very close to Ipswich, so we ended up back there. I'd done two years of school in Adelaide and I'd played Aussie Rules and loved it. I had also played indoor cricket because proper cricket wasn't really for five-year-olds. But in Ipswich there was no Aussie Rules so I took up rugby league.

I would always get a cricket ball or a football for Christmas; I think I got my first cricket bat when I was four and I used to love watching cricket on TV. I got my passion for the game from my dad who loves his cricket but he'd dislocated his right shoulder when he was about 14 so that knocked out his sporting ambitions. Then, of course, there was backyard cricket. Our neighbour on one side used to go crazy. We had a wooden fence and every time I played cricket I used to knock the base of a paling out; I was scared of the guy because he always had to knock it back in again. My old neighbours are still there and I'm sure they remember—I drove them up the wall.

My mate Steve and I played backyard cricket all the time. We'd have a piece of paper and we'd pick our team with our heroes—Allan Border, Mark Waugh etc. etc.—and we'd write down our score. You never really think that one day you could actually be playing with some of those blokes. But we were kids and we had our dreams, like any other kids—I was just very lucky that mine came true.

I joined a cricket club down the road, and when Dad started coaching I was in the Ipswich Under-12 team he looked after. Another boy and I were the better players in the team and we shared the captaincy. I suppose Dad could have given it to me on my own, but he didn't want to be seen playing favourites. That sense of fair play and doing the right thing was strong with my parents. Dad's always been very close to what I've been doing but he never put pressure on me. In fact, unlike some other kids with sports-mad parents, I never felt any pressure from my family to be successful. But they always made sure I worked hard at whatever I wanted to do, and that included getting a good education behind me as well as playing sport.

And they made sacrifices for me. We were by no means a wealthy family, but I never felt like I missed out when I got opportunities such as going on cricket or football tours. The downside was I think our shared interest in sport—my parents and me—really got to my sister Nicole and she rebelled against it. It can't have been easy for her; I was getting driven around all over the place for this practice and that game—taking up a lot of Mum and Dad's time—and then that's all we'd talk about at the dinner table. So for a while, especially when we were kids, she hated sport with a passion. But we are very close now and have been for years. As soon as Nicole saw I had a chance of realising my dreams and ambitions, she became an amazing support. These days she loves watching me play and helps me with my day-to-day business. She enjoys seeing me succeed but she also feels the pain when things don't go right too.

There's a fantastic set-up for any kid in Ipswich who's interested in cricket. Every Saturday there's a coaching clinic at the Len Johnson Oval in North Ipswich and anyone can go there—boys and girls—as young as they want up to about 12. It runs for two and a half hours; you get put in your age group and there are volunteer coaches to teach you the basics. It had been going for at least 20 years before I showed up and it's still going now. Even when I got picked for the Ipswich Under-11s, one of our training sessions involved going to the coaching clinic on Saturday morning; we did half of that with all the other kids and then we did our own training.

It was mostly boys, but a few girls came along. Melissa Bulow, the former Queensland women's cricket captain, used to turn up. I don't know if they have that kind of set-up anywhere else but they should. I still keep in touch with them and I try to help out as much as I can, even though I live in Sydney, by buying them caps and things, because those grassroots gave me such a brilliant base to turn the dreams I had at that age into what I'm living right now.

My heroes back then were Craig McDermott and the Broncos' stars Allan Langer and Kevin and Kerrod Walters—Ipswich legends who'd been through the same structure as me. Langer and the Walters brothers were leaguies who'd also played cricket. I would stay back after the coaching session to look at their photos on the wall. I'd say to myself, 'He's playing for Australia now.' And looking at those photos I'd think maybe I could do that too some day.

My first proper team was the Ipswich Schoolboys Under-11s, and I loved it. It was a really big thing for a young kid and my weekends were soon taken up entirely with cricket. But it was only when I got picked in the Queensland Under-12s that I first thought I was measuring up against other people around the country.

Even at that stage I was an all-rounder and if that was a taste of things to come, so was what happened next . . . only in a bad way. Playing for the Under-12 Schoolboys up in Darwin I got my first stress fracture in my back, meaning I couldn't bowl. I was still picked as a batsman—I batted at number three and had scored a lot of runs—but bowling was out because my back was killing me. So I went and saw the Queensland Bulls physio in Brisbane.

At that stage they could have put me in a brace—a full-on cast. But they ended up ordering me to take 12 months' rest and to give up rugby league, which I loved and had played from the age of eight. But it never entered my head that maybe I wasn't built to be a bowler. At that age you're fearless.

It was at least a year before I started to get back into it but after only about three months of bowling I broke down again.

That was the first time it really hit me hard. I remember sitting in the doctor's surgery after getting a bone scan that showed I had another hot spot—another stress fracture. I was shattered, thinking I might not be able to do what I had always wanted to do.

I cried all the way home, then lay in my room just sobbing my heart out. Every kid has disappointments in life—many much bigger than mine. And plenty of boys would be happy to have done what I'd already achieved. But I had a dream and it had looked like there was a real possibility of it coming true . . . now it seemed it could be over.

Dad came up to my room and said he wanted to have a chat to me. He took me out the back, underneath our big willow tree. The willow is famous for two things, weeping and cricket bats, and there I was, heartbroken because my dreams of being a bowler seemed like they were over. But Dad told me how proud he was of what I'd achieved already and of the things I'd been able to do. Like playing for the Queensland Under-12s—a thing he'd not done because he was never quite good enough. He told me not to give up; I still had my batting—I'd even won a bat for scoring a century for the Ipswich Under-12s. That pep talk kept me going, because at that stage I could have easily have packed it in. I remember that moment like it was yesterday—sitting there with Dad, still crying but talking it all through. The tree's not there anymore, but I'll never forget that day. It's the kind of thing you'd put in a movie.

The Queensland Under-13 Emerging Players had videoed me and said the reason I had a back injury was because my technique was pretty bad. But trying to change your technique as a 13-year-old is hard. You don't really think about what you're doing; the only thing you're sure of is that you want to bowl fast—you want to be a Craig McDermott or a Merv Hughes. I copied Craig when I was younger. He was different to the others, definitely more side-on with his shoulders. Later, at the

Cricket Academy, I would analyse lots of bowlers' techniques, trying to work out why they were so good, why they were fast, all that sort of thing. So Craig was my model when it came to bowling and I tried to bowl as much like him as I could.

When you're batting, you always try to emulate someone. For me, it was probably Steve Waugh, a very compact batsman. Even better, I wanted to be a combination of Steve and his twin brother, Mark. Mark was so elegant—how easily he timed the ball—whereas Steve was hard and tough, but everything was so effective. If you could bring those qualities together, you'd be some batsman.

The other thing about Steve was the whole psychological toughness thing. Even as a young kid, I was very much into that in my own way, especially when I was bowling. I was always trying to test the limits of what we could and couldn't do. In the Under-14s and 15s, you weren't allowed to bowl bouncers, especially not in school cricket. But I'd always slip one in and the umpire would be onto me immediately. I'd pretend I'd forgotten, but I knew what I was doing. There was a fair bit of sledging too and, yes, I was always one of the guys heavily involved in it.

I'm not the kind of person who goes looking for trouble. Right from primary school, I never intentionally broke the rules but I've always been very competitive. I want to win and I know what the rules are; sledging was part of the game that was allowed and I was right into it.

But don't get me wrong—I was confident on the field but I wouldn't say I was cocky. And the thing about going beyond age-group cricket is that you start playing with guys a little bit older than you. I think I played my first game against men when I was 13 or 14, and I was smart enough to know not to pick a fight with them. I saved my sledging for age-group cricket. The first time I really copped it myself was when I went to play for Tasmania. It was really nasty but that's a story for later.

In Queensland, they did try to get us ready for 'real' cricket. At the Emerging Players level—Under-13s—they'd put us in against the Under-15s. They were the best bowlers in Queensland for their age and they were fast. They were men really—at least that's how it felt to a 12- or 13-year-old. I remember one big guy, probably over six foot but it felt like he was ten feet tall. Imagine you're 14 years old and this giant is thundering in towards you. I did okay but, to be honest, my reflexes weren't up to it.

They didn't bowl bouncers, but we were getting exposed to pace. It hurts when you get hit even now but as young kids we were petrified. And there's always the chance of a 'mistake', so we would wear helmets, but I tried to put off wearing a faceguard because I thought it would impair my vision. Turned out you just had to get used to it—but it wasn't until I was 15 or 16 that I wore a full faceguard.

After a couple of years I had outgrown schoolboy cricket and if you were serious about getting picked for Queensland, it was best to be playing grade cricket in Brisbane. So I was 15 years old and I had a decision to make. We talked about it as a family and it was decided I'd try to get into Easts/Redlands, because that's where Damien Mackenzie, my best mate from the state Under-17s, played.

They were willing to give me a chance to play second grade, maybe a couple of one-day games for first grade in the first year. I could have played somewhere closer to home, but I wanted to go where I was a bit more comfortable. However, that meant Mum or Dad would have to drive me an hour to training once a week and then, when we played, they had to drive an hour each way to drop me off and pick me up.

That was a huge commitment, especially for Dad. He would come home early from work to take me to training and that went on for a year and half until I got my driver's licence. But I needed to make that step up to establish myself and progress to the level I wanted to be at. If they thought it was worth the sacrifice, I wasn't going to say no.

This was the real thing—playing tough competitive cricket against real men, real players with no restrictions on what you could and couldn't do within the rules. Later, when I was 17, I played a couple of first-grade games against Andrew 'Roy' Symonds and Matthew Mott, and with Jimmy Maher. I even played against Ian Healy when he was playing for Australia—so, if nothing else, you got to play against your heroes. That was a big deal for a young bloke.

The other important thing was the coaching. There was always a grade coach to help you out. There was a New Zealander called Roley, an older guy who'd had polio and who just loved being around the club; he gave me tips whenever he could. But the real coaching came from Queensland Cricket. As emerging players up until 15, and then if you were playing for the Queensland Under-17s and 19s, that was when you really got your best coaching, whether it was in batting or bowling.

Cricket was my great passion—I was always saying I wanted to be a sportsman, a cricketer. Mum said that if that's what you want to do that's great, but you need something behind you, just in case. So I always worked very hard at school. Mum worked for the accounts department of my high school, Ipswich Grammar, which meant we got reduced fees, making it easier for my parents to afford them. Mum was always there and involved in other ways.

Whatever I do in life, I give it everything I've got. Those were the values instilled in me by my parents. But I was no angel; in fact, I was a bit of a shit really, especially when I was younger, and mostly to Mum. Dad worked nine to five, so it was Mum really bringing us up and I was a little terror. If I didn't get my way, I'd crack it and that made it really tough for her at times. I think I had started high school before I finally snapped out of it.

I was 16 when I had my next stress fracture; the Queensland Cricket doctor now warned me I needed to back off a bit with my bowling. Rugby league had gone, but I was still playing rugby union and had represented Queensland Country at Under-16s. To begin with I was a flanker, but then I went to hooker; I remember the first time I packed down in the front row of the scrum—jeez, that was a wake-up call. Anyway, I had to give that away too because of the pressure rugby puts on your neck and back. And the doctor said I couldn't bowl fast because my back wasn't built for it. End of story. So either I didn't bowl or I bowled spin. I batted on and did really well. But when it came to spin bowling, it was more like the batsmen saying, 'You throw it up here and I'll see how far I can hit it.'

The problem with bowling—and fast bowling in particular—is that it's a totally unnatural action. You're running at close to full pace, then you go sideways, jam your front foot into the ground and catapult the ball with a straight arm. No wonder quicks usually have a limited sporting lifespan and the ones who last a long time do so because they have a different kind of action. Glenn McGrath's weapon was his accuracy rather than raw speed. Richard Hadlee and Dennis Lillee both extended their careers by changing their actions. But when you're a kid, all you want to do is thunder in and bowl at a million miles an hour.

Grade cricket was a very special time for me. As a teenager, you're looking around and you can see all sorts of influences, good and bad. There was one guy at Easts/Redlands who was an unbelievable batsman. He would regularly get 100 before lunch in grade cricket. But he had an alcohol problem and would turn up drunk for matches, that sort of thing. Apparently when he was coming up he was super-talented—better than any of the guys who went from the club to play for Queensland—but he never made it.

Dad would say, 'Look at this guy—look how talented he is but, thanks to booze, he's stuck at this level.' Dad made me realise early on that you've got to do everything you can to give yourself the best opportunity to achieve what you want. Dad wasn't a non-drinker—he might have a couple of beers at the weekend—but he was never a big drinker, and never really drank during the week.

That said, I was no wowser either. I loved the social side of being part of a club. That's a huge part of cricket and, when I was 16 or 17, I wouldn't have had the chance to go out in Brisbane if it wasn't for cricket. I actually got into the old City Rowers when I was only 17. All the Queensland cricketers had drinks cards and you could go there and just drink whatever you wanted.

Once, when we won a one-day final for Easts/Redlands, Jimmy Maher took us out there and got me in. The idea was, once you were in, to drink as much as you possibly could. Jimmy was someone that I really looked up to. He had been a very good player for Queensland and had played a few one-dayers for Australia; so I thought, 'Okay, this is how it works.'

The social side of cricket was an eye-opener for me. I never went to parties in high school because I always had cricket the next day and I never used to smoke pot like everyone else. I loved playing cricket and I wasn't interested in anything that might interfere with that. As for girls, when I was at school I suppose I was always a bit of a nerd in a way. We weren't that well-off and I never had all the new fashions. Also, whatever my dad wore, I thought was cool. I guess I was an under-achiever on the social side.

On the other hand, I wanted to do something so that people knew I existed. I was going to make a name for myself in whatever way I possibly could, and the obvious way was through cricket. The first time I saw my name in the paper felt strange.

When I was about 11 or 12, the local paper wrote some articles and ran a photo of me. Mum still has them; she collects everything.

I copped it a bit at school, but I think that's partly because I didn't handle being noticed that well. Kids would pick on me and Mum and Dad would say it was jealousy, just to make me feel good about myself. But I would never fight at school—even if someone hit me. I'd say to Mum 'I really want to hit this guy', but she'd tell me it wasn't worth it.

So I never went looking for trouble and I never tried to start a fight, but sometimes trouble comes looking for you. I had decided to make a career in cricket and, so far, all my problems had been physical. But I was about to make a decision that would cost me the friendship of a good mate and make me a lifelong enemy.

THE KIDS ARE ALL RIGHT...

The idea of technical coaching for cricket must seem a bit alien to some people. Playing cricket is as natural to most kids as swimming or riding a bike—you just do it and then get better as you keep doing it. Once you get past the basics, what else is there?

But, just like swimming, you can improve a lot if the basics are right and then you learn the things that make you more consistent and efficient. If kids copy what they see players do on TV and they go for their lives, they'll be halfway there... but only halfway. I got my base at the coaching clinics on Saturday mornings in Ipswich and that's how I know it's important to teach kids the fundamental skills.

It's very important to have the really basic stuff right from the outset, and that goes for everything, from your grip to your stance. I remember the way I batted from the age of about ten to 12—my hands would go well away from my body, and the coaches would all say if you want to progress up to the next levels, you can't have your hands out because your bat will be too slow and your balance won't be good. So I batted a certain way until I was 11 or 12, and then for a couple of years my batting didn't really go anywhere because I had to change my technique. Of course, this was bad news for a 12- or 13-year-old: I just wanted to go out there and hit the ball and not worry about the technical things.

But think about it: Don Bradman, the greatest batsman who ever lived, practised with a cricket stump and a golf ball against a water tank. That has to help your hand–eye coordination and your reactions. So you do what you can and try to have some fun. I had one of Mum's stockings with a cricket ball in it hanging up on our willow tree so I was able to work on those little things myself without needing Dad to throw me balls or wait till Saturday morning to work on it at coaching.

I must have just absorbed the idea of bowling with a straight arm because I can't remember my dad teaching me to keep my arm

DRINKS BREAK 1

straight and I never, ever 'chucked'. I see young kids coming through now and the only way they can get the ball to the other end is to throw it; but for some reason it was never an issue for me. Keeping your arm straight is so important when you start bowling, even from a really young age. The correct bowling action is so unnatural that the sooner kids master it, the better.

If you try to learn it too late, you'll have an uphill struggle. And some people just aren't built for it. A young guy called Aaron Bird, a fast bowler for New South Wales, grew up with a bit of a bent arm, which meant his bowling attracted more scrutiny than most people's. Poor bloke kept getting reported, and eventually had to give up the game at the age of only 26.

The first time I came across a real cricket ball was when I was about five and got one from my grandad. He'd played a bit and he had both a really old cricket bat and a ball that had been some kind of a trophy. I remember sitting in the house and shining the ball, or trying to at least. I wasn't really shining it—it was a really old ball—but I'd spit on it and rub it on my pants, and then get a red stain on them. Mum just could not believe it!

Those balls kids can buy now—that are half tennis ball, half shiny—are great. We used to adapt tennis balls using electrical tape on one side so they would swing a bit in the air. Swinging balls are harder to hit as a batsman and, for would-be bowlers, they help you learn what you have to do to get the ball to go either way. As well, they teach you that you don't have to bowl at 150 kilometres an hour to be really effective.

The series I played in the English summer of 2010 was the first time I ever totally concentrated on swinging the ball. The type of ball they use in England—the Duke—and the conditions there make it easier to swing the ball all day, whereas with a Kookaburra it stops swinging after about 15 or 20 overs. The difference is the type of leather; with the Duke you can polish one side up so it's totally shiny, but Kookaburra balls lose their shine and therefore lose their effectiveness. The most successful I've ever been as a bowler has been when I could swing the ball all day. It was a time when my pace was nowhere near what it used to be, but I could move the ball and it paid off with wickets.

For kids who want to be the next Shane Warne, there are also balls with spots on them to show you exactly where your fingers are supposed to be. I think it's great. Anything that makes it easier to get the basics and still have fun gets my vote.

CHAPTER 2 **TAKING A CHANCE**

The next step up for a young bloke in grade cricket is the Australian Under-19s and the Cricket Academy, which back then was at Henley Beach in Adelaide. Rod Marsh had been the coach at the Academy since 1992; as a player and a coach, he had seen the greats of world cricket, and just about everybody who's gone on to play first-class cricket and then play for Australia has gone through the Under-19s. In the same squad with me were Michael Clarke, Mitchell Johnson, Chris Hartley, Nathan Hauritz, Andrew McDonald, Adam Voges, Phil Jaques and Paul Rofe, who was playing for South Australia until recently. So we had a very good squad.

I remember being at home in Ipswich when I got the call from the Academy. I thought, 'This is the first time I can really be a cricketer full-time.' I decided I was going to give it all I had. The year before I'd been full-time at university but I had deferred study so I could learn everything I possibly could about cricket.

Rod Marsh liked how I worked, and probably how committed I was. I went through the academy for four-and-a-half months and I worked flat out on everything I did. I got a great part-time job, working around the residences and doing a bit of driving and admin. The rest of the time it was cricket, cricket, cricket. We had all the best coaches in Australia—whether it was batting, bowling or fielding—and all the resources you could possibly imagine to be able to get the best out of yourself. I was obsessed with it, no question.

For instance, Rod said the best way to work on your catching was to practise with a golf ball off a brick wall. So I would spend hours out the back of the gym, chucking a golf ball as hard as I could and catching it, trying to develop 'soft' hands. Everything that anyone said to me during that time, I did. It was like gospel. It was what Ricky Ponting and Glenn McGrath—all the greats of recent times—had been through. I thought, 'If they did it once, I'll do it a thousand times.'

At the end of it all I knew my skills had improved, but I hadn't seen any results in the games we played. I hadn't enjoyed many rewards with my batting and I hadn't taken many wickets. The other irony was that my back was holding up. This was the first time I had really got into my gym work and I was as committed to that as I was to everything else. Troy Cooley, later to be the Australian bowling coach, was a strength training and conditioning coach in my first year at the Academy. When I first went there I was bowling medium pace, about 115 to 120 kilometres an hour, because I didn't want to put any pressure on my back. But at the Academy I got a lot stronger and improved my core strength, so by the time I came out I was bowling 135 kilometres an hour. That's when I stepped up my bowling and I was able to hold it together because I didn't have too much back pain.

My accuracy was okay, but I wasn't a front-line bowler. I was there to provide impact—a change-up when the strike bowlers needed a break. But I was so obsessed with the technical side of things that everything was very mechanical in my bowling action. I was so hung up on the intricacies of every part of it to make sure I didn't injure myself again. But at the same time I wanted to be as good as I could possibly be and become really successful.

It was the same with my batting. As anybody who plays golf will tell you, you have to get all the elements of your swing right; but then you have to relax and let it happen—it's hard to concentrate and relax at the same time. You can train a lot harder on batting as it's not as physically demanding. Later on, the more I played first-class cricket the better I got.

At the end of my time at the Academy we went out and played against Second-11 teams around Australia. We played the Queensland Seconds, which was interesting for me. I was always talking to Troy about how few opportunities there were in Queensland back then, even though I felt I was getting better and was starting to score some runs. But I knew I wasn't going to play for the Bulls any time soon because they were so strong and they had plenty of good young players, a bit older than me, queuing up to get into the side. Thinking back, I wasn't overstating their strength. In the 12 Sheffield Shield or Pura Cup finals played between 1995 and 2006, Queensland were in ten of them and won six. They appeared in eight one-day finals over the same period. They had already started this run and I could see this was a team that was only going to get stronger.

As Queensland were super-strong, there was little opportunity for a young kid to make the side. I was just starting out and they really didn't need what I had to offer. I wasn't complaining—it's just the way it was—but this was when I began to think that, apart from playing for the Academy, I was going to be stuck playing grade cricket for the foreseeable future. Elsewhere in Australia, young blokes were getting a start. Michael Clarke was playing for New South Wales and, even though he wasn't really at the Academy that long, I always compared myself with him. Obviously he was more developed than me because he played first-class cricket earlier, but that was who I was aspiring to be.

I saw all these other guys getting opportunities to play first-class cricket and wondered when my chance would come—if it ever would. My biggest fear was that sometimes, when you stick with a strong team, it can skip a generation. When a team starts to age after years of success, they can overlook the guys who've been patiently waiting in the wings for a long time and go for the younger blokes coming up behind that group.

The last Academy game just before Christmas 2000 was against Tasmania Seconds. I didn't get many runs, but I got four wickets in each innings. I didn't realise that Greg Shipperd, the Tasmania coach, was there watching the game. He was really good mates with Rod Marsh and Troy Cooley and they must have had a word with him because, as soon as I got off the plane from Hobart, I got a message from him asking me to call back as he had something he wanted to put to me—so I did. He said, 'I'd like to offer you an opportunity. What would you think about moving down here and playing the last five Shield games and the last five one-day games and then we'll see what happens from there?'

Jeez! That came right out of the blue. This was my shot at a professional career—which was great—but it also meant turning my back on Queensland, which, to be fair, had expended an awful lot of time and money on helping to get me to that stage. I talked to Mum and Dad and they were supportive, in that 'whatever you do, we're behind you' way. I rang Rod Marsh, because he understood professional cricket better than just about anyone I knew. 'Look, it gives you a jump on everyone else your age as well as the guys you went to the Academy with,' he said. Dad wanted to talk to him as well, and Rod made him feel really good about the opportunities in Tasmania and the prospects beyond that.

As I said, I wasn't playing for Queensland yet—or I wouldn't have been considering the offer—but I had played for their Colts and, fair's fair, they were still looking after me. I had already made my mind up, but I rang Bennett King, the coach of the Bulls at that time. I said, 'Look I've been made this offer—what do you think?' He said the best way to learn was staying right there in Queensland.

'You don't want to go somewhere else where the facilities for coaching and the cricket culture aren't as good. You want to stay here to get the best out of yourself.'

When I told him I had more or less decided to go, he asked me if I knew who my first game would be against. I said I did—Queensland.

'Well, you'll get what you deserve, Sunshine.'

That didn't seem very generous, but he was pissed off that I was going to go somewhere else. However, if I thought Bennett King was dirty on me, I hadn't yet spoken to Stuart Law or Jimmy Maher, the current and future Queensland captains.

Stuart Law had been at one of the 'culture camps' when I was in the Queensland Second-11 squad and had spent an hour or so with me, helping me with tips and advice. He was bitter about me leaving. Jimmy Maher had been a good friend and he'd looked after me through club cricket; while he was very pissed off with me, he eventually cooled down. But Stuart wouldn't let it go and it eventually led to a really nasty showdown between us.

Most of the people in Queensland cricket hated the fact that I was leaving. They didn't care that I couldn't see how I was going to get a start in the first team. They reckoned you should only want to play for Queensland, because that was the state with the best cricket culture. That was the reason the Bulls were so successful through that period—their single focus. It was a tough school.

The other downside of leaving Queensland and going to Tasmania was obvious. Tassie was a bit of an afterthought, and not just in cricket. At least half the Tassie players were imports. There were some home-grown guys, but a lot of the others were players who had missed out on opportunities elsewhere, like Dan Marsh, Rod Marsh's son. When Victoria dropped David Saker, he moved down to Tassie and finished off his playing career there. He would later become England's bowling coach leading up to the 2010–11 Ashes—he clearly knew his stuff.

The next shock for me was a good one: the money. I wasn't offered a full contract initially because I was going for just the last few games of the season. But at that stage the Sheffield Shield match payment was $2500, which was serious money—all I was earning at the Academy was $100 a week, which was just enough to be able to save up for the weekend and go out with the boys. Tasmania never guaranteed me a contract, but I knew I'd get a post-dated deal—including additional money—if I played three Sheffield Shield games. It added up to $27,500 once I'd played those games.

It was crazy! I went down there on $100 a week and all of a sudden I started to see my bank account just go nuts. How did this happen? Even accommodation wasn't a problem. The Tasmanian Cricket Association had a house across from Bellerive Oval, their home ground, and I rented it from them for about $60 a week. Adam Griffith came from Launceston, via the Academy, so we moved in there at the same time. He was a bit older than me so he showed me the ropes. I got a huge buzz out of going to K-Mart to buy the basics like bedding and an electric blanket (it was freezing there)—and all with my own money.

A lot of guys would have run out and bought a car, but I thought fancy cars were a waste of money and I didn't get myself anything new until 2005 and then only after I'd paid off my house. Until then I still had the same car Mum and Dad had bought me, an old Mazda 323.

Meanwhile, Mum's advice that I needed to have something behind me, just in case it all went wrong, persuaded me to do an accountancy course by correspondence. I was good at maths in high school so I agreed. I still can't believe I did it—I hated it. I kept it up for another two years, until I started playing one-dayers for Australia. Then I thought, 'Okay, I need to devote my whole time and energy to getting the best out of myself.' It sounds like an excuse, but what a relief that decision was.

In my first game, against Queensland, my old mates did me a huge favour—although helping me out was the last thing on their minds. The sledging started even before the game. Stuart Law said in the local paper the morning of the first match that if I had been any good, Queensland would never have let me go. I'd never got a grade century, I wasn't up to Queensland standards and Tasmania could have me for all they cared. It was pretty clear that it was war and this was just the first shot. I didn't read it, but Stuart wrote an article in a newspaper later on, saying that the only reason I went to Tasmania was for the money. He knew as well as anybody that I'd gone for the chance to play first-class cricket. I can understand his irritation but, jeez, he went on with it.

As for the game, it was the best initiation I could ever have imagined. I had to be tough to begin with and get a lot tougher in a hurry, otherwise I would have just gone to water. I batted at seven and bowled a few overs, and all the time I got the absolute living daylights sledged out of me. The match was being broadcast by C7, the cable sports channel, so Mum and Dad were watching on TV and they were picking up some of the stuff the Queensland players were saying to me. Like Stuart Law, talking about the time he'd chatted to me at the cricket camp, saying, 'That's an hour of my life that I can never get back, you little prick.'

Jimmy Maher nailed me as well and I really copped it, verbally and physically. They bounced the shit out of me and it didn't help that Tassie got flogged. I think I got 27 not out and 24 not out—not great scores but at least they didn't get my wicket. But that didn't matter; we lost badly. Payback was my first wicket—Jimmy Maher, of all people. Funny thing, it wasn't a very good ball but he just missed it. I remember that very well—wonder if he does.

The Tassie guys around the place and the support staff saw and heard exactly how much I was copping it and maybe it made them realise I had something going for me. I didn't fire up, I didn't sledge them, I didn't say anything—I just copped it all, because I had to. I think that impressed the Tassie selectors because the next game I was moved up the batting order to four. It was a brilliant introduction to first-class cricket and I wouldn't have wanted it any other way.

Because we'd been beaten in three days, the Queensland mob had a break before the Mercantile Cup one-dayer. Trouble was, with the Saturday off, they had too much time to celebrate their win while maybe congratulating themselves on all the crap they'd heaped on me that . . . well, let's just say they weren't at their best. The other gratifying thing about the one-dayer was that it was on Channel 9, so Bill Lawry and Ian Chappell and guys like that were commentating when we flogged them by seven wickets. I got 16 not out, and played a pull shot after facing my first couple of balls.

When I saw the TV replays and heard the commentary, with commentators like Bill and Ian saying some good things about me, I felt I was on my way. It was like all those backyard cricket games when my mates and I would commentate on ourselves—only it was coming true.

After that I moved up the order in Pura Cup matches (as the Shield was known then) and I felt I was getting better with every game. Most importantly, I felt I belonged at that level. All that work I'd done in the Academy was now starting to pay off. I was playing the guys who had been, at some point, among the very top players in the country: Brendon Julian, Shane Lee, Darren Lehmann and Greg Blewett are just a few who spring to mind. At least once a year all the Test players are back with their states and it's the luck of the draw who you play with and against. Against one of the stronger states, you could be facing half the Australian Test team and the other half would be former or future internationals.

There were a couple of hiccups. I was getting to 20 and losing my wicket, but I was batting really well up to that point. I thought it might be a concentration problem or bad shot selection, but Greg Shipperd said it was shot execution. Basically, I just needed to relax and allow myself to play my shots.

Sure enough, I got 50 against Western Australia the next time I played and followed that up with 60 against Victoria, in a team that included Paul Reiffel. Then, in my last game of the season, I got my first 100. I can still remember being 87 not out overnight. I didn't sleep that whole night—I was 13 runs away from doing something I never thought I would ever do. I was rapt that I was playing first-class cricket, let alone being on the brink of a century.

By the way, the whole thing about 87 being a bogey number is a bit of a myth. I know plenty of cricketers who are superstitious about other things, but 87? Look at the stats—it's just another number. Every run closer to a century is more pressure than 87, so what was keeping me awake wasn't being on 'the devil's number' but the excitement of my first first-class century being so close I could taste it. That's the biggest mental barrier—in your mind you're already raising your bat to salute the crowd when you should be concentrating on the next ball.

Next day I just went out and played carefully rather than

cautiously, and the century rolled around in due course. It was the last match and the icing on the cake as far as that initial spell with Tassie went. I felt strong in every possible way. I was still picking up a couple of wickets whenever I bowled and my body was standing up to the stresses. At the end of the season I had averaged 50 with the bat and 29 with the ball across those five games.

And I was being well looked after. I was very, very lucky to have David Saker around. He was getting towards the end of his playing career—he moved down to Tassie the same year I went there and became very much a father figure to me. I was 19 and he must have been about 34 or 35, but we would hang out and talk about almost everything—values and morals as well as the game and its players. It was good for me at that stage of my career to meet someone who was prepared to talk about those things, and not from a 'holier than thou' point of view.

David had been there and done it all; he'd seen all sides of life. He'd gone off the rails in his early twenties, and didn't play first class until he was 27 or 28 (in Victoria, where he did very, very well). He'd had a marriage break-up. He was really good mates with Shane Warne and Darren Berry, who was one of the biggest sledgers around, but he was phenomenal for me. He was always advising me about my batting and bowling, but he also showed me how to cook, and that's a passion I still have today.

The Tasmanian team at that time were about half and half local and imports. Jamie Cox was a Taswegian and I played for his local club, Lindisfarne. That was when he was at his absolute best, getting 100s all the time. Dene Hills was Tassie-born, and Michael Di Venuto was a local. But Sakes and me, Damien Wright, Dan Marsh and a couple of others were ring-ins. Most of them were glad we were there and did everything possible to make us welcome. Jamie Cox was the captain and he invited me round to his house the second night I was there. Damien was from New South Wales originally and became a very good mate.

One person who wasn't keen on me was Shaun Young, another Tasmanian, who was an all-rounder too. He was an unbelievably talented player—he'd bat beautifully and get runs one day, and then take five wickets the next. But he only played one Test for Australia. Why? My guess is it was because Shaun was a prickly character. He barely talked to me at first, except when I batted with him, and that would only be a brief bit of conversation, and that was it. He saw me as a threat, pure and simple. He thought I was there to take his place as an all-rounder, so why would he welcome me with open arms? The irony is I was there to bat more than anything. But it didn't worry me. I had a lot of very good mates there.

Shaun retired a few years ago, pretty bitter with the world from what I hear. He played his one Test in England in 1997 because he happened to be there when someone got injured. It didn't go too well. I think he scored a duck and four and didn't take any wickets although, to be fair, he only bowled one over. Anyway, he never got another chance.

One of the things I was learning back then is how important it is to get along with the other players in the squad. Even if you're a brilliant player, if nobody likes being around you, as soon as there's an opportunity, you're gone. That's another thing David Saker always instilled in me—which brings us back to Stuart Law.

Despite what I said before about not letting stuff get to you, by the next time we played Queensland, I'd had it with Stuart. I'd expected a lot of sledging the first time we played, but when it was still going on even a year later, I was over it. I remember lying in bed at night thinking, 'Tomorrow I'm going to go out and kill Stuart Law.'

Don't get me wrong—I had a lot of respect for him. He was

the first Queenslander to captain the state side to a Sheffield Shield win; he had led them superbly for years and meanwhile had a good solid record in one-day internationals (ODIs) for Australia. But there was a question mark over him. Back in 1995 he'd played his one and only Test for Australia and scored 56 not out on debut. That is an outstanding debut, by any standards. So how come he never played another Test match? This, I thought, could be the weak spot.

Sure enough, the next day he starts up again on me—really nasty personal stuff. So when I was bowling, I gave it to him. I said, 'Stewie, one Test, 56 not out, and you never got asked back. What went on there?' He chucks it back at me: 'You'll never play even one Test, shithead, so don't worry about it.' Next time, I hit him with this: 'Want to know the reason you never got picked again? Because you're an arsehole, and the other blokes didn't want you in the team.'

Now, fair's fair—I was just making it up as I went along. He could have been injured after that first Test, for all I knew, or scored too slowly, or maybe it was just that he had replaced Steve Waugh who missed the Test due to injury, but had come back. Whatever the reason, that really pushed Stuart's buttons and he went nuts at me: 'You have no idea . . . You're just a kid . . . You'll never know . . .' And I just smiled. Gotcha!

Three balls later I stuck a short one up into his ribs and I could see it really hurt. I stood there with my hands on my hips and laughed, 'Ha . . . ha . . . ha!' Like a kids' pantomime character. A couple of overs later I got him out, caught behind. I thought that would be game over, but in fact the whole thing kept going for a couple of years before it died down. But at least I got a few shots in.

The flip side of being seen as 'difficult' is that, if you are a really good team man and everyone gets along with you, you can get a little leeway, especially early in your career when you're having to adjust to the higher standard of cricket. Take Ricky Ponting in the 2001 Ashes. Earlier that year in India, batting at six, he'd scored three ducks, six and 11 in the Tests, then nine and 23 in the one-dayers before he hit 101 in the fourth ODI.

When he got to England, he was smacking the county players all over the place in the tour matches but couldn't get past 20 in the Tests. However I remember reading in the papers that Ricky was very skilful and a great team man and he was gonna come good. Certainly the selectors were giving him every chance to prove himself and, sure enough, in the fourth Test at Headingley he scored 144 and 72 and developed into probably the greatest batsmen Australia has had since Bradman. David Saker would always tell me that an important part of your development is making sure you find a way to get along with everyone in your team.

For me, moving down to Hobart was the best thing I could have done in terms of growing up as a person as well as a cricketer. Hobart is pretty quiet and a relaxed and chilled-out sort of place, so it was a good way of moving out of home. I'd done enough over those five games to get a contract with Tasmania, so I signed a three-year deal and for a young guy, not even in his twenties, it was very good money. The base contract was $50,000 for the first year, going up $5000 a year after that, with match payments on top.

Looking back, my biggest regret about my time in Queensland was how I treated one of my earliest mentors. His name was Barry O'Connell and he was one of my schoolteachers at Ipswich Grammar, as well as my rugby and cricket coach. Barry was among the first people who suggested I might have to move states to get ahead in the game. He had played Lancashire League cricket in the UK and three or four times a week he would take me down to the nets to practise my batting. That gave me an incredible technical foundation and was the reason my batting was better than anyone else's my age.

Barry could clearly see I had potential and one day he suggested that we talk about signing a contract so he could manage me. Obviously he expected to get paid and that freaked me out. I guess I was a bit immature, but I've always been wary of people trying to take advantage of me. I'm sure now that he wasn't, but I just cut him off. Looking back, he didn't deserve that. He'd given me so much of his time and experience; even if I hadn't made him my manager, we should have talked it through.

By the time I signed my first full-time contract with Tasmania, I probably needed a manager. Luckily I had my sister, Nicole, coming round to the idea that maybe cricket wasn't such a bad thing after all. And I needed all the support I could get if I was going to take the next big step . . . into the Australian cricket team.

CHAPTER 3 **STEPPING UP**

The next season, 2001–02, I started to think realistically about getting into the national side. This was no longer just a dream, it was a realistic aim. The only question was whether or not I was good enough.

One of the best things about playing for Tasmania was having the chance to get to know Ricky Ponting pretty well. Although he was away with the national side a lot, when he was around he looked after me and would ask me out for dinner with his wife. I was still fairly young—just 20—but some of the things he dropped into conversation made me think I was definitely on the national team's radar.

During that summer, Australia didn't make the finals of our own triangular one-day contest for the first time ever and that was the last time Steve Waugh captained Australia in one-day cricket. Changes were in the wind. Ricky was about to take over as one-day captain and I remember him telling me the guys were talking about me as a prospect around the group. It was nothing more than that but, man, to hear Ricky saying it was just amazing. This was a dream that was maybe, just maybe, about to come true.

When Ricky played for Tassie he saw the best of me, the

side of me that has a go no matter what. Whether we are about to win or lose, I'll always give it everything I've got. Greg Shipperd had coached Ricky since he first came into the Tassie team, and I suppose Greg saw a little bit of him in me in some regards, maybe in the way I batted or took on the opposition.

In my first year with Tassie Ricky played a one-dayer in Adelaide in a pre-season tour and Greg worked it so that I roomed with him. That was the first time I'd ever met him. Can you imagine walking into your hotel room and one of your heroes is right there? I hardly slept that first night because I couldn't believe Ricky was in the same room. But he was totally cool about it and he would take me for coffee and a chat, always keen to know how I was going and what I was up to.

In my second year he played a four-day match against New South Wales at the Sydney Cricket Ground, in which he got 100 in both innings against Glenn McGrath and Stuart Clark. It was phenomenal to watch. I couldn't have known it then, but I would need his support through the tough times that lay ahead.

Another Tassie legend that I got close to was David Boon, who gave me advice on everything from technique to cricket bats. I saw a lot of him because he was media manager at Tassie cricket. But he was an Australian selector too and he often filled me in on what was going on. One morning in late January or early February 2002, I was at home and he gave me a call. 'I have something to talk to you about,' he said. 'Can I come over?'

I was thinking, 'What have I done wrong?' He came in and said, 'We've just picked the Test team to go to South Africa. We normally take 14, but we've added another one to the squad and we want you to come along. You're not there for the Tests; we want you to get to know everyone, with the prospect of maybe playing a part in the one-day series. Are you interested?'

Interested? I was just blown away. I had Tassie training that same morning, right after he told me. I was bursting, wanting to tell everyone, but I didn't want to boast. I needn't have worried. Greg Shipperd gathered everyone together and told them I'd been picked to go on the tour and everybody seemed genuinely pleased for me. I did my training, but as soon as I turned my phone back on I had about 20 messages from journalists, family and friends.

These were the days before Twitter, but it had been released in the media and gone nuts from there. A lot of the people trying to get in touch with me were big-name journos and media identities wanting to be the first to do an interview. All the big newspapers... all the major TV channels... radio stations... news agencies... it was mind-blowing to think that so many people wanted to talk to a kid from Ipswich.

I did an interview on the *Today* show on Channel Nine with Steve Leibmann. I always used to watch him when I was growing up. He talked to me about the Baggy Green, which I didn't have yet. But to be talking to a genuine TV celebrity—wow! Mum and Dad have got a tape of it. It was amazing, but nothing close to the buzz of going on tour with some sporting heroes and bona fide legends. This made all the crap I'd had from the Queensland boys worthwhile

Here I am, 20 years old, it's 13 February 2002 and I'm on a plane to South Africa with Steve Waugh, Mark Waugh, Glenn McGrath and Shane Warne, just to name a few. These were my absolute idols. The first time I met some of them was at the airport, just before we got on the plane. Some were more friendly than others. Steve Waugh, who was still captain of the Test side, went out of his way to be really nice to me and said, 'If you ever want a chat, my door's always open.'

I'd met Shane Warne previously, through David Saker. Warnie was amazing—taking me under his wing and looking after me. I never really socialised with Warnie but, sitting down and having a quiet chat with him, you realise he's an absolute cricket fanatic. He has the most amazing passion for the game and would talk to you about cricket all day, every day—he loves it that much. Me? I was happy to listen.

There's no doubt Warnie is the best captain Australia never had. He's a genius—technically as a bowler, on the field as a leader, and as a thinker about cricket. Later, when I was playing under him in the Indian Premier League, I saw first-hand what a great captain and competitor he was. Brett Lee was another guy I got to know very well. So, as well as Ricky, I had a few allies in there to start with.

Travelling overseas with the national cricket squad is a strange mixture of business and pleasure. For the younger guys, like me, it was an adventure; but most of them were fairly relaxed. There are a few guys who keep themselves to themselves a bit more, but the majority have played together for a very long time and they are a very tight group. Some of them I struggled with, because they were 'old school'. There was a sense of 'Who's this young punk, coming in and getting an opportunity, and he hasn't done anything, while I had to do so much to get into the side? How come he's getting picked?' That only lasted for a short while, but these guys were the best of the best in the world—they weren't going to let anybody 'into the club' unless they'd earned it.

Mark Waugh was a good example. For years I had loved everything about the way he played, but at the start of the tour he wasn't all that friendly to me. He wasn't cruel, but he took the piss out of me a bit. I knew it was his way of sussing me out, seeing what I was made of, so I didn't take it too personally. It wasn't until I played a tour match against the South African A team in Port Elizabeth that he came good. I got a couple of wickets in the first innings; when we batted, all the guys scored runs so, when I came in at seven, I had nothing to lose and I went out and played my shots. I eventually got 100 off 97 balls.

It was amazing to be able to do that, especially in that environment. Afterwards, Mark went out of his way to make me feel part of the group; he sat next to me and asked me all about myself. It was a big deal for me to finally have him on-side.

Otherwise, I was someone in the background really. Wherever these guys went, everyone knew who they were and they'd always be asked for photos and autographs, but of course I never got asked. I had it easy. I enjoyed all the best things about being on tour with the Australian team but I didn't have to worry about not having much personal time and space, so I got the best of both worlds.

When you're on tour, you work with the guy who is the official twelfth man for that particular match—which would have been Stuart MacGill or Darren Lehmann mostly—organising the drinks and so forth. But, even if that's all you do, it's something else to be on the inside when the team is playing.

In the dressing room for my first Test match I saw Adam Gilchrist when the crowd were really sticking it to him because of some pretty sick rumours in the papers about his wife and family. Gilly's a real family man, a lovely caring emotional guy, and it really did affect him. But when he got out in the middle, it was phenomenal to watch. If the crowd was trying to put him off his game, it was having the opposite effect. It was like he could lose himself in his cricket and nothing else mattered; he scored a Test double century.

At my next match, in Cape Town, I saw Warnie play his one hundredth Test. That performance just blew me away too. I reckon he bowled 40 overs straight from one end. All the other guys bowled well, but he must have got six or seven wickets. Physically, it's not that demanding bowling spin for short spells. But 40 overs? And then there's the mental concentration that goes into what he does. I reckon he hardly bowled a bad ball throughout that whole spell.

It's really hard to maintain the highest standards with leg spin, because it's so difficult to do in the first place. I remember seeing him after he came off, and he was mentally and physically wrecked. He couldn't do anything because he was so tired. It was something that truly inspired me, to see someone at the top of their game able to do that and rip a team apart.

People always used to ask why Warnie was preferred over Stuart MacGill. There was a time when Stuey's figures were actually better than Warnie's, but he didn't have the consistency over a whole Test match. When I played Shield games against Stuey, you always knew he could bowl a few balls that could get you out, but then every so often he'd give you an easy boundary.

Whereas, facing Warnie, he never let up—every ball was on the money. His variations were subtle and, on top of that, his comments were all over you. Not exactly sledging, more making observations that you knew were right—messing with your head, planting little seeds of doubt that made you change what you were doing or caused you to lose confidence. You knew you were in an absolute contest with every single ball that you faced.

Stuey was a great bowler; but Warnie was like the soul of cricket, and every over was a master class. It must have been tough for Stuey, being one of the very best spin bowlers in the world and not even able to get a game.

Warnie's ability to read the opposition was unbelievable. Once, when he was bowling to Carl Hooper, the West Indian batsman was going really well and every so often he'd come down the wicket and smash the ball back over Warnie's head to the boundary. Warnie was getting frustrated, because he couldn't see it coming. So he focused not just on the ball he was bowling but on any changes he could see in the way Hooper was playing the shot. Finally, he worked him out and I asked him how he did it.

'Whenever he's going to pump it back over my head,' he told me, 'he's got this huge smile on his face.'

We played three Tests in South Africa and won two of them, so I was there for four weeks all up. As a non-Test playing squad member, the biggest new experience for me was being part of the celebrations when we won. The party was like the best day of your life. The first one was in Johannesburg, in the change room of the Wanderers club. We won in three days and everyone had a whale of a time, including the ritual burning of our match tickets that wouldn't be needed for the last two days. Even better was the party after the Cape Town Test, when we had won the series. We went up to the top of Table Mountain and sang The Song:

Underneath the Southern Cross I stand,
A sprig of wattle in my hand,
A native of our native land,
Australia, you f---ing beauty!

This was something Ian Chappell and Rod Marsh had brought into the team, but the story is it goes way back to a guy called John McMahon, who played his cricket in England mostly after the Second World War. Ian and Rod brought it back into the modern dressing room and since then the team has had a songmaster, who decides where and when it will be sung. It went from Rod Marsh to Allan Border, then David Boon, then Ian Healy, then Ricky, Justin Langer and Adam Gilchrist. Mike Hussey is songmaster now and when he leaves the team it will get passed on to the next bloke. I did it in Brisbane when Mike was injured—what an honour. I love that kind of tradition and to see it all first hand, to be part of it all, having some beers and sitting down and talking to your idols—life doesn't get much better than that . . . Unless, of course, you're playing.

I didn't play the first one-dayer of the series, but on my debut I got two off the bat in the second one at Pretoria's Centurion Park and my bowling went all right till I got smacked into the stand by Lance Klusener. Who hasn't? My first three overs went for about eight runs and then my next few went for a lot more. Lance just kept hitting me into the crowd. In the third game I scored eight and went for 40 runs off six overs, so I was rested for the fourth and fifth matches. My run scoring wasn't crash hot and I did get hit a bit when I bowled; but that's all part of the learning process—the reason I was there.

In the final game in Cape Town, I batted at three and Shaun Pollock took the piss out of me, working me over till he got me out. I got 16 runs and my first international wicket—Nicky Boje—and we lost the game; but we'd already won the series 5–1 (with one tie).

Looking back, my one-day batting hadn't developed yet but I've always been patient—something that's paid off since I started opening the batting for the Test side. Not taking risks is suited to the longer version of the game, especially opening the batting. Rotating strike and taking risks to hit boundaries or big sixes, as you have to do in the short forms, wasn't my strong point at that time. When I was in the team, because our side was so strong, I was always down the order, which meant I only got a few chances to bat. Even then my role was to go out there and slog, which I couldn't really do.

So I was expected to be on a fairly steep learning curve. If my bowling didn't improve quickly, no doubt I was going to get dropped for someone else who was better at hitting sixes than me. I was there because of my bowling and I had to get up to speed—in every sense of the word—and try to be a lot more effective.

My pace was my weapon in Shield matches, but I was only bowling probably 140–145 kilometres an hour at best and most of the fast bowlers in the world bowl consistently over 150. I wasn't moving the ball, my consistency wasn't great and I didn't really have big changes of pace—so once guys got in against me, they could take me down. To begin with it didn't matter so much that I didn't take many wickets because Glenn McGrath, Shane Warne, Brett Lee and Jason Gillespie could make it up if I didn't produce the goods on a given day. This was a development phase for me. Management was giving me time around the team to develop and hopefully, when those guys moved on, I'd be able to take over from them.

When I needed guidance or coaching, mentally and technically, John Buchanan was my go-to guy. But I began to get frustrated with John when he couldn't give me the answers I needed. There was no batting or bowling coach, just John and the physio. Later on, Tim Nielsen came on board as an assistant coach so we started to get a bit of batting coaching. But at that level you are expected to know your game so well that no more coaching is required.

It's funny. Just about every other sport has specialist or individual coaches—soccer teams have goalkeeping, fitness and skills coaches; union and league have defensive coaches—but the Australian cricket team had one guy, who was mainly there to help with teamwork, fielding drills and tactics.

It's true, everyone helps each other out, but only up to a point. Your first priority is to make sure your own game is in order. You don't necessarily want to spend hours trying to help out some young punk. So, when I knew I wasn't pulling my weight with either the bat or ball, I had to try to work it out for myself. The only thing I could think of was to develop a slower ball out of the back of my hand. I got that working reasonably well in the nets so it gave me a little bit of variation and that, later on, turned out to be the key to hanging in there.

I hadn't set the world on fire in South Africa, but I was

progressing enough to keep the selectors happy; so when the Aussie cricket contracts were announced on 1 May, three weeks after our last match in South Africa, one of them was offered to me. I was ranked highly in both the long and short forms of the game, so I was offered a multi-year contract with money that I couldn't imagine. The base contract was $180,000 plus match fees. This was unbelievable.

My dad at the absolute peak of his earning power had been pulling about $50,000 a year, and he had a wife and two kids to look after. This was a huge change to the money I was used to; but I'd like to think my values never changed. However some things would change, whether I liked it or not. Suddenly I was public property, in a way. Along with fortune comes fame—and if you don't know how to deal with it, you had better learn fast.

THAT'S ME IN THE SPOTLIGHT...

DRINKS BREAK 2

When you step up to international cricket, you don't get much in the way of advice on how to deal with the media, which is surprising because marketing and promotion are such big parts of the game these days. A lot of media guys talk to you about what you can or what you can't say—especially when there's some controversy going on—but I never got any coaching about the best way to portray myself without looking like a goose. For example, you might feel like you're saying the right things and trying to sound positive and keen, but then, when you see yourself in print and on TV, you realise you look like you're up yourself.

It's something I had to learn for myself. I didn't have any problem doing press conferences, because I'd done a public-speaking course at high school. But that's only part of it. You need to know what to say, and what not to say, especially when fans are reading every word. I didn't pay that much attention to how I was coming across at the time, but later on I realised I'd created an image of myself as an arrogant young bloke, someone who wasn't really me, and it took me a number of years to be able to turn all that around.

I'd never been the type to talk myself up but, before I went away to South Africa, someone wrote that the only thing missing in the Australian team was a genuine all-rounder and I decided I was going to be that player. I was trying to show that I was confident and wanted the job, even though deep down I knew I had a long way to go. Freddie Flintoff was making a big impression for England and he'd proved the value of all-rounders in the modern game, so I said I wanted to be Australia's answer to Freddie Flintoff. Big mistake!

People immediately jumped on that and started comparing me to him, even saying I thought I was as good as him. I wasn't but that didn't matter to some reporters. Suddenly they were saying Freddie's done this and that—and this young bloke's done what? I was talking about my dreams and aspirations. You can aim to be as good as this player or that one, but you should let someone else make the comparison.

I'm not one of those players who doesn't read the papers. I love sport, so how am I going to keep up to date if I avoid the cricket pages? I knew I was going to find out about positive or negative reactions from my family or my friends anyway, so I'd grit my teeth and hope for the best. But it was hard. You could go from being praised and feeling good about yourself to being smashed about your performances. Sometimes you feel like you can't win.

I don't blame journos. It's their job to analyse and speculate, and at that point I wasn't much to write home about. I've had my fair share of supporters too; but as much as I liked the positive headlines more than the negative ones, I didn't take what people wrote all that personally. Of course, if you're in a bit of a slump, the whole situation turns in on itself. It's hard to pick yourself up when the papers are saying 'Watson must go!' or something like that. It's part of the challenge of playing for Australia in a sport that's so well loved and high profile throughout the country and around the world.

I remember talking to Ricky about some of the tough times he went through and to Warnie, when he was in the headlines. They gave me good advice but, until you go through it yourself, you can't really comprehend what it means. The thing that keeps you going, whether it's during injury or a form slump, is knowing that all of the best players in the world have been through it and they've had to find a way to turn things around. That, I reckon, is the mark of a champion.

When I came back from the seven weeks in South Africa, things had definitely changed. Down in Hobart I started to get recognised a lot more in the street. Hobart is a small place and there are not that many high-profile people there. The footy players go to Melbourne or interstate, and it's the same with actors and musicians. So if you are looking for sport stars, chances are they'll be playing cricket; back then that meant me, Ricky and David Boon, who is still adored down there. I've never been over-keen to draw attention to myself, so that was the first time I had to get my head around people recognising me.

DRINKS BREAK 2

I remember, soon after I got back to Hobart, it was the first time anyone had ever given me any stick when I was out having a few drinks with my mates. This drunk fronts me and says I'm no good and all that crap and I remember thinking, 'Why am I having to deal with this?' I was in my new home town, going out for a quiet drink and this muppet decides to have a go. I was pissed off well and truly, but I'm not a fighter and, even if I was, it would be stupid to mix it with some drunk in a pub. You can't win, either way. You could get injured and more than likely the brawl would end up on YouTube, if not in the papers and the courts. So you just have to cop it and back away. I thought, 'This is not what I signed up for', but I knew I had better get used to it.

The other down times were when I had an injury and I was self-conscious about going out at all in case someone recognised me and asked me about it. People mean well, but when you're struggling with injuries and you're trying to get on with your life, it's hard to take people coming up to you every five minutes asking 'How's the back? What's wrong with you this time?' And I suppose for a while I was obsessed with trying to turn people's opinion of me around. You're never going to please everyone, but to get the majority to say they appreciate what you do, whether they like you or not, that's worth aiming for.

There would come a time when I would get pats on the back in public and in the press, but they were a long way off and I had a few hoops to jump through before I got there.

CHAPTER 4 **BACK TO BASICS**

The trip to South Africa had been only a qualified success: I got on well with the others in the squad, but I needed to lift my game if I wanted to cement my position in the one-day team, let alone make the step up to the Test side. I was prepared to work as hard as I could to make it. What I didn't realise was that the harder I worked, the less chance I had of staying fit enough to achieve my ambitions.

After I got settled into my new flat in Hobart, I was off again in September 2002 to the Champions Trophy one-day series in Sri Lanka. That tour was the flipside of what can happen when you are playing for Australia. We made it to the semi-finals but we had a long break before we played, more than a week, so we took four days in the Maldives. It was sensational, just hanging out with the guys in such a beautiful place.

We possibly relaxed a bit too much because we got flogged by Sri Lanka in the semis. The ball was turning square and, to give you an idea of how bad it was, Warnie was top scorer with 36. I only got seven and we were 162 all out. I didn't bowl. We were in bad shape and desperately trying to restrict their scoring. Ricky clearly didn't have all that much confidence in what I could do to help and this was no place for an 'improving' bowler.

The next series was the 2002–03 one-dayers against England and Sri Lanka, starting in January, and leading up to that series I played some state cricket. I was trying to find my best form, but in October my back started to get really sore. I knew that it wasn't great but I had no choice, I needed to get into the team for the upcoming one-day series, to play well then make sure I was in the squad for the World Cup in South Africa in February and March the next year, just four months away. I was hoping I could battle through and still be able to perform. Once the World Cup finished, I'd have all the time I wanted to deal with any injuries.

A couple of games from this VB one-day international series really stand out for me. In the second one-day match at the Melbourne Cricket Ground, England's Nick Knight was taking Glenn McGrath down and it was the first time that had happened to 'Pigeon' in a long time—Knight kept cutting the ball off the stumps. Earlier Gilly and Ricky had both got centuries in a total of 318, but England was now threatening to make a fight of it. I had been copping it from the media, as I should have been because I wasn't performing—I only scored nine, batting at number seven. Anyway, Nick Knight was powering on with 70 off 68 balls when I got him out to my new, slower ball. Even though I only took one wicket, I stopped the England fightback and that was when I finally felt I had contributed.

Next up was a game in Hobart, which came right down to the wire. Damien Martyn had scored 101, Michael Bevan got 52, my old mate Jimmy Maher got 49 and we were looking good at 271—not brilliant but useful. But then Marcus Trescothick and Nick Knight came out and scored over 80 runs each, and Nasser Hussain, especially, and Alex Stewart looked like they were going to get them over the line.

I kept looking up at the scoreboard, watching them get closer and closer and I realised I was probably going to have to bowl. This was my home ground and there would never have been a better chance to do something heroic in front of my own crowd during my first summer playing for Australia in Australia. It was also the first time the whole crowd was chanting my name as I was running in to bowl. What they didn't know was my back was sore and I was feeling a really sharp pain every time I bowled a ball.

I got Stewart with the second-last ball of the forty-eighth over—leaving them with two overs to get 20 runs. Nasser was on his way to his 50 and, when I came to bowl the last over to him, I knew I really had to put in. He took two off me and was looking to score ten off the last four balls—very do-able for a player who's got his eye in—but then he missed a ball that wasn't quite a perfect yorker and I bowled him. Caddick only scored two and it was all over.

That was my first experience of being on the back page in the papers. Walking through Melbourne airport, I saw in the *Herald Sun* all about me 'Winning the Game for Australia'—it's funny how the previous 49 overs of hard graft get forgotten thanks to one ball that got through.

I knew I was getting closer to where I wanted to be as a player, but my back was just about to go. I went and saw a doctor in Melbourne. He said it was a stress fracture, but he and the team physios thought I might be able to play with the help of pain-killing injections and carry on through to the World Cup.

The next match, against Sri Lanka in Brisbane, I only made four runs and didn't take any wickets. I got an injection before the following game in Adelaide—it lasts for about three or four hours and for a while you're not actually feeling much. The problem is your body doesn't protect the injury, because it doesn't know it's there. Okay, I took two good wickets and held up one end while Michael Clarke got the winning runs but, needless to say, my back was worse than ever after the game.

I had a crack right through a facet joint on my left side—facet joints link the spinal discs and allow movement. I knew I was really struggling and it was affecting my bowling and my running in the outfield. In my last game at the MCG, against Sri Lanka, I bowled three overs; but I could hardly run in and my pace was way down: about 115 to 120 kilometres an hour. I didn't get smashed or anything, but I couldn't go on. I missed the finals of the one-day series and was ruled out of the World Cup. At the time it was disappointing, of course; but I'd had stress fractures before and I knew I just had to modify my technique again and be as safe as I could with my body.

Back pain is nothing out of the norm for cricketers. Many fast bowlers have sore backs a lot of the time but no one really knows it's a stress fracture until it's properly diagnosed. The doctor said to me I had to be in a back brace for at least three months to let the bone heal because with a stress fracture in your back there are two ways to heal: either bone on bone—which is the best you can get—or the bone doesn't really come together and you get a fibrous, soft-tissue repair that can open up and is harder to get rid of. In fact, I was in a back brace for four months down in Hobart and I couldn't run for six months.

A lot of people thought Andrew Symonds got my place in the team; but that wasn't really the case. Roy was there to replace Darren Lehmann, who had been suspended for five ODIs. It was Ian Harvey who replaced me as an all-rounder so I thought there was still maybe an opportunity for me once I was fit again. Watching the World Cup from home, I was amazed to see how much Andrew had improved. Previously he had looked very scratchy, but now every single shot he played seemed to come off the middle of the bat. He got 143 not out against Pakistan in the first match. I wondered what he did and who he worked with to be able to do all that against some of the best bowlers in the world. He later told me he'd worked on one little pre-movement and it meant everything else sort of lined itself up and he went from there.

Whatever happens in my life, I try to take the positives out of it. In this case I thought I could go back and work on my batting, which I felt had gone down a little bit technically. It was getting more flawed the longer I went on, so this was my chance to get back to basics, to get some good coaching and to do some serious work on it. So as soon as the back brace came off I went back to the Cricket Academy and worked with Bennett King.

My biggest issue with my batting was not being totally in control. I didn't know exactly what I was doing, so I couldn't fix it when it started to go wrong and then it just got worse and worse. A lot of it came down to balance—my bat swing was not consistent because my balance wasn't good. The best answer to a problem like this is to break your technique right down and build it back up again.

Bennett King and I worked five days a week for two months, pretty much starting over. I shortened my bat swing to make it more consistent. That also means you're taking away some power and rhythm and timing—but at that time I was willing to make these sacrifices to gain some consistency.

I changed my pre-movement, before the ball is even bowled, to be more balanced when it's delivered. So it was really a total reconstruction of my batting, which was fine by me. I love all the technical things. At that time I was a bit of a robot—I was a bit mechanical, but I was effective.

Meanwhile, I still stayed very fit. I walked for two hours a day, including up sand hills at the Academy, to try to build my back up again. I was okay as long as I didn't put any stress on my back and didn't even try to run.

After about six months I batted in a couple of pre-season games, but my first Pura Cup game was against South Australia at the beginning of November back in Tassie. To avoid my back getting re-injured straightaway, I didn't bowl; but I got 103 with the bat, which felt good.

That was the start of a very successful year during which I hit 987 runs. Finally, about 11 months after my injury, I started bowling again, in the second innings against Queensland (of all teams) in Hobart. I got two wickets, including my old sparring partner, Stuey Law, clean bowled. Yes!

I topped it all off with a 300 for Lindisfarne Cricket Club after the Pura season had finished. That was a real celebration. I was so happy with how I'd been batting throughout the year; I'd scored many more runs than I thought I would ever get in a Shield season so I just went out and tried to hit every ball to the boundary. I batted the whole day and it was one of those innings when everything you try comes off—premeditated shots, the lot. To put the icing on the cake, I also took seven wickets.

During the four months my back had been in a brace I'd had three scans, to make sure it was fully healed. It did heal very well, but I still built up my work load very, very slowly. I started with walking and worked up to bowling in January of 2004. Along the way, I had to make some drastic changes to my bowling technique, so even by the end of the season my bowling was still a long way off peak performance and I got very frustrated at times, because I couldn't yet do what I wanted to do.

CHAPTER 5 **CROSSROADS**

My first tour back in the Australian team was to Zimbabwe in May 2004, a year that saw a lot of changes in my life. Tassie had been great for me and really got my career on course; but, when you've seen a bit of the world, Hobart (lovely place that it is) feels small. I was a young bloke in my prime and I wanted to be where there was a bit more life. I decided it was time for me to move back to Brisbane.

Going back and playing for Queensland was something I'd always dreamed of doing. I knew how good the facilities and coaching were—definitely a step up from Hobart. They now had the Centre of Excellence—this was the new name for what used to be known as the Cricket Academy. In 2004 it had moved from Adelaide to Brisbane and Bennett King was up there, so the facilities for cricket would be a lot better. Being close to my family was another big thing, but mostly I felt like I was ready for a change.

I needed to get to a bigger city and expand my horizons as a person too. I always have been, and still am, so grateful to Tassie cricket for giving me the opportunity they did—it was a big risk, no doubt, to pull me in halfway through the year and give me a chance. I realise how lucky I was and I still thank all the guys who were part of that. I was with them for three-and-a-half years and it was the foundation of my professional career.

But this isn't like professional football, where you sign a contract and then you can be traded for money. The way the Cricket Australia contracts work, every year when your contract comes up for renewal, all you have to do is nominate your state. So you don't actually sign a contract with the state association—it's just when you're only playing state cricket that you sign a contract with the state. So in the end all you've got to do is let the old team know your reasons for leaving. They've got to be okay with it as well, but I can't see any of them saying no. Nobody wants a player who'd rather be somewhere else.

The year before I left, even though I was happy playing in Tassie, I started talking, very informally, to Queensland and they were really keen to get me back home. Actually, Victoria were interested too. Greg Shipperd had moved from Tassie to be the assistant coach for Victoria and David Hookes was the head coach. So they talked to me seriously about moving to Melbourne and playing there. The other option was to try to get out of my contract a year early to go back to Brisbane. In the end I knew the right thing was to repay Tassie for giving me the opportunity, so I stayed there and let my contract run out.

I'd been around the Tassie team quite a lot because of my injuries, but I'd been getting a bit frustrated with the coaching set-up there. At the start of the 2003–04 season David Saker retired from playing and came on as a bowling coach and Dene Hills was taken on as a batting coach. That definitely created a better environment and I really enjoyed my last year with Tassie. Even so I felt it was time for me to go home to Brisbane.

Having done the right thing by Tasmania, I now felt I had a chance to repay Queensland for everything they did for me when I was growing up. But first I had to go to Zimbabwe. It felt good to be back in the national squad after a year away.

Once again I had some back pain, but it wasn't anything too drastic. Like I said, all fast bowlers get back pain—it kind of goes with the territory—it's just that for some players it's only general soreness while for others it's a sign of something more serious. I got a game in the third match in Zimbabwe and it was nice to be back.

In the end I didn't really bowl that much because I wasn't really needed—all the other guys were taking wickets before me—so it was a perfect way to ease myself back into the one-day team. Zimbabwe was always one of the Australian team's favourite tours in the early to mid-nineties because of how beautiful the country was. They went on wildlife safaris and to Victoria Falls and really enjoyed their time. But in 2004, which turned out to be our last tour there, we couldn't leave our hotels. The old hands said Mugabe's influence was a lot more obvious than it had been on previous tours. It was only a couple of years since they had been suspended from the Commonwealth, and then quit altogether—they weren't too happy with us Aussies for the role we had played in those events.

The crowds weren't great and the teams seemed to be mostly young African kids developing their games. From there I went to Hampshire for a few weeks and I met a couple of guys from Zimbabwe who had gone over to England to play county cricket just to get away from all the political issues in their country. Some of them talked about how their families' farms were taken off them and how dangerous it was and one guy, who'd played international cricket from the age of 17, was fed up with everything that was going on with his country.

In Hampshire the contrast could not have been greater. This was my first time in England and my initial impression was how similar it was to Australia, at least in terms of the British people, and it made me appreciate my roots. We are just about identical—apart from a few slight differences in how we are brought up. It got me interested in history, as one of the things that strikes you in Britain is how old things are. Here in Australia, European culture is just over 200 years old. Some of the buildings you see in the UK are four or five times as old as that. It makes you realise how young post-colonial Australia really is.

I'd been asked to go to Hampshire to replace Warnie when he was on Test duties and to play alongside Michael Clarke. Warnie had been there from 2000 and he pretty much ran the show. Everything that happened within the team was down to his influence, even when he wasn't there. All the structures and the foundations and philosophy that the team played by were from Warnie.

For instance, we played aggressively. A lot of the other counties that we played against might be pretty happy with a draw and let the game peter out; or, if a batsman was in and scoring freely, they would put a lot of people back on the boundary and not really try to get him out. Whereas Warnie's way was that we had to keep the game moving forward—back yourself, be smart, get through the tough periods and, when you're bowling, you've always got to be looking to get a wicket, no matter what the situation is. That year we did pretty well. Hampshire were definitely on an upward curve and I loved my time over there.

I got injured again, so it cut short my initial spell and I had to cop sledging from the locals about the overseas player getting injured on debut. I was able to keep batting but, for the last couple of weeks, I didn't bowl because I'd strained a hamstring. The Brits in the team were a bit wary of me to begin with but, after I scored some runs, they seemed to like having me in the team. Most teams I've been involved with seem to enjoy the way I play. I was always having a go and I scored some good runs through that time.

The other thing is, I was getting better as a player. Before my injury, I had never really found my feet in terms of how to bowl on English pitches. I did okay—I didn't get belted or anything—but I didn't get too many wickets. Just by playing more I found there were little things I could improve, both with my batting and my bowling.

The other bonus was that I was living in Shane Warne's house. His whole family was over there, so I moved in with them for about a week or so before he went back to Australia for the Sri Lanka series in Darwin and Cairns. Simone and the kids went to Spain for a couple of weeks while Warnie was back home but, before they went, I was able to get to know the family really well. They looked after me very hospitably. I had a great time and stayed there for six weeks, all up.

Meanwhile I was playing all over England. My first game was a one-dayer against Lancashire at Old Trafford and I played a few games at the Rose Bowl, Hampshire's home ground in Southampton. Then there were Twenty20 games at the Oval and Lord's. I didn't get around all the grounds in England, but I was able to see some pretty special ones. Okay, you could tell that football was the main sport, no matter what, but the majority of people seemed to still love cricket.

I've been going back and forth now for the last seven years, and I think there's a bit of difference, depending on how well the England team are performing. If they aren't going very well, interest sort of dies off a bit, whereas in Australia we've been very successful over the last ten to 15 years so the crowds still come out, especially for the big games.

The stay in Hampshire was a success for me, particularly as a batsman. It had already occurred to me that, if the worst came to the worst, I could maybe still get into the Australian side just with my batting—but it would take me a lot longer. Guys like Matthew Hayden, Damien Martyn, Justin Langer and Adam Gilchrist were still around, so there was no shortage of world-class batsmen. If I lost my bowling, it would just put me in the back of the pack with all the other very good batsman around Australia. The year I got 987 runs in the Pura Cup there were four or five other guys who scored similar figures. I knew all along that the best way to keep myself in the mix was to stay an all-rounder.

My back was in pretty good shape because I had already modified my bowling, although I wasn't really charging in as fast as I had been before my injury. Also my batting had really taken over as my major contribution to a team so in that first-class environment it wasn't the be-all and end-all for me to be bowling 145 kilometres an hour.

In August I was in the squad for a one-day mini-tournament against India and Pakistan in the Netherlands, but the first match against India was abandoned halfway through because of rain and the second match against Pakistan didn't even start because of the weather. Australia won the final against Pakistan, but I wasn't in the side.

In early September, we played a one-off one-dayer against Pakistan at Lord's. Andrew Symonds got 104 not out and I got seven not out off six balls in what turned out to be a fairly tight ten-run win. I was also in the squad for the Champions Trophy held in England later that month and played in the second match against New Zealand, but we won comfortably and I didn't even get to bat. We were knocked out by England in the semi-final.

As the Test team was getting ready to travel to India, it became apparent what my role with them might be. They really needed an all-rounder to be able to provide another bowling option, just in case they wanted to play two spinners. That's why I got picked for the Test squad for India in 2004. I was edging closer to that Baggy Green and, with less than a year to go till the next Ashes series, I started to allow myself to believe my luck was turning.

TOO STRONG FOR MY BODY

As a professional sport, cricket was pretty late coming to the party on fitness training. But the days are long gone of the old pro only swatting fours because, if he took a run, he'd need a taxi to get back to his crease. You have to be an athlete these days, with all that entails.

This is especially true for bowlers, given that it is a really unnatural series of movements under extreme stress. No wonder bowlers get more injuries than any other cricketers. Freddie Flintoff—my role model—saw his international career come to a fairly abrupt end when his body couldn't handle the workload anymore.

My problem, as I would only discover years later, was that my injuries were being dealt with in isolation. A sore back was a sore back. The strength and conditioning coaches would talk about building up my legs and shoulders; if I had a side injury, a minor hamstring injury or a quad strain, for instance, they would fix what was there—massage the part that was hurting and try to get it right. But that was it. They never asked *why* it had happened.

Also the strength and conditioning philosophy at the time was: if you get bigger and stronger, you're going to bowl faster. I'd done weights from the age of about 16, both for my cricket and rugby, and I continued throughout the Academy. Everyone kept telling me if you get bigger and stronger you'll bowl faster. That seemed to make sense and bowling faster was exactly what I wanted to do.

Through 2003–04 I was big. Genetically, I suppose I'm programmed to build muscle, so when I really get into weights I do bulk up. I'd be in the gym three times a week and for two-and-a-half hours just doing weights; then I'd do my fitness workout as well. For a cricketer, I was very big.

In the Australian team there were a few guys who were gym junkies, like Matthew Hayden for instance. Damien Martyn was also going through a period when he was really, really fit. But ironically, the bowlers wouldn't really train all that hard in the gym. Brett Lee would do a bit, but Glenn McGrath and Jason Gillespie wouldn't—they'd do squats and that sort of thing, but nothing like what I was doing. And this is where my logic let me down a bit.

I thought these guys must be the best in the business, otherwise they wouldn't be in the Australian team. But, rather than doing exactly what they were doing, I thought I'd work harder in the gym and that would help me to be as good as them. I would only discover later that this was the worst thing I could have done.

But I was young and impressionable. I believed everything the coaches told me, because they were the experts. I did whatever I was told to the finest degree. If I had a day off from playing or team training, I'd be in the gym getting bigger and stronger. Hindsight has 20–20 vision, but it was only when I met Victor Popov three years later that I discovered I had been doing the worst thing imaginable for withstanding the stresses of fast bowling.

Just before I met Victor I had done about eight weeks of superintensive heavy power weights. And then, as soon as I tried to bowl, I strained my hamstrings. I'd done all this work and I was the strongest I'd ever been—bench pressing 100–120 kilograms and squatting 120, all pure power work. Abdominal strength, which is core strength, was something you did only if you had time at the end of your session.

In the end, I had so much power in my legs and upper body that, as soon as I tried to put that together—which is through your core—I was gone. I just fell apart. When all the injuries started mounting up, John Buchanan said I was too strong for my own body. At the time I thought it was a ridiculous thing to say . . . except I now realise he was 100 per cent on the money.

If a young cricketer asked me right now what was the single best exercise they could do to improve their fitness, I'd say Pilates. Core strength and flexibility are your foundation—the most important things to start with. If I had my time again, I would have started my weights when I was 16, like I did, but I would have definitely done Pilates as well as weights. If you don't have good core strength, it doesn't matter how strong you are in your upper body and legs: you can't put it all together. Your body will be out of alignment and it will literally tear itself apart.

You still need to be strong and very fit to play professionally. Even rock stars do fitness training before they go on tour these days. It's a question of recognising the demands that will be placed on your body and then putting yourself in the best place to deal with them.

You should run, but only every second day. In fact, whatever you do, you've got to give your body a day to recover. Running is important and for me, coming back from hamstring injuries, steady pace running for 20 minutes or half an hour every other day was what my body needed to be able to gradually build up its endurance and tolerance at that sort of load.

Everyone's body is different. Some guys are more natural runners than others, but running is important because you've got to do things in training that you do on the field. You do a fair bit of running as a bowler; even as a batsman, you've got to sprint between wickets—so you do have to run quite a bit. Aerobic fitness training is important, whether it's on the road, treadmill, bike or rower. It's vital to be very physically fit.

And you need to have a balanced diet. As part of the whole package with Victor, I went to see a specialised doctor called Michael Artmann who could analyse what my body was lacking and then get it to be as balanced as it could be. Whether it was diet or supplements, he told me what I needed to make sure my body was in balance. For instance, I'm a little bit low in magnesium, which is why I used to cramp a lot—I still do occasionally. So I take a supplement for that all the time. I've got a minor blood condition called Gilbert's syndrome, which causes a high level of bilirubin in my blood, and this means I can get a bit of jaundice if I'm fatigued. It's not dangerous or anything like that, but I've got a liver tablet to try to stabilise it.

I take a multivitamin to cover all the bases, just in case my diet isn't up to scratch—no matter what you do, no one has a perfect diet. The one thing Michael emphasises is getting the acidic balance in your body right. He reckons bad things grow in your body when it's acidic and that comes from a number of things that you eat—sugar, alcohol and chocolate, for instance—so you need to balance it out with some alkali. Now every day I take an alkaline solution to try to level out my body's pH level. Michael has had some success with cancer patients. His thinking is that cancer only builds in an acidic environment, so he tries to neutralise it.

That may seem a bit 'out there', but I know I feel a lot healthier, and a lot more balanced in general. It's not just food and minerals, it's attitude as well. I have been very, very intense in the past and that was creating a stressful acidic environment within myself. He talked to me about finding ways to avoid building up tension, because it increases your chances of getting injured.

Admittedly, aggression and intensity have been part of my character as a player. But there's a fine line between intensity and anger. I used to get angry in order to bowl aggressively. Now I'm intense, but I don't get angry as often as I used to.

I used to get really angry every time I got out. Now it's only the odd occasion. I just think how lucky I am to be in the position I'm in—out there, backing myself and playing how I always dreamed I could play. That keeps the Furies at bay.

CHAPTER 6 **OUT OF INDIA**

In October 2004 I went with the squad to India. I didn't play but it was something else just to be able to see the guys in action at close range, operating under the most hostile conditions, and winning in India for the first time in 30-odd years. I saw Michael Clarke make his Test debut and get Man of the Match—which could only be encouraging for me—and to see Jason Gillespie, Glenn McGrath, Michael Kasprowicz and Warnie bowling was phenomenal. They were at the top of their game and they really worked over the Indian batsmen—and all in 40-degree heat.

The wickets were very flat and turning a lot, but even so Damien Martyn got a couple of 100s in that series and batted unbelievably well. In the end, 2–0 up in the series and with one to play, they didn't need the extra bowler, so I was shipped home to play some cricket. I didn't expect to get my first cap, but it was disappointing to miss out on the celebrations.

This wasn't my first taste of India. I'd gone over there for two weeks in 2000 with Paul Rofe, Troy Cooley and Dennis Lillee, who had set up a school for fast bowlers in Chennai. Every year Basil Sellers, a wealthy Australian businessman, sponsors two guys from the Academy to go over and work with Dennis and train flat out for two weeks. I'd already met Dennis when he was involved with Pace Australia's coaching clinic in Brisbane, but that had been just for a couple of days.

To be able to work with him intensely for two weeks in India was amazing. He's a great man; he would talk to you about bowling, about cricket in general, and enjoy a few drinks with you as well. Dennis's feedback was always very positive and gave me that inner belief that maybe I did have something special.

It was an amazing experience to see India itself. It was so confronting! We arrived in the middle of the night and there seemed to be thousands of people standing around the airport—young kids, older people and everyone in between. I thought, 'Why are these people here? They should be in bed!' Driving from the airport and seeing people lying on the side of the roads sleeping, I thought, 'What's going on here? How is this a way of life? This is very different to what I'm used to.'

I realised that the main goal for the people around where we were staying at the Madras Cricket Club was simply to find a meal for themselves and their families—it was mind blowing. My goal was to play for Australia but their ambition was to feed their families every day, and that was a really big achievement. I struggled with all this for a while. I tried to put myself in their position and realised how lucky we are in Australia to be able to reach our dreams, whereas for a lot of the people I saw in India there was nothing there for them beyond survival.

There are rich people in India as well. I saw that when I was invited to the home of the guy who owned MRF, the sports goods and tyre company that backed Dennis's bowling school. There the extravagance was unbelievable—a huge contrast with the sheer poverty and misery I saw elsewhere.

After India, I went back to where it all started for me—Queensland—but I wasn't too worried that there would be any lingering resentment from the time I'd left a few years earlier. Stuart Law had retired the year before I went back up, and that definitely made the transition easier for me. And I'd played one-dayers for Australia with Jimmy Maher, who was now captain of Queensland. That had given me a chance to sort things out with him.

When Jimmy and I were in South Africa, the first time I was there, Queensland were playing Tasmania in the Sheffield Shield up at the Gabba, so Jimmy would keep chipping away at me: 'Who are you going for? Queensland or Tassie? You will be happy with whoever wins either way.' It was fine, no big deal, but he mentioned it every single time he saw me. At the end of the tour, we'd gone out and had a few drinks and he was still being a smart-ass, so I just gave it to him. I said, 'I've had enough of all your carry-on. It's time to give it a rest.'

To his credit, he did agree that, if I hadn't moved to Tasmania, then I probably wouldn't have been in the one-day team. After two years of me absolutely copping it, he was honest enough to say that he thought it was the best move I could have made. From then on things sort of died down a bit and he didn't give me shit anymore.

So there I was, back home and playing for Queensland. Matthew Hayden was playing non-stop for Australia and had been for a few years. A few of the more experienced guys were at the end of their careers, so I suppose they felt I was always going to provide good batting and bowling options. I also really enjoyed going back to my old club, Easts/Redlands—it was where I had started my journey and they'd always followed my career closely. To be able to come back as an Aussie cricketer—in the one-day team and part of the Test squad—was nice for them as well as for me.

Initially I moved back in with my mum and dad because I still had to find a house, and I was there for a month or two. It was good living in Ipswich, but fighting the traffic every morning and night for an hour each way made me appreciate the sacrifices my folks had made, ferrying me around all the time.

But it was great to be home. I used to get up early for training at six or seven and Mum would have my breakfast ready and want to know how my day was yesterday and all that. Sadly, I'm not at my best first thing so the most she got was a few grunts of 'Okay'.

Things had changed a bit at home—well, I had. I love my food, so I used to cook a little bit at home for Mum and Dad, because I wanted to eat something really nice. Mum's always been good with diet and knew to stay away from fatty foods but I reckon by the time I found a place for myself in the eastern suburbs of Brisbane, my family had had enough of 'Shane's Kitchen' and I'd certainly had enough of the commute, especially compared to how close everything was in Hobart.

My first match back in the Queensland team was in Adelaide and I was batting at three. I did okay, scoring 17 and 61, and took seven wickets across the two innings. But against Western Australia at the WACA my batting came together and I scored 136 while Andrew Symonds got 126. Being able to do that for Queensland meant a lot to me. I'd left Brisbane as a raw youth player and come back a fairly polished product, getting a century in my second game. I was rapt.

The game eventually petered out to a draw, but I remember one moment vividly. I was batting with Roy and Brad Hogg was bowling. I tend not to take spinners on in the longer form of the game, so I was playing him fairly cautiously. At the end of the over, Roy walked up to me and said, 'If you don't get me on strike to George [Hogg], I'm gonna run you out.' So I got him on strike and he hit the next ball for six. Roy was awesome to bat with. He hadn't had an opportunity in Test cricket yet, but his time was coming soon.

Nobody likes to run a team-mate out. I've unfortunately got a reputation for it in recent years, but you would never do it deliberately. I think probably one of the worst things, as a batsman, is if it's a bad call and you turn your back on your mate—you go back into your crease and they run through. It looks bad and, frankly, it is bad. It's a shocking thing, and you never want it to happen because you'd feel really selfish.

Of course, if you're the recognised batsman and the guy at the other end is a genuine tail-ender, your first responsibility is to not get yourself out. A lot of it comes down to concentration. If you know that the guy you are batting with is either inexperienced or not a great judge of a run, you've got to concentrate harder to call for him.

A couple of times when I was playing for Hampshire, I played with a younger guy. I wasn't fully concentrating and he was really nervous; it was a bad call and I was run out. After that, I realised I just had to concentrate more and say 'no' when I thought he may have called it wrong. You practise your calling when you're a kid, but in the heat of a Test match or an ODI, when the crowd is going off and the fielding team is yelling at each other, it's nearly impossible to hear a call so you just have to watch your partner.

There's one call you never want to miss—and that's the one from the Test selectors, telling you you're in the team.

COUNTY VERSUS SHIELD

The first thing that strikes you about playing domestic cricket in England is that the overall quality is a bit lower, most probably because the available talent is spread more thinly than ours—they've got 18 first-class counties plus all the minor counties. We've got six states. In every county team there are probably only two or three players who are really good cricketers. I'm not saying the rest are rubbish players—they're good, but they're just not world-class.

That means in every team you play, there's always one or two bowlers you know you can score pretty freely off. And as a bowler, you know that if you have a good day you can get quite a few of their batsmen out. But there's quality right across the county scene too and, if they cut down the number of teams they had and brought all their really good players together, it would be as good as, if not better than, our competition. But that's not going to happen because of English County tradition, which is a shame because there's enough talent there to make it the best competition in the world.

We are lucky in Australia. The very best players are playing with or against each other or they're in the national side. It's changing a bit now and the standard of Sheffield Shield cricket has fallen off slightly, possibly because of a desire to get young cricketers into the first-class set-up as soon as possible.

That means some players who are over 30 and have been very, very good cricketers for their states are being pushed aside for 18- to 19-year-olds who are good prospects but not quite there yet. This is prompted by fears that the national team is ageing. Inevitably the standard has dropped a little, with younger guys getting opportunities to play first-class cricket sooner, based on what they might do rather than what they have done. But that also means there are fewer senior players with experience to pass on and the competition is a bit weaker.

We've also lost a lot of experience because of players being banned after they joined the Indian Champions League. That cut short the careers of guys like Jason Gillespie, Jimmy Maher and Matthew Elliot, to name a few. They would probably have had another two or three years if they hadn't had to choose between playing first-class cricket for Australia and lucrative contracts in India. It was like a retirement fund for some of them and there were a few who quit state cricket earlier than they might otherwise have done to go and play there. Ironically and very unfortunately, a lot of them didn't get paid when it all fell apart.

So that's a chunk of experience gone that would otherwise have been handed on to the younger players. Meanwhile, with the increase in international fixtures, state teams can't count on their international players coming back too often. When I was younger and I was only playing one-day cricket for Australia, I'd have a five- or six-week training block and then I'd have a three-week one-day series here and then the same again overseas. The Australian players used to turn out for at least one game a year for their state but in 2009 I didn't play one game for the state and only two in 2010. Ricky Ponting says it's been getting like this for the past ten years.

It's good to come back and play for your state, but playing Shield games in almost empty stadiums is very different to playing in front of big crowds. We can hear everything that's going on and our on-the-field talk echoes throughout the ground. When you're playing big matches, the things that can really get you going are firstly the situation in the game, and then the intensity of the crowd. However much you try to block it out, it really does get you hyped up. You get even more anxious when there's a bigger crowd, so you learn to use that to lift your game. However, it means that, when you go back to play Shield or county cricket, you've got to gee yourself up. If there's no intensity in the game and there's just one man and his dog at the ground, you've got to find some way to get your mental state up to a level where you can perform.

Sometimes, if I need to get myself going, I get into an argument with the opposition. I suppose it's an ego thing—not to get beaten. So I start a fight that I hope I won't lose. This is more so when I'm batting.

DRINKS BREAK 4

Your concentration has to be spot-on, otherwise you can get found out, so that's a way of getting your mind into the place where it needs to be. You'd think it would be different, and that a bit of a verbal stoush would be a distraction rather than a help. But you need an edge and it will usually give you that. In any case, I've been very lucky over the last year or so to play most of my cricket in front of decent crowds.

CHAPTER 7 **THE CALL**

After I'd played a couple of games for Queensland in November 2004 and the first ODI against New Zealand at the Docklands Stadium in Melbourne, I went off to have a Christmas break on Hamilton Island. Michael Brown, head of Operations for Cricket Australia, called me—he's normally the one who lets players know when they've been picked, so I knew something was up as soon as I heard his voice. I mean, team management don't just call you on your holidays for a chat.

They had decided to play two spinners—MacGill and Warne—in the final Test against Pakistan at the SCG, and that meant they needed an all-rounder to bowl a few overs of pace, if need be. This was phenomenal. I'd always dreamed of getting my very own Baggy Green and playing for Australia and, before I knew it, I was at the SCG, surrounded by my heroes, doing exactly that.

Apart from that, it didn't exactly go to plan. Coming downhill from the Paddington end for the very first time in a Test match I was so nervous that I must have been trying too hard and after I released the ball I started to fall over. I tried to stay up but I had too much momentum and kept falling. I felt like a complete goose and the crowd let me have it. What a start to my Test bowling career! When I went out and batted, I only got 31 but even so I felt like my batting was in a really good place. Ricky got 207 in his first innings. He was in the middle for more than eight hours and was still at the crease when I came in, still batting beautifully.

I can't totally remember all the details of this match, but I do remember getting my first wicket. The ball was going a little bit reverse and I was bowling to Younis Khan; I had one close lbw call refused after a big shout and Billy Bowden, who was umpiring, calmed me down a bit.

'If you can just get it a little closer, I'm keen to get you your first wicket.'

He wasn't promising anything—what he was really telling me was to take it easy, get it right and everything would flow from that. A couple of balls later, I got it perfectly on line and that famous crooked finger went up.

By the way, the tactic of playing two spinners and two quicks was pretty successful. Stuey MacGill got eight wickets over the two innings; Warnie got five. Glenn McGrath got four and we won by nine wickets.

A first-up win and my first Test wicket were just icing on the cake for me. It was hard to believe I'd finally made it to my dream. Later that summer, we played the VB one-day series against Pakistan and the West Indies. I did okay—my bowling was all right but, as I've said, to come in at seven and try to slog was definitely not one of my strengths.

In the second of three finals we were cruising when, in the second-last ball of my fourth over, I felt my side go. Darren Lehmann had to finish the over for me. I was gutted. I had strained my side and that put me out of the squad for the tour of New Zealand. Playing the Kiwis would have been the perfect place to try to consolidate my place in the Test team. I had only played one Test and I was on the treatment table once more.

Brad Hodge from Victoria came in and did well, so I thought I'd missed the boat again. It was frustrating and, to make it worse, this was an Ashes year. I remember Ricky saying I was really close to getting picked for the squad and he was keen to have me there, but unfortunately it just didn't work out that way. I did get picked in the one-day squad to go over to England, but it wasn't much of a consolation. I was missing a big opportunity and, until that injury, had been in a good position to make the most of it.

On the way over to England we stopped in France and visited the battlefields of the Somme. That was the first 'in-your-face' reality check I had about what it meant to be Australian. To see all these headstones of young Aussies—18 or 19, a lot younger than me (I was 24)—lined up, and when they didn't know who the soldier was the inscription would just say *Known unto God*. It was very eerie and very powerful to think of the sacrifice they made, and we didn't even know their names.

John Buchanan arranged it; he had done something similar in 2001 when he took the team to Gallipoli on their way over. I know how big Gallipoli is for Australia and New Zealand because of Anzac Day, but I never fully understood what it was all about until I started reading up on the history of it. I wasn't on the Gallipoli visit, of course, but going to the battlefields of the Somme was continuing that tradition and reminding us that our fairly friendly rivalry with the Poms started with a dark page in our history. It was supposed to inspire us, and it did, I suppose; but more significantly it made me think about the whole thing and now I'm reading up on it, because I love history.

Ironically, I suppose, we were playing the first one-dayer of the NatWest Challenge series against England in Leeds on 7 July when the London bombs went off, killing 52 civilians and the four suicide bombers. The first three explosions went off in the London Underground during the morning rush hour just before nine o'clock, and the other one went off on a bus about an hour later. Reports were coming through while we were getting ready for the game and then all day after that.

Few of us had ever experienced anything like this and we were shocked and a bit scared, to be honest, out there in the middle wondering what the hell was happening. There were a lot of radios in the crowd, so the news was buzzing all around us. In the context of all those deaths, this seems petty in hindsight but we had a very difficult decision to make. We were due to travel back to London by bus that night and there was a big discussion about whether we should go or not. All the players came together with our security officer, the coaching and support staff, and we decided what we should do. It was the general consensus that the damage had been done and hopefully there wouldn't be any more.

It was times like this when you'd see Ricky's leadership come to the fore. He didn't speak for the players without getting their views first. He would make sure he got all our thoughts and then he would relay that to the security officer and the team manager. All the senior players said exactly what they thought, but in the end it was Ricky who conveyed that to the team management—he was the voice of the players.

Eventually it was decided pretty much unanimously that, even though London was hit, we were as safe there as we would be anywhere else. So we drove down and arrived at the Royal Garden Hotel in Kensington High Street, which is in the heart of the city, at the other end of Hyde Park from Buckingham Palace. It was eerie driving into the centre of London with police on every corner and almost no traffic, whereas normally it's heaving. It's really scary to see London at a standstill like that—*that's* when you know something serious has happened. The atmosphere was awful.

A couple of days later we played a game at the Oval and

some people couldn't get to the ground because the Tube stations were still closed. It wasn't a good time to be in England. I remember being driven in the team coach to the ground and seeing a big red bus pull up next to us. You felt like diving under the seat because of what had happened a couple of days earlier. It flashed through your mind: imagine what it did to people who were there when it went off.

The best answer to terrorism is to keep doing what you're doing—otherwise they have won. Our team security was tightened up, of course, and basically we were confined to barracks and not allowed out. But we got on with our cricket, although I didn't do myself justice in the one-dayers. I bowled fairly well, but I didn't get much of an opportunity to bat, because most of our guys played really well and I wasn't needed. In any case, with two games to go I strained my quad, so I didn't play the last couple of games.

Instead, I went straight into the Hampshire team—purely to bat, at first, because I wasn't fit to bowl. My first game for Hampshire was a quarter-final against Surrey at the Oval in the Cheltenham and Gloucester Trophy one-day knock-out competition. They got 360 and I got 139 as we chased them down. Every time I go back it's one of the first things that people mention, especially the chairman, Rod Bransgrove. We are really good friends now—still enjoying the memory of that day, and where it took us.

That six weeks, my second spell at Hampshire, was a special time for me because I continued to see substantial development in my game. I batted well and, once I had recovered, I bowled well too. It was also the first time for ages that I got through injury-free and my body got used to bowling again. That was the exciting part about it: we jammed a lot of cricket into the time I was there and I got through it all really well. Looking back, I now realise what was making the difference—we were playing just about every single day, so much so that I didn't have time to go to the gym. That's what saved me from more injuries.

Also Andy Bichel was the other overseas player there then, so I spent a lot of time with him. He didn't have his family with him for his short stint so we spent all day, every day chilling out and talking; we'd have lunch (often at Pizza Express—I was addicted) or dinner, and go to a couple of pubs and just hang out. That was a special time.

We played at Lord's in the final against Warwickshire; it was sold out and the majority of the crowd was cheering for us. Warwickshire was a pretty good side, with a few England internationals like Ashley Giles, Ian Bell and Nick Knight. I didn't really get many runs—only 25—but Sean Ervine, the Zimbabwe international, got 104 and we won by 18 runs (16 of them scored by Andy Bichel). I also got three wickets, including Ian Bell's, so all in all it was a good day at the office.

In fact, it was a phenomenal experience. It was so special for all our guys because Hampshire hadn't won anything for about 15 years. And for it to happen at Lord's, it was amazing. I didn't think that I would play at Lord's in front of a sold-out crowd predominantly cheering for my team ever again, so I relished every moment of it.

All this time the Test series was going on and it was such an intriguing series that, whenever I got an opportunity to watch, I did. Towards the end of the series, because of the amazing stuff Freddie Flintoff was doing as an all-rounder and because I was doing well for Hampshire, there started to be some whispers in the local press that I might get called up for the final Test. Now there's never any mileage to be got from having such thoughts in your mind. You know it's just speculation on the press's part and wishful thinking on your own; but if you have a passion for the game, you can't help imagining yourself striding out at the Oval to help win the Ashes for Australia.

To add fuel to the fire, there were reports that John Buchanan had said there was a chance they might call me up. I had also messaged Glenn McGrath to see how he was going, because he had an ankle injury and the last message I got from him was 'I'll see you soon'. You try hard not to get your hopes up, but I was match fit and confident. In the end I got a call from John Buchanan, who apologised and said it was just a media beat-up—my services were not required. But one good thing to come out of this was that Freddie showed what a big difference a world-class all-rounder can make to a team.

Freddie took four or five wickets just about every time he bowled, which was often, and at serious speeds up around 145 kilometres an hour. Each time he got the ball he looked like he was going to get a wicket. Then, when he batted, he went out and took on the Aussies. Whether it was Warnie or McGrath, he took them on and more often than not he'd take them down. Even if he got 60 or 70, it would be at a run a ball and he got a century in one innings. He was skilful, aggressive and brave, and gave us Aussies a taste of our own medicine.

In the last Ashes series in England, as soon as Freddie came on to bowl, the crowd totally got behind the England team. The team relied on him, but so did the crowd, because he was so competitive and so good at what he did. He got the crowd going, every ball he bowled and every boundary he hit. For me I knew the tide was starting to turn. Our guys realised an all-rounder could play a big part. And it was likely to be Warne and McGrath's last Ashes tour, so the door was starting to open.

THE (NOT VERY) GREEN GRASS OF HOME

Every stadium in Australia has different characteristics and one benefit of playing Shield cricket is that you get to play on all the Test grounds. The Sydney Cricket Ground is easily my favourite, mainly because of the heritage, being out in the middle and looking back at the Members and Ladies stands . . . they are beautiful. I can remember seeing them in the background on TV when I was a young kid watching the World Series, with Richie Benaud commentating. It's an extraordinary feeling to play there and know that Bradman and all those other legends of the sport went before you. You really get that sense at the SCG.

The wicket itself is an absolute dream to bat on, even if it does turn compared to other wickets in Australia. It's not like an Indian wicket that dusts up totally; it turns but it's not an outrageous turn. From the bowling point of view, you can get the ball to reverse in Sydney because the wicket's quite abrasive. There's also a bit of pace and carry at times as well. So it's got something for everyone and you get out what you put in.

The Gabba is very different to any wicket in the world now. At its best, it's fast, very bouncy and, due to the humidity up in Brisbane, the ball swings a lot more than it does anywhere else in Australia and it can seam quite a bit as well. So you've often got three things working for the bowler there: swing, seam and bounce. Ironically though, the Gabba is probably my least successful ground in Australia. For whatever reason, I haven't done that well there. Also the heat is a factor and with the humidity it can get pretty stifling at times, especially if you're out there toiling away for not much reward.

The MCG is a different wicket again: a lot of the time it is quite low and slow and there's not much bounce there at all. It can be very hard to score. On the bowling side of the ledger, it's hard to get a bouncer up over the batsman's head, but the ball does reverse swing. Even in the Boxing Day Test in 2009, the ball reversed in about ten overs. It doesn't really turn much, but Warnie had a lot of success at the MCG, so I suppose it depends on who's turning it. Either way, the stadium is the most fantastic place to play and I've had my moments there too. Like the SCG, the heritage is there for you to see. The history is amazing and, again, to see all those names on the honours board is just unbelievable.

The WACA is a different story again. When I first played in Perth, the wicket was faster and bouncier than the Gabba, but the ball didn't seam or swing much because the Fremantle Doctor would take the moisture out of the air and there would be too much of a breeze anyway. The wicket used to be flat and dry, but fast. For whatever reason, over the last five years it's slowed down and lost some bounce. Even when it did bounce, it was like a low tennis-ball bounce. However, it was a very good wicket during the 2010 Ashes.

The WACA used to be a favourite ground to take touring teams and pound them with fast bowling, but not quite so much now. It does bounce a lot more than in India or even at the SCG but, funnily enough, the nets are still like how the wicket used to be, really fast and bouncy. If you go to the nets and forget that, it's a wake-up call because, before you know it, the ball hits your gloves when you think it's going to hit the middle of your bat.

Hobart has changed over time but it's probably more like the MCG now, for the simple reason that they've had the former assistant groundsman from the MCG working there. It's not quite as slow as the MCG but the ball does reverse there very quickly. It's a bit better to bat there too because the ball comes onto the bat a little quicker. Bellerive is one of my favourite grounds, and why not? When I played for Tassie, I scored quite a few runs there. Now that they've installed floodlights, they can play day–night matches. Great idea in theory but, jeez, it can get cold at night down there.

Adelaide is one of the better grounds to bat on. It's a really true wicket, it has a nice pace—not super fast—and the square boundaries are really close, so it's easier to score fairly quickly. It does turn—it's a little bit like the SCG in that respect. The ball definitely does reverse there too, so there's enough in it for the quicks. But on the first three

DRINKS BREAK 5

days of a Test it's one of the best wickets in the world to bat on. It's also a really beautiful ground, particularly now that they've knocked all the western side down to improve the facilities and increase seating. I love the new stand and it's one of the few grounds, along with the WACA and Bellerive, that still has a grass hill under the scoreboard.

I played one game out at the former Olympic Stadium at Homebush in Sydney. I think, because it's basically a footy field, the grass structure is a lot different—perfect if you're wearing football studs but, without them, it's like running on glass and you slip over all the time. I played a few games at the Docklands Stadium in Melbourne and that is exactly the same, if not worse. That said, the drop-in wickets there were very good. In fact, drop-ins usually are good, but occasionally they get it wrong and the ball just rolls along the ground. The ones I played on at Docklands Stadium were really fast true wickets, like the Gabba, so when they get it right—especially for a one-day game—it's perfect.

I've also played in Cairns; the wicket block and everything is very similar to the Gabba, so it's fast and bouncy. Darwin, when I played there for an Australia A series, had a drop-in wicket which was like the MCG's drop-in wicket—a bit slower, so it's harder to get out once you've got settled.

But if you think Australian wickets vary, it's nothing compared to what you face when you go overseas.

CHAPTER 8 **TESTING TIMES**

In September 2005, straight after Hampshire, I went to Pakistan with the Australia A team. Pakistan seemed a bit less crowded than India, at least when we were in Islamabad. That's where all the government officials are based and we were very well looked after, visiting a few of the embassies.

Islamabad felt very safe; there were also a lot fewer cars on the road for a capital city, compared to India, which is generally teeming. The people were lovely. I got to know a few of the hierarchy in Pakistani cricket and found it very interesting getting their views on the world and how they saw September 11—a different point of view, which opened my eyes.

Then we went to Lahore, to play three one-dayers over five days. The atmosphere in Lahore was a lot more intense, with a lot more traffic. Despite what had happened in London, this was the first time I felt unsafe on tour, certainly compared to how I felt in Islamabad. It turned out I had good reason to—two bombs went off; one fairly close to the hotel and the other about 40 kilometres away. We were all petrified. It was the most scared I'd been on a tour. I think we all wondered if we were going to make it out of Pakistan unscathed.

We really didn't want to stay; we didn't want to play the

game, we just wanted to get out. But England were due to come there in November and it would be the first time one of the big cricketing nations had played there for a while, so there was a lot of political pressure to keep us there. We felt like we were pawns in a game, to make sure that the England series went ahead for Pakistan. The Australian team management would have been under huge amounts of pressure to stay and play the matches.

Most, if not all, of the players were saying they wanted to leave. Mike Hussey was captain of the team and he was the one who passed on the message: just get us out of here. The situation seemed to be out of control and we didn't know how good the security was that we had at that time. Even so, in the end the decision was made for us—we were going to stay and play the three games.

Four years later, when I saw the footage of the attack on the Sri Lankan team bus, I realised the landscape had changed. Previously, people had said that cricketers were safe because everyone in Pakistan loves their cricket so much that they wouldn't do anything to reduce the chances of other countries coming to play there. The Sri Lanka attack put paid to that myth.

As it turned out, the authorities cleared the roads for us to make sure we got there safely, and the whole ground was surrounded by police. They even moved the game to a bigger stadium so as to be able to patrol it better.

Funnily enough, after going through that experience, I don't worry about security anymore. You could be anywhere in the world but if you're in the wrong place at the wrong time, that's just how it's meant to be. Obviously in Pakistan it's slightly different because of the volatility, but in India, for example, I don't feel worried at all. I love what I do, and that includes travelling to India and playing the Indian Premier League.

Much later, before I went to play the IPL for the second

time in India, the recommendation was that Aussies avoid going there because one of the big terrorist groups had targeted the Champions Trophy, the hockey, the IPL and the Commonwealth Games. But I talked to one of our owners and he said the security was brilliant, that we had a whole unit of commandos guarding us, as well as three of the South African security officers that we had in the first IPL. During the inaugural IPL, bombs went off in the old section of Jaipur, our home city, and two or three of our baggage guy's friends were killed. Since then our security had been bumped up. The South African guys were excellent and I knew if we had them on board we would be very well looked after.

Look at the Delhi Commonwealth Games—there were no security problems. It's too easy for political groups to say we're going to attack here and blow up such and such. And you can't live your life in fear of what might happen otherwise you might never leave your house.

Getting back to cricket, I bowled really well throughout the series in Pakistan and was probably one of the better bowlers in that tour, with four wickets in one match. Mitchell Johnson, Stuart Clark, Nathan Bracken and I did most of the heavy lifting, and I was getting the ball to reverse more than most. My batting was a bit up and down—two 1s in the first game alongside a 50 and a 44; so not great, but not terrible either.

When we were in Islamabad the squads were announced for the ICC Super Series that was to be held in Australia in October; it was billed as the Best Team in the World (that was us) playing against a team of the World's Best Players. Trevor Hohns, the Chairman of Selectors, told me I was in both the one-dayer and the Test squads—and they were looking for me to play in the Test because they wanted an all-rounder in there.

When we arrived back in Australia, the one-dayers against the ICC XI were on first and I picked up where I knew I was at with my game. I got three wickets in the first game and four in the third; in the third game I also scored 66 and contributed to a partnership of 145 with Mike Hussey that got us out of trouble. We won all three games.

I got two Man of the Match awards, which was hard to believe, considering we were playing against the likes of Brian Lara, Chris Gayle, Virender Sehwag, Rahul Dravid, Jacques Kallis, Shaun Pollock and Daniel Vettori and, of course, Freddie Flintoff. That was when I knew I was getting closer to where I wanted to be—on the world stage and performing against the best players in the world.

Meanwhile I played in the big Test match, but my long-form game was still developing. I didn't really bowl that well and I didn't get many runs. Muralitharan got me out lbw for 24 in the first innings and Freddie got me out for ten in the other. That was the first time I'd faced Freddie in a proper game. He's a big man and he bowls good pace, so you've got to keep your wits about you. He's always going to go hard, so it's pretty daunting.

Freddie doesn't say much on the pitch but he definitely tests your mentality. He's very competitive and aggressive, so you know every ball he's trying to either get you out or do some damage to you. On the other hand, he's a really class act. When he went up and commiserated with Brett Lee at the end of the Edgbaston Test in 2005, when Australia lost by two runs and the England team couldn't believe they had won in an absolute nail-biter—to even think about an opponent at such a time is the mark of a truly decent person.

You could tell how competitive and aggressive he was on the field, but I'd always heard what a nice bloke he was off the pitch. After that Test match against the World XI, which we won, I had a couple of drinks with him and guess what. It's true!

This was shaping up to be my big summer. I'd been dreaming of an opportunity like this—to make my mark and then consolidate my place in the Test side. And for all the doubters—and that included myself at times—it was a chance to show what I could do. Even better, my next Test match was against a struggling West Indies side at the Gabba, in front of my home crowd.

Mum and Dad were there, so it was a pretty special time. I didn't bowl at all in the first innings; but I came on at first change in the second and got Chris Gayle out, just when he looked like he might be settling in to do some damage. The Windies were chasing 508 and, when he went, they were gone for all money.

But my celebrations were short-lived. I was fielding out at mid-on when I ran and dived to stop a ball. The Gabba is sand-based so, when I put my arm out and tried to slide, it just dug in. My shoulder didn't pop out, but it made an awful noise as my whole body weight went through the joint. It was a grinding, crunching sort of noise so I knew I was in trouble and, as the other blokes ran up to me, I said, 'I'm gone.'

I didn't want to move it, because I knew it would just fall out. A surgeon who was at the ground came over and said I should try to move my shoulder to see where I was at. But it just kept clunking and grinding. It was awful; so I went and got a scan, and it showed I had a fair bit of damage and I needed surgery.

I flew down to Melbourne the next day and saw Greg Hoy, a Melbourne-based orthopaedic surgeon who had fixed Warnie's shoulder and spinning finger. I had the operation done immediately and started the rehab. I was very lucky that it was my left shoulder—if it had been the right one, I would have been out for at least 12 months, because I wouldn't have been able to bowl or throw. Greg did a wonderful job and I was back playing within two months, which was phenomenal.

It was at this juncture that Andrew Symonds came back into the team for the next three Tests against the West Indies, and then the three-Test series against South Africa. I was sitting at home watching this and thinking, 'Oh no, I've missed another opportunity and I might not get another one.'

Australia won both series and Roy did okay. He got a 50 in quick time in the Boxing Day Test and that was one of the few times in my life I've found it hard to watch cricket. The more I watched it, the more I thought, 'I've missed this opportunity—why does this have to happen now?' But in the end you just have to get over it and play the hand that you're dealt.

On the upside, within ten weeks I got picked to go to South Africa and played some one-dayers there. I bowled pretty well in this series and I stayed away from diving in the field. I used to throw myself around everywhere before I did in my shoulder but, knowing what an impact it had on a big opportunity in my career, I'm a lot more careful nowadays.

WICKETS OF THE WORLD

If you think wickets and grounds in Australia vary, then wait till you see what you get overseas. We talk about English wickets or Indian wickets but, of course, just like here there is immense variation between one place and another within those countries. New Zealand isn't so different—it reminds me of Hobart—and the wickets there are definitely more bowling friendly.

But it's very different in India, where you get a couple of distinctly different surfaces. The red soil wickets are normally the big turning wickets, like in Mumbai. Although some have pace and bounce, mostly they are slow and low—lower and, especially, slower even than the MCG—but the ball can turn massively on them, so they are far from easy to bat on. Usually, within half a day there are big, deep footmarks where the bowlers' spikes have ripped the soil out and balls just explode out of nowhere. That's probably one of the biggest challenges Aussie players face, because you never see that kind of wicket until you go over there.

That said, I enjoy it because it's such a big challenge. I don't enjoy it as much as Andrew Symonds, who smacked the spinners everywhere; or Matthew Hayden and Adam Gilchrist, who would really take them down. But going over there and facing Harbhajan Singh on those turning wickets is different from anything you'll get in Australia.

The other type of wicket in India is on a kind of light clay, and those can be good wickets to play on. I'm thinking of grounds such as Bangalore and Mohali, which are along the same sort of lines as Adelaide, the truest batting wicket in Australia. The ball comes through pretty quickly and reliably, although it does reverse and it does turn. So those grounds are a bit more like what we are used to in Australia.

But the biggest challenge in India is how well-suited their players are to those conditions. We all know they've got very skilful spinners and that's what we've struggled with over the years; but their quicks are very good at getting the ball to reverse early in the match—often after only ten overs—and that's a huge weapon because the bowler's action is the same but it is only after they release the ball that you can pick which way it's going to move and adjust accordingly.

Pakistani wickets are quite similar to Indian ones, although I haven't played at the major grounds. But they do have red dust wickets there, and they too can be lower and slower than we are used to. As far as Sri Lanka goes, before the 2011 World Cup I had only previously played there in an Under-19 World Cup in January 2000. They take a bit of getting used to.

English wickets vary a lot. The Oval, for example, is more like the Gabba at its best (though not like in the 2010 Ashes Test). It's fast, bouncy and doesn't really swing much with a brand-new ball, certainly not compared with somewhere like Headingley. The Oval is probably the closest to Australian conditions that you'll get in England, both in terms of bowling and batting.

The Lord's wicket is quite Australian-like with pace and bounce, but the slope brings in an extra dimension. It's a big gradient that goes through the whole ground, and across the wicket block. Everything is on that slope, so the batsmen and bowlers can feel like they are playing on the side of a slight hill. The first time I got there I couldn't believe how big the slope was. The same ball can either run away down the hill or hold up. It's different from anything else you are used to. In 2010, playing against Pakistan, the ball was swinging and seaming; and occasionally it would do something else up and down the hill. They were just about the hardest conditions I've ever batted in because of that added dimension.

Strangely, the slope doesn't affect your bowling as much; although you definitely feel like your feet are landing at different angles when you're running in to bowl and it takes a few balls to adjust. If you're bowling from the Pavilion end, down towards the Nursery end with its space-age looking media centre, it feels like everything is pushing you down the hill.

But that's only one of the amazing things about Lord's. It's a fabulous stadium and the Pavilion, where the dressing rooms are, is just the most beautiful building. To look back at that from the ground is simply breath-taking. In 1989, the first time I ever watched the Ashes on TV, it was a Lord's Test and I remember seeing that building and the dressing-room balconies, where the players sit to watch the game.

Being there is unbelievable. It's the home of cricket, after all. It's a sports arena, all right, but it has a totally different feel to any other. You can sense the history when you walk down the Long Room and have the members all there standing up and clapping. And yes, I've got my name up on the honour board now—but not for batting, and not for an Ashes Test. That's an ambition I still have to fulfil.

At Headingley, the home of Yorkshire cricket up in Leeds, the wicket is pretty normal, just a standard wicket. It can seam a bit more, but what stands out is that the overhead conditions dramatically change the way the wicket plays. If the sun's out and there's not a cloud in the sky, the ball goes through beautifully—there's no real swing and it doesn't seam. But if there's cloud cover, the ball starts to really swing and seam. I'm not sure about the science of seaming. All I know for sure is that, when the clouds come over, the Headingley wicket changes significantly and the ball behaves differently. That can happen a lot in England and it's very different from anywhere in Australia.

I haven't played that much at Old Trafford, Lancashire's ground in Manchester, but I do know the sun sets at one end and, if you're batting at the Brian Statham end, it can be right in your eyes. However, there's a major redevelopment of the ground under way and that's supposed to include a reorientation of the wickets to north–south. They're aiming to be ready for the Ashes series in 2013 and I can see why they want to do it—there is such a glare that it is hard to see the ball coming out of the bowler's hand.

Old Trafford is very near Manchester United's stadium and it makes it obvious how much bigger football is than cricket in England. It's chalk and cheese, really. We watched a Manchester United game in 2009 and the facilities there are out of this world—everything to do with the ground is all brand new and high tech, whereas at the cricket ground it was all a bit run down. You see the extreme contrast when they are so close to each other, although the gap won't be so big when the redevelopment is completed.

Edgbaston in Birmingham is a quirky ground. Running in to bowl, you've got to jump into a massive hill to get up to the crease. It's like they have top-dressed and re-laid the wickets, but haven't levelled it out around the pitch; so the wicket keeps getting higher and you have to step up to get onto it. It takes a bit of getting used to. Otherwise the wicket there is a little slow and there's not heaps of bounce. That alone makes it different from any Aussie wickets.

The West Indies were very different from what I always imagined. All you see on TV is the best parts of the Caribbean, with everyone having fun on the beaches and having a big party at the cricket ground. But one thing that struck me there was just how poor the countries are—apart from Barbados where we played, which had a lot of British and American money coming in to develop it. Even so, there and elsewhere the cricket facilities at the grounds could be quite ordinary and the training facilities in the West Indies often aren't too great.

That said, it's one of the most enjoyable and relaxing places to go and tour because everyone seems to be so chilled out. I suppose it's island life—they never seem to get annoyed. After a week or so you realise there's no point in getting worked up if, say, something you've planned looks like it's not going to happen. Eventually you realise it's going to happen in due course and they don't care anyway—so the trick is to go with the flow. These big Afro-Caribbean guys and girls are lovely people, and they love their cricket. It's something that brings all their countries together.

The atmosphere in the grounds is legendary, although the World Cup I played in during 2007 didn't have great attendance due to the high price of tickets. But the crowds at the Twenty20s I played in 2010 were unbelievable. It was just a huge party, with people drinking their rum punches and dancing away. It was something else!

They often have a disco going in the crowd, but it stops as soon as you start your run-up. Then, when the ball goes dead, the music starts again. So it's a bit wild but, at the same time, they're mindful that there's a game going on out there. At the Twenty20 World Cup, well-known reggae artists came in and staged concerts after the games, so people would go to watch the cricket and then stay on for the music. One game we got to see them while we were doing our post-match warm-down. Watching the crowd dance and generally go crazy was entertaining in itself.

South African grounds are probably as close as you'll get to Australian conditions, including the climate. In Durban it's like Brisbane, very hot and humid, but in Johannesburg it's a little different because it's at altitude and the wicket's a bit like the WACA was when it was super fast and bouncy. The ball swings, but it goes through the air quicker. When you're batting, it definitely travels a bit further than you expect. Running in to bowl is a lot harder and at times we get breathless because of the altitude.

Cape Town is all over the shop, the conditions change so much. I remember we played a one-dayer there and we were told that the team that bats first in a day–night match always wins. We thought they were exaggerating—surely it couldn't be that predictable. After we lost the toss they batted and made 280 on a beautiful batting wicket. Then the sun went down, the lights came on and, all of a sudden, the wicket turned into a seaming, swinging minefield. I think we were 4 for 0 at one stage—it was a huge contrast. So Cape Town goes from one extreme to another, but overall the wicket is a bit slower and less bouncy than Jo'burg or Durban.

The climate and the landscape in South Africa is very similar to Australia in some ways and Cape Town is one of the most beautiful cities in the world. It's a shame about the crime in Jo'burg and throughout South Africa because it's such a wonderful country with all those fantastic wild animals. We did a couple of safaris in game parks and saw elephants and rhinos. You feel very privileged.

The best safari I did was when we had a tournament in Kenya in 2003–04 and played some games against Pakistan and Kenya. When we had a few days off, we went to a luxury safari resort in the Masai

Mara. We arrived in this tiny, dodgy aeroplane onto this little runway, and the first thing we saw were two lions—one was trying to mate with the other—and that was just driving into the resort. It was the most amazing thing I've ever seen.

We saw zebras and wildebeests and the next day we went out and, while we didn't actually see a kill, we saw the hierarchy of life in the wild. Some lions were feeding on a kill and hyenas were waiting for them to finish. Vultures hung around for their turn and then a couple of little jackals came in—all that happened in just over an hour or so.

To see the food chain illustrated right in front of us, in the animals' natural environment, was pretty special. Meanwhile, at the risk of drawing too long a bow, there's a food chain and a bit of the law of the jungle in all sport—and cricket is no exception.

DESTINY: Christmas Day, 1983, aged two and a half. Note the cricket set—is this where it all started?

JUST A GAME: With cousin Ben (left) at our Brunswick Heads holiday home in January 1988, aged six and a half.

UP FOR IT: Eight years old in 1989—all set up for my first day at the local cricket club in Ipswich.

ON THE ROAD: Me and Dad about to leave for the Ipswich Schoolboys Under-11s North Queensland Cricket Tour in 1992.

TEAM PLAYER: My first Ipswich representative team—the schoolboys in the 1991 McCasker Trophy. I'm far left in the middle row.

YOUNG GUNS: The Youth World Cup squad for Sri Lanka, 2000, with me on the back left and a few now familiar faces, including Paul Rofe, Andrew MacDonald, Mitch Johnson, Shaun Marsh, Nathan Hauritz, Michael Clarke and Rod Marsh.

DEBUT: Bowling in my first one-day match for Australia in South Africa in 2002.

INSPIRED: A memorable visit to the First World War battlefields of France in 2005, with Mike Hussey, Brett Lee and Andrew Symonds.

BREAKDOWN: Glenn McGrath, Brett Lee and Simon Katich are the first to learn I've badly injured my shoulder playing the West Indies in Brisbane in November 2005, the year I broke into the Test team.

HARD YARDS: Pacing ourselves on a trek through Beerwah State Forest during the notorious boot camp in 2006.

FLYING: Giving my all in the ICC Champions Trophy against England in Jaipur in 2006.

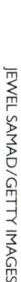

MORAL SUPPORT: Glenn McGrath has a quiet word as I leave the field injured during the Super Eight match against Bangladesh during the 2007 ICC World Cup in the West Indies.

CELEBRATE GOOD TIMES: Enjoying our win at the ICC World Cup in the West Indies in April 2007.

BODY BLOW: Injured again, this time against Sri Lanka in the Twenty20 Cup Super Eights in South Africa in September 2007.

HEATSTRUCK: David Hussey shades me with a towel on my way to my first one-day international century against the West Indies in June 2008.

CHAPTER 9 **OPENINGS**

Getting back to 2006, although I'd been in and out of the Test and one-day sides over the years, I'd never actually been dropped from the one-day squad. Since the first time I got picked, if I was fit I was named in the squad, but across my career, of course, that's been a big 'if'.

The first time I felt like I got dropped from the Test team (not through injury) was after we played the one-dayers in South Africa, when I had come back from my shoulder reconstruction. I had bowled pretty well, but I didn't get much opportunity with the bat and there were three Tests straight after that. The Test team was pretty settled, so it was between me and Andrew Symonds for the all-rounder role and I hadn't played a lot of cricket.

Roy, on the other hand, had played in the Test side throughout the summer, but hadn't really scored many runs. It was head to head with him to get in to the Test squad and I missed out, so that was the first time in my career when I felt I was dropped. It was a very different feeling to getting an injury, which is an unfortunate fact you just have to deal with. Getting dropped means someone doesn't think you are as good as another player, and that's harder to accept. It feels less like a matter of fact and more a matter of opinion but I knew I hadn't had enough good performances leading up to it. Even so, it still stung.

Instead of playing in South Africa I was going back to domestic cricket, where Queensland were about to play in the Pura Cup final. As soon as I knew that I thought, well, I'm going to go back and score runs. The final was against Victoria at the Gabba and I set my mind to showing the national selectors what they had missed.

I'd batted at three for Tasmania, but when I moved up to Queensland I batted at four behind Martin Love. He was a phenomenal player and there's no doubt that in any other era he would have played many games for Australia. He scored a lot of runs; he was a good technician and he timed the ball so easily—like Damien Martyn. No matter who was bowling, Martin never looked like he was being rushed.

Martin's last Test for Australia was against Bangladesh up in Cairns, where he got 100. I think he was misunderstood because he was very quiet. He's a country bloke and can be a bit shy around people to begin with, and some folk misread that as being stand-offish. But once he gets comfortable in an environment, he's a really witty guy with a good sense of humour. He's also very intelligent and a trained physiotherapist, but I think in the Australian set-up he came across the wrong way, as if he wasn't a team player or something, which wasn't true. Whatever the reason, he didn't get the chances he probably deserved and that was sad because he was hugely talented.

Anyway, when we got to the Pura Cup final, the wicket was probably the flattest Gabba wicket that I've ever played on. We bowled Victoria out for around 300 in the first innings, which was a great result because the wicket was so good for batting. Then we got 5 for 900—yes, 900! Jimmy Maher got 223, Clinton Perren got 179, Martin Love got 169; I got 201 not out and then strained my calf right at the end of the innings.

It felt great to score those runs. Meanwhile, Roy didn't score too well in the three-Test series and he certainly didn't have the impact he would have in the future. So everything had gone to plan, except I had another injury.

Thanks to that, I missed the one-day series in Bangladesh in April 2006, although I was told it wasn't a bad one to miss: the temperatures were in the mid-40s, the hotels were very basic, and they had to drive an hour and a half each day to the ground, where the facilities were less than world class. But I'd still rather have been there, and having played there since, it wasn't so bad—although it was really hot.

The domestic season was over and I was injured, so all I could do was try to get my calf right. When we were younger, Mum and Dad had a holiday house near Byron Bay—just a little shack a few minutes' walk to the water—and we'd always gone down there whenever we had the chance, like on school holidays. I've always loved the beach and so I moved down to the Gold Coast. It was just me—I was single, I wanted to find a way to escape and enjoy my life away from cricket, which was still my great passion; but it seemed that, with all these injuries, maybe cricket didn't love me as much as I loved it. I needed something else in my life, just in case.

At first I tried to learn to surf, which took quite a while (and is still a big work in progress). But it was round about then that I thought, Hey, I love music, and I learned to play the guitar when I was about seven, so why not have a go at that? Mum and Dad thought it was a good idea, to broaden my horizons. I was okay at it as a kid, but then I got to a stage when playing guitar wasn't the cool thing to do—so when I was ten or 11, I remember saying to Mum that the one guitar lesson I had a week was taking time out from playing sport. So I let it go.

Here I was at 24, picking it up again; but I had to pretty much start from scratch. Yet it was something I really wanted to do and, like everything else in my life, I worked very hard at it. For the next two months all I did was train, try to learn how to surf and re-learn how to play the guitar. It was a real change of direction in my life—everything up until then had been put on the back burner so I could totally concentrate on my cricket. But I'd reached a stage where I realised that I had to pull back a little bit; I had to have more in my life; I had to be less intense about my cricket which, until that point, had been all about winning and losing, being picked for a team or not, being fit or injured.

I rarely sat back and thought how lucky I was to be able to travel around the world, seeing places some people never see, meeting people that everyone else only reads about, doing what I wanted to do more than anything in the world and getting paid for it. It was like a light had been switched on—I could still be passionate about cricket, but I could have other things in my life too. In this case, it was music.

I was just learning pop songs to begin with; but the more I got into it, my taste in music totally changed. I started getting into more rock 'n' roll and the old stuff. Funnily enough, when I was in Hobart, David Saker would always take the piss out of me for listening to pop—he'd say there was no music in it, no guitars. I wouldn't take him seriously, because he was a real big Rolling Stones fan, but he was right. The stuff I was listening to then was just background music, really, and very different to what I'm into now.

I started reading books on musicians and buying guitar magazines to find out where the guitar culture all came from. I soaked up all I could—about the guitars these musicians used and the earlier musicians they had learned from. That took me back to the mid-sixties and the British Invasion, and that's when my musical tastes started to change drastically—by listening to guitar-band albums, and studying what the lead guitarist was doing or how a three-piece band worked.

Pretty soon I was totally engrossed in learning everything about it. I think the moment I first really got it was listening to 'Brown Sugar' by The Rolling Stones. The Keith Richards riff at the beginning is pretty simple, but it's an iconic piece of music and that's when I started to read more about the Stones and what their roots were, which then led me back to blues music.

I absolutely love blues and Eric Clapton is a hero of mine so I was trying to play this stuff and read more, to understand exactly how they played. Jason Krejza is another big Eric Clapton fan and an absolutely superb guitarist himself so he's been a big inspiration, especially when we're on tour together.

I suppose you could say I have a tendency to become obsessed; it's how I've always been. My parents instilled in me that, whatever you do, you want to give it everything you've got and do everything you can to be as good as you possibly can be. I'm sure my folks would draw the line at becoming obsessed, but it is a pattern in my life—it's how I'm built now. If I've got my mind set on something, I want to know everything about it.

That's generally a good thing, but there's no doubt I paid the price in my cricket. I was a perfectionist and I over-trained, and had to cut back. Before that, if I didn't hit the ball exactly how I wanted to, I'd keep hitting balls until I got it right, even if it took hours. It was the same with my bowling. Then I'd go into a game and I'd be fatigued without knowing it. The lay-off period changed my thinking. Previously my mindset was that if I hadn't achieved the things I wanted to in my cricket career then I was a failure in my life. That's a very tough way to live, with very high standards to live up to—but it gives you an idea of how intense and obsessed I was.

There's no doubt this affected my relationships. I had girlfriends, but most of them found the going too tough. I was too intense and I was relying on other people to provide the fun in my life. But you have to give as well as take, and that was one reason I was often single.

With new people that I don't know, I'm a bit shy. I'm comfortable talking to people, but if I don't know much about them or if I haven't got much in common with them I'm pretty quiet. That's how I've been all my life. With new crowds I was always standing in a corner—not hiding away, but definitely not the life and soul of the party. These days I'm a lot more confident and I know how to enjoy myself, but I'm still a bit shy with people until I get to know them more.

Another reason I was fairly quiet and reserved at this time was I always thought some people were thinking I shouldn't be out enjoying myself when I was injured. I didn't want to be seen to be living it up when the rest of the team were off doing battle in Bangladesh or wherever. I was frustrated with my injuries of course, and that's really all that mattered. So I had to find ways of being able to branch out and enjoy myself without looking as if I was having too much fun. Surfing and playing the guitar pretty much covered those bases—they're both solitary pursuits, and I could be as obsessed as I needed to be.

The next cricket tour on the horizon was a tri-series against the West Indies and India in Malaysia before the Champions Trophy in India. I was fit again, but I didn't know if I would be called back into the squad. In any case, before it was announced a couple of things happened to me that were life-changing.

Most importantly, I got to know my wife, Lee, for the first time. I met her initially through Brett Lee; Liz, who's now Brett's ex-wife, met Lee at a charity ball one weekend. She rang me and said, 'I met this girl who would be absolutely perfect for you.' Liz said she'd try to arrange for us all to go out for dinner. I discovered a few more details about Lee before we went: she was in the same edition of *Alpha* magazine as an article on me and my ex, Kym Johnson, with whom I had gone out for two or three years before it all fell apart. So I was able to read about Lee and the things that she liked. She was a *Fox Sports News* presenter, loved golf and tennis, and was a big fan of cricket. I thought, 'Wow that's brilliant—that might give me a foot in the door!'

It was 1 or 2 September 2006, just before I went away to Malaysia for the tournament against the West Indies and India, and then came back for a week before the Champions Trophy. I was living in the Gold Coast at this stage so I flew down to Sydney and stayed at Brett's place. We went out for dinner and I met Lee. I already knew she was very attractive, but the first time I met her I was struck by how unbelievably sweet she was. Often the really attractive girls you meet don't have a genuinely soft side. That was what drew me in—how sweet she was.

At the dinner Lee was very quiet—I found out later they had been to the races that day and she was feeling a bit crook, but she was persuaded to come along and see how she felt; she had no idea I was going to be there or what was going on.

I had a game plan based on my experience from a youngish age, which was not to seem over-keen, but I got her number through Brett and Liz. Throughout the Malaysian series I ended up getting to know Lee over the phone. She had only recently started at *Fox Sports News*, so she was on the early shift. But we were talking for three or four hours a night and her mum would come in and say, 'Lee, get off the phone—you've got to be up early in the morning.' She had the 5 to 11.30 am shift for the first two or three weeks, but she didn't get a lot of sleep thanks to my phone calls.

Just talking to her and getting to know her, we realised we had an enormous amount in common. All the things I loved in life, she enjoyed as well. In 2006 she was only 21 and I was 25. She was switched on and knew what she wanted, and was very driven as well. A couple of days after I got back from Malaysia she came up to the Gold Coast and spent some time with me. And it all gradually progressed from there.

But even before that, there was another controversial and potentially life-changing development that became pretty notorious in the Australian cricket team's recent history: boot camp.

CHAPTER 10 **BOOT CAMP**

The cricket 'boot camp' was the brainchild of Australian cricket team coach John Buchanan. He knew the Brisbane Broncos had done it when Wayne Bennett was coaching and they got some really good results out of it, particularly for bringing people together as a group. John thought it would be a good thing to do in the lead-up to the Ashes so he approached the company who ran the Broncos' 'Harden Up' camp.

We didn't know what to expect and I know quite a few people were trying to get out of it before they had any idea what it was going to be like. They suspected, rightly, it was going to be tough. Some guys in the team who were at the end of their careers—like Shane Warne, Glenn McGrath and Stuart MacGill—didn't want to risk getting injured doing this and missing their final Ashes series.

I wasn't too worried; I had got through a fair bit of cricket. I didn't want to get injured, either, but it sounded like something I might enjoy. Warnie was less impressed and was worried about whether he could take his smokes or if he would have to go cold turkey.

We met up initially at a big warehouse near Brisbane where we were given a backpack and told that there were only certain things, like underwear and a toothbrush, we could take with us for the four days of the course. They gave us khaki overalls and two T-shirts with a number on them; you weren't to be known by your name, just your number. That was about it. You couldn't take any food and you had to pack your sleeping bag in the backpack they provided.

The whole combined Test and one-day squad of about 25 players went, and quite a few of the support staff from Cricket Australia—our fielding coach, the team manager, our media manager, the assistant manager—more than 30 people, split up into groups of about six. Some of the group selections were quite funny; you were deliberately put with people you might not be too comfortable with.

Shane Warne was put in John Buchanan's group—which was always going to create some tension—and I was also in that group along with Jason Gillespie and Philip Pope, the British-born media manager, who was not an athletic specimen whatsoever. Every group had a team leader, usually an ex-SAS guy, and you could see they were testing you out every single moment they possibly could.

On day one we were driven to the middle of the Sunshine Coast and given a steep climb up a huge hill, with each group having to carry two big jerry cans full of water. We worked as a team, passing the cans around so as to share the load, and then we had to get down by a certain time or we wouldn't get our food. That's how the day kicked off and it gradually panned out to be the most intense test of endurance that any of us had ever done.

The next challenge was to navigate our way to a certain place. A car was waiting for us on a dirt track and we had to push it, so we took it in turns—someone would steer and everyone else had to push. It was a long haul and it took about an hour with no real food—just one sandwich.

Then we had to carry a stretcher loaded with four jerry cans full of water, about 20 kilograms each, something like 10 kilometres. By the end of the day we were in the middle of a pine forest and we rolled out our sleeping bags, all very tired. We were given a couple of cans of chunky soup that tasted suspiciously like dog food which we had to eat cold with some bread, and that was it. They said: 'Go to bed, get some sleep.'

In the middle of the night, I was so tired I was having this dream about war, imagining there were all these bombs going off. Then all of a sudden I woke up and there was a big flash and a huge bang, and I realised it was real. Another flash went off, followed by a powerful stun grenade. This was about midnight; we had to put our stuff together in a hurry and get out of there. We had no idea this was going to happen, of course, so a lot of guys had left their stuff in a mess and didn't know where it all was. It was pitch black—you couldn't see anything—but we had 10 minutes to find our kit, and get ready to go. We walked for probably an hour in darkness to get to our new 'camp ground', which was really just two deep tyre tracks—we all had to sleep in two long lines, head to toe.

I remember Warnie sitting there with his sleeping bag all done up, because it was pretty cold, with his cigarette in his mouth in the middle of the night. He said, tongue in cheek, 'One thing I've realised today—I'm soft. I'm as weak as piss. I've had enough and I wanna go home.' He had a point.

After that, the next couple of days were big treks through this wilderness area that had a story behind it. Back in 1937, a plane travelling between Brisbane and Sydney crashed into the Lamington Ranges, but an aerial search failed to spot any wreckage. Nine days later a grazier called Bernard O'Reilly set out on foot; he used his bush skills to find the crash site and, amazingly, two injured survivors. He then trekked back to civilisation to lead a rescue party to the plane. So we did a trek up to the crash site to get a sense of what an amazing achievement it was.

Another challenge was to navigate through a semi-cleared pine forest in the middle of the night. It was pitch black and all you had was a glow stick and a compass. Without getting too carried away, you got a sense of what it must be like for Army special forces, creeping around in the dark, trying to see without being seen. The discipline had a military flavour to it too.

If something went wrong—like a few guys left things behind when we all had to pack up in the middle of the night—you had to do a certain number of push-ups as a group. If someone let another guy down, everyone had to do the punishment together. Everyone in your group had to do it, so that made everyone accountable for each other. It might sound like a load of BS, but after a while we started to bond.

A very different aspect of boot camp—for some, more of a challenge than the physical stuff—was that you had to sit there and tell people about yourself. Eventually you started to get an insight into people's situations and I began to understand a bit more about where John Buchanan was coming from and an appreciation of what he was doing. You got to know people on a totally different level.

Forget the physical discomfort—the exhaustion, hunger and the thought that you had to sleep on hard ground—getting young blokes to open up and talk about themselves is taking them well out of their comfort zones. Just ask any young woman how often her husband or boyfriend talks about his feelings. Take it from me, if that bloke is a sportsman, it's even less easy.

One exercise took four or five hours one night. We all had to take each person in turn and say three positives and three negatives about them. Then they were read out to everybody, which was extremely confronting. The positives were okay, but the negatives were hard to take.

One for me was saying I was a whinger. That hurt a bit. I reckon I just say what people are thinking. Did that mean I was more of a whinger? My immediate reaction was to think, 'Maybe I just won't say anything at all then.' But how will problems get resolved? That night I went to bed a bit miffed: I didn't think I was like that. Another criticism was that I was too intense—I guess I have to pay that one.

It was a very confronting few days. We couldn't shower for the whole time we were there and, after all the physical things we were doing, we were absolutely reeking. On the third day we went into a creek just to get wet. The food rations that we got every morning were pretty slim: two sandwiches, a piece of fruit and a protein bar—and that was to do us for the whole day till dinner time. Brett Lee would smash his rations down right away and then try to get through the rest of the day; but when he'd get to lunch, he'd be hungry and he'd be looking at everyone else's food, hoping they'd give him something.

At dinner you'd get one piece of steak and a slice of bread. Some guys would trade off. Warnie didn't want steak as much as he wanted bread, so he would try to find someone to swap with. I was only eating small amounts compared to what I would normally eat, and it was very basic food. But in the end you survived—you were tired, but you had enough energy to keep going. It made me realise that you can get through a lot more than you think you can, and what we experienced was only a minor inconvenience compared with what soldiers have to put their bodies through.

One thing we did get out of it was that we became much closer as a group than we had ever been before. It was amazing. The guys who came in later as they weren't contracted yet missed out on this amazing experience that everyone else had been a part of. You had so much more respect for our fielding coach and team manager because, after the first day especially, they were hurting but they pushed on. Some were ex-athletes, if well past their prime, but even the players were exhausted. It created this respect within the group—we appreciated what they endured.

Everyone helped them out. There were times where we were walking up a hill on a trek and Philip Pope, our media manager, was 'gone'—he couldn't walk anymore. People were taking turns to get behind him and push him up the hill. That happened with different people in all the groups.

I was a bit sceptical of the boot camp idea to begin with, but by the time we finished I was a convert. Initially everyone was saying, 'I don't want to do this; this is ridiculous; why can't we eat?' In the end I loved it. The leaders of the groups, the SAS guys, gave you nothing at all. They were really hard on you. Anything happened, they knew and you had to do push-ups. You weren't allowed to call them anything but DS. There were no names, just numbers—no personalities or egos in it at all.

At the end of the course, when the group leaders were saying their goodbyes, their whole demeanour changed; now they were smiling and friendly. When this happened, our guys said, 'You've been absolute arseholes—you treated us like shit throughout this whole time and now you're trying to be our mates. No way!' But in the end we realised they were there to test what we were made of and we couldn't blame them for loving what they were doing. And if the idea was to build a team, it worked. Everyone understood we were in a team environment. We just had to look after our mates—we couldn't leave someone behind, because then our whole team would suffer.

Even Warnie tried to give it his best—as he always does—for the first day, at least. He didn't want to let his team down and he has amazing powers of concentration when he's got his mind set on something. But after the first day his knee gave him a bit of grief—or at least he said it did. It most probably did hurt, but it was also pretty smart of him too, because he didn't have to go on some of the treks that we went on. Whatever his excuse, he wanted to make sure he didn't injure himself, because it was very physically demanding and it was his farewell Test series. But he was always there at the night-time sessions, which were as tough mentally and emotionally as the days were physically.

And it could be fun. One day was like SWAT training. You had to work as a team in a warehouse full of different rooms. There were a couple of 'bad guys', who had paintball guns, and a couple of hostages. You had to simulate an attack to try to bring out the hostages. Warnie did all those sort of things. That was another test of working as a team because, if you only looked after yourself, you got shot. It was really interesting to see what soldiers might have to go through in combat. It was fun but also nerve-racking.

I was one of the baddies. I had a dummy pump-action shotgun with three cartridges of paint pellets, and I was just waiting for the attack. I knew I would get shot eventually, because I had a hostage behind me, but I was trying to take out as many as I could before I was taken down. You knew you weren't going to get hurt—you had paintball masks and other protection—but it was still a rush.

Apart from the trainers, each day the groups had a different leader. They would say, 'Okay, you're the leader and so and so's the second in charge.' Everyone had a go at being group leader for a day and then at being second in charge—some people are better at that than others. When I was leader, John Buchanan was my number two, but he was the one issuing orders. There were no negotiations—he's a forceful person, but in a nice way. He's a coach and he expects to be listened to. One of the things that exercise taught me is that leadership is as much about listening to other people as it is about telling them what to do.

And now that I'm vice-captain of the Australian team, I think that's something I can take back with me.

In fact, if someone suggested another boot camp for the squad, I'd say 'Bring it on'. It's an amazing way to get everyone together. It provides an unbelievable sense of unity within a team and I'd be there, boots and all.

BAT AND BALL

Having seen both sides of the batting and bowling divide, I have to say that batsmen get the best of it. For a start, being a batsman is not physically very hard at all—that's why batsmen can have such long careers. Okay, it's tough psychologically on batsmen because you only make one mistake and you're gone. You might not even make a mistake—just be unlucky. But if you have more good days than bad days, you can play for 15 years.

On the other hand, if you have a bad day as a bowler, you have to keep bowling because you have to do your share. If you're bowling crap, the crowd and the selectors get to watch you bowling crap over and over again. And you're still putting your body under the same physical stresses, only with no result. Whereas if you have a bad day with your batting, you face one ball and you're out. You can go and sit on the couch and that bad shot is forgotten after a couple of replays on the TV. It is so different.

Bowlers generally don't get much praise from the media. After bowling 30 overs on a hot day, they might only get two wickets and the sports writers won't even mention it. Also, they don't get big bat contracts and nowadays those are very lucrative for the top batsmen. Some guys are on well over $300,000 a year just to carry a certain brand of bat. Bat manufacturers aren't going to fall over themselves to sponsor a bowler who comes in at the end of matches and averages in single figures.

Bowlers don't have any choice about what brand of ball they use. In Australia it's only Kookaburra, so it's not as though they can get sponsorship from the manufacturer. Shoe sponsorship might get them $50,000, whereas a bat contract for the big guns can bring in ten times that. Glenn McGrath always used to joke, 'We do all the hard work, and the batters sit there and score a few runs and they get all these things that we don't!'

DRINKS BREAK 7

In days gone by, batsmen would put stickers from one brand of bat onto another one to fulfil their batting contract. Even when I started, the bats from certain companies weren't great at all. But there was a guy called Paul Bradbury, who was a really good batmaker in Perth, so the guys used to get his bats and put other people's stickers on them. Now no one in the Australian team uses a bat that isn't what it says on the tin. There is so much good wood and so many good batmakers—and so much extra scrutiny!

Like most batsmen, I am very particular about my bats—about their weight, balance and quality, and how the ball comes off them. When I started using Gunn & Moore bats, they weren't really what I liked: they had a very traditional English way of making bats. Bats are a lot bigger and better now compared to 15 years ago, but they're not that much heavier thanks to the techniques they now use.

Gunn & Moore at first struggled to get their heads around what I wanted. They made me a bigger bat all right, but it was really heavy. Then, once I went to Nottingham, where they make their bats, we sat down and they finally understood what I meant. I was able to give them an example of what I wanted and from then on they were able to make perfect bats for me.

Now they make some of the best bats in the world; that's the input that guys who are on these sponsorships have. It's all very well to take the money, but you still have to do the business on the field. So the players give the batmakers the feedback, and the bats get better and better for everyone. All the guys are very particular about their bats, because it does make a big difference. If you've got a good bat, you can mishit the ball and it still goes for six.

CHAPTER 11 **ANOTHER OPENING**

The short three-way contest in Malaysia in September 2006—involving ourselves, India and the West Indies—wasn't only unusual because of its location; it was the first time Cricket Australia had taken an extended squad overseas. I think there were something like 17 people on tour, although a few people came in and played a couple of games and then flew home. There was a real mixture of old and new players. Mark Cosgrove, I remember, played one game and he was gone. Matthew Hayden played, but that was the last time for a while. Cricket Australia were clearly trying out new players and different combinations, away from the glare of a major Test or one-day series. The most significant thing for me was that it was the first time I got to open the batting for Australia.

I had opened before—for Tasmania in my second year of first-class cricket—and I knew I was batting well, so I was delighted to get a real chance to bat in the top order. The downside was that I didn't have a great game plan in one-day cricket—I still didn't know exactly how to approach it.

In the long form, the openers are expected to take the shine off the new ball and deal with the opening bowlers while keeping the scoreboard ticking over. In the one-day game these days, you're expected to do all that *and* push the run rate up at the same time. That's what Matthew Hayden and Adam Gilchrist had been doing for years.

In my first game I was a little bit wild—I don't think I let a ball go and I hardly played a defensive shot. I was aggressive, and then some, and I made 79. It turned out to be perfect timing for me. Because Matthew hadn't had a great run in one-day cricket, they were looking at changing the order to fit everyone they wanted into the team. My bowling had continued to improve. It was very humid, but I wasn't really swinging the ball; I was just running in and trying to deliver a good length at pace. We won the final against the West Indies by 127 runs and, all in all, the Malaysian series was another big stepping stone for me.

We came back home for a week before heading to India for the Champions Trophy, which is a mini one-day World Cup involving, in 2006, the top six teams in the world plus two qualifiers from the next best four teams. It's the biggest one-day tournament after the World Cup, but Australia hadn't made it to the finals in four attempts, although we had got to the semi-finals the two previous times (in England and Sri Lanka).

In India, we had a tough group—India, England and the West Indies—and we didn't start well, losing to the West Indies in the first game. I was opening the batting with Adam Gilchrist and determined to make a good impression. Would you believe it, I went for a third-ball duck.

But I followed up with the scalps of three of England's top order, including Freddie Flintoff, in the next match. And then a 50 and a wicket in the match against India. Most importantly, we won both, and that got us into the semi-final against New Zealand, which we also won—despite another duck from me—and went on to face the West Indies in the final.

Apart from my bad start in the first match, the Champions Trophy worked out unbelievably well for me as I started playing a big part with the bat. I got two 50s and a few wickets. I felt I bowled really well throughout, especially against India and England and in the final against the West Indies. But, more than anything, the chance to open with Gilly was amazing.

The best thing about batting with someone who is aggressive, no matter the situation, is that it takes the pressure off you to score, so you can bat the way you would normally. If I'm batting with someone who doesn't take on the opposition, it means that I've got to take a few more risks myself. Batting with Gilly was absolutely brilliant. He took them down no matter what— these were some of the best bowlers in the world and he was just smacking them everywhere. Even if he only got 30 or 40, it was way quicker than a run a ball and he was always getting the team off to a good start.

He's a pretty chilled-out bloke and when you're batting with him, he's very relaxed and supportive, which is great. Some people say the wicket-keeper batsman has a slight advantage because he spends all day watching balls come flying down the pitch. But with Gilly it wouldn't have mattered if he'd seen one or one thousand balls—his instincts were so sharp and his skill level so high. He just went out there, cleared his mind and backed himself. Where Gilly was so good was that he was able to put pressure on bowlers straightaway, no matter what the situation of the game.

I was so lucky that my opportunities came when they did. The Champions Trophy was the first big final I'd ever played in for Australia, and don't forget this was the same Windies team that had beaten us in the first game. They were quick out of the gate, scoring about ten runs per over with Chris Gayle flying, scoring 37 off 27 balls with two sixes and six fours—only one single. But Nathan Bracken bowled him on 37 when the score was 88 and we rolled the rest of them—including Brian Lara— for just another 50 runs by the thirty-first over.

We only had to chase 138 and we were pretty confident. But in the third over we started to wobble a bit. Gilly got out and Ricky was only in the middle with me for one over before he was on his way back to the dressing room. To make matters worse, there was rain in the air and lightning flashes that seemed to be getting closer. We stopped for the dinner break after ten overs, needing just over 90 runs; to be honest, I think we'd have preferred to stay out there and get it over with.

Sure enough, the rain rolled in. There was a delay and, by the time we got back out there, the chase had gone from 94 in 40 overs (2.35 runs per over) to 70 in 24 (2.9). It was a fraction harder, but still very achievable. In the end, Damien Martyn and I were both not out, me for 57 and him for 47, and we won by eight wickets with seven overs to spare. We had a very good team—including Gilly, Glenn McGrath, Damien, Ricky, Mike Hussey, Michael Clarke, Brett Lee and Andrew Symonds—but I got Man of the Match in the final.

That whole series was leading up to the 2006–07 Ashes and there was a lot of talk around the team about who was going to get the number-six spot. The selectors told me I was one of the front-runners because of my form in the Pura Cup final and opening in the one-dayers. Opening the batting, you get a chance to show what you can do every time the team plays. If you are down the order and the openers do well, you could be sitting in the dressing room half the time. For instance, Michael Clarke and Andrew Symonds didn't get a bat in the Champions Trophy final. So I was well-placed to grab that vacant spot in the team. Michael Clarke had been dropped from the Test side and Roy was the nominal all-rounder, but he hadn't really done much in Test cricket.

So Michael and I felt like we were vying for the place even though we were very different players. I was an all-rounder and he was just a batsman, albeit a very, very good one. Michael had had a phenomenal start to his career, but he was getting frustrated, batting seven at that stage and not getting a chance to show what he did best. Meanwhile I was doing all right as an opener and probably bowling the best I ever had, so I knew if I got an opportunity in the Ashes, with both bat and ball, I was in a good position to take full advantage.

When we got back, it was announced that I was in the Ashes squad, ahead of Michael; previously there had been a Shield game and I had bowled probably the best that I had in domestic cricket, against the likes of Justin Langer, Damien Martyn, Gilly and Mike Hussey. I picked up two wickets with an economy of better than 1.8 in both Western Australian innings, so I was in pretty good shape for the Tests. There was some discussion about whether or not I should play the one-day game that followed, but I think the selectors wanted to have a good look at me before naming the team, so on I went.

I was doing okay with the ball, but in my sixth over disaster struck—I felt my hamstring go and I knew I was in trouble. I was rubbing the back of my leg and Mitch Johnson and Jimmy Maher came over; Jimmy told me to get myself off the field and get some treatment. It wasn't a big injury, but it was only six days before the first Test and I knew my body well enough to realise it probably wouldn't be able to heal in that time. That was the start of what would turn out to be the most frustrating period in my career, not knowing what was going on with my body and not being able to get any answers either.

I'd felt bad during the previous couple of summers whenever injuries kept me out of action, but every year you play, you get better and you improve and feel ready to make the most of your opportunities. This time I felt I was playing better than I ever had; I was in the squad for the biggest cricketing contest any Australian can face and I was ready, mentally and physically, to make the most of my opportunities. Unfortunately it wasn't meant to be. It was only a three-week injury, max, but it stopped me getting into the Ashes team and allowed other players to get a grip on the series.

The scans showed that there wasn't that much there at all, only a little bit of damage, but scans can confuse the situation because in the end the most important thing is what you're feeling. If you feel pain, then it doesn't matter what the scans are showing. The advice I got was I might be okay; I might be able to push it—there was a 60 per cent chance I might be right. Sixty per cent? This was the Ashes! I felt that, maybe for the first time in Test cricket, I had earned my spot but now someone was telling me I had only a 60 per cent chance of getting through.

Even so, that was enough for me to think, 'Okay, I'm going to see if I can get it right.' It wasn't the ideal preparation—all the other guys had been training flat out, and only three days before the first match I still wasn't even jogging—but Ricky and the selectors were willing to give me every opportunity right up to the day of the game to prove my fitness. I pushed myself as hard as I could but I felt some pain in my hammy whenever I pushed my running or started to bowl—it just didn't feel right. So I pulled out and Michael got back into the team.

We thumped England in the first Test. Ricky scored 196 and Michael got 56 in the first innings; Glenn McGrath took six wickets and England collapsed for 156. They did better in the second innings, but the damage was already done. The second Test was straight after that, in Adelaide, and it was a real seesaw match with England declaring at 550 with a double century from Paul Collingwood and 150-plus from Kevin Pietersen. We replied with 513, including centuries from Ricky and Michael, and this time the England collapse was in their second innings. We eventually won by six wickets. Even though Australia was playing so well, I knew there was still an opportunity to get into the team if I could get myself fit.

After Adelaide, there was maybe a week in between the second and third Test and the selectors said I had to play a Sheffield Shield game before the third Test if I was going to get picked. I went back to Sydney and worked with the New South Wales physio, who got me to a point where I was able to run just about flat out and change direction, which was all good. So I went and played the Shield game in Adelaide in the hope that I could get through, but I knew deep down it hadn't had enough time to heal. I started well and got two wickets in my first over but I was still very nervous running in to bowl and I knew I was a long way off being able to get through the game.

Suddenly, when I was halfway to the crease, I felt my hamstring go again. I knew there and then that that was the end of this Ashes series for me. I was never going to be part of it; I didn't have enough time to be able to come back. It was all I'd been aiming for—to play with some of the greatest cricketers ever and to wear the Baggy Green in the ultimate contest against our oldest sporting enemy. This was the kind of dream every kid with a bat and ball plays out in their backyard—and it was all over.

THE BOWLER'S RUN-UP

As a bowler, one of the elements of the delivery is the run-up and people wonder if it really makes that much difference. Different bowlers have different run-ups, depending on how athletic they are and how they've been trained. As young kids we all saw Merv Hughes and Craig McDermott have really long run-ups, so we thought that was how you had to do it.

There's no doubt that the forward momentum of a long run-up helps, but Mitchell Johnson, for example, could bowl at least 130 kilometres an hour off three steps if he wanted to. On the other hand, if I bowl off a couple of steps, I can't bowl that fast—I've got to get my momentum up. So some guys need their run-up more than others.

Some just put it on for show. Shoaib Akhtar's normal run-up is very long, for instance; but in a one-dayer that I played in, he bowled off four steps and still hit 150 kilometres an hour. He obviously didn't need such a big run-up—but he's psyching you out. To watch him building up a head of steam as he comes in from the boundary can be quite intimidating for most batsmen.

Brett Lee can bowl fast off a few steps as well: genetically and athletically, he is built to do that. But he needs momentum to bowl extreme pace. For my part, I always had a long run-up as a young kid because I thought that was how you bowled fast—running as fast as you can and bowling as fast as you can.

When Glenn McGrath first started out he was definitely faster than he was in the most effective part of his career. But as he developed, his pace wasn't the reason he was so good—his accuracy and bounce were his big weapons. When guys get bounce, the ball is often not where you think it's going to be and that's when you edge it.

Any ball that does something off the wicket—whether it's seam or extra bounce or low bounce—is harder to adjust to because it's a later movement. At least with swing (unless it's really, really late swing) you can see it early and you can adjust early. If the ball seams, it gives you less time to adjust, so it's much harder to play.

DRINKS BREAK 8

CHAPTER 12 **MISSED CHANCES**

After I strained my hamstring again, everyone panicked, as they do, and took the conservative route, which is to keep you out of cricket completely, in my case for eight or nine weeks. This was a new low for me physically and emotionally; all I could do was keep plugging away and hope that the next time I got a chance, I'd be in a position to take it. Even though I was playing for Queensland, I was staying in Sydney with Lee and I thought I'd just make the most of it. Meanwhile I worked on getting my hammy right.

That's the hardest thing about being injured—it isn't so much getting over the injury as the missed opportunities. When you're out injured, you worry if there's going to be another opportunity when you're fit again. Injuries are part and parcel of any sport, but it's what happens while you're not in the team that can be hardest to deal with.

In my case, Michael Clarke—a world-class batsman—had come back into the side and batted at six, the slot we'd both been in contention for, and got a 50 and then two centuries, batting beautifully as he does. He'd started his career as the boy wonder, with a century on debut in India; then he hit a slump in form, but now he was finding his feet again. It felt like an opportunity missed for me. Then it happened again: after the second Test in Adelaide, totally out of the blue, Damien Martyn retired and Andrew Symonds came in to replace him. So Michael moved up to five, Roy went to six, and all I could do was sit at home and watch.

With the Boxing Day Test at the MCG coming up, Lee and I had gone to a health retreat for a couple of days to get away from everything. I tried not to watch, but I had to find out what was happening. Under pressure, when the team was in trouble, Roy batted beautifully and took on the English bowlers, getting more than 150 runs with Matthew Hayden at the other end. They went from 5 for 84 and added 280 runs before Matthew went for 150-plus. It was a masterful performance but, from a totally selfish point of view, I was very disappointed. It's hard to take when you know that either of two slots in the team could have been yours.

I was happy for the team, though, and Roy and Michael deserved their success. They are very good players, so there was always a good chance that they were going to cement their places in the team. But I had missed another two opportunities and those don't come around that often. Michael was locked into the batting order and Roy was playing Test cricket as brilliantly as he did the one-dayers.

On New Year's Eve 2006, just before the final Test, I was invited onto a boat on Sydney Harbour chartered by Rod Bransgrove, the chairman of Hampshire. It was a pretty impressive guest list, with David Gower, Michael Holding and Ian Botham all on board to see the fireworks.

I'd bumped into Ian before, when he was commentating while I was in England, and he and Rod are great mates. But this was the first time I'd managed to talk at any length about his cricket career and achievements. He was incredibly generous with his time and spent about an hour with me; what he said would turn out to be hugely prophetic. He knew I would have been in the Test team but for injuries, and he told me I was doing too much gym work. He said, 'I know the game has changed, but my gym work was bowling.' They played a lot more county cricket in his day, because the international schedule was a lot less hectic. Okay, he'd had his share of back injuries and a big operation at one point, but that was how he got fit—bowling in matches and in the nets. He said he avoided gym work because it tended to tighten up your muscles, and that's when you get injured.

Having been kept out of the Ashes series because of a pulled hamstring, I was listening to this and wondering if that was my problem. But the experts around me, then and previously, had told me the opposite. They said that the bigger and stronger I was, the faster I would bowl. So who should I listen to?

All I knew was that talking to Ian Botham made me more determined than ever to play county cricket in England that next northern summer, because it was when I was playing cricket back-to-back without a break that I was most free of injuries. And he was confirming something that a lot of people—including my family—were now saying: spending too much time in the gym was causing my injuries.

I have to say that the message still wasn't getting through yet, but the seed had been planted. It was something some of the older guys were saying too—even Dennis Lillee, who was one of the first Australian players to use gym work to get fit. But then I'd look at Mitch Johnson as an example. Here's a guy who works hard, does everything the strength and conditioning coaches tell him, is a supreme athlete and then goes out and bowls and bowls for years almost non-stop, and never seems to get an injury. Okay, there's only a couple of people like him in the world—physically gifted and lucky in the way they are built. They don't realise how lucky they really are.

Back to the Ashes series, this was the last time all those legends—Glenn McGrath, Warnie and Justin Langer—played Test cricket. I went to watch the last Test in Sydney, because it was the end of an era and I wanted to see these guys play together for the last time. I remember at the end of the final day, I was halfway home when Brett Lee messaged me and said to come into the change room. I didn't really want to go, because I thought I'd look like a hanger-on—but if I didn't go, I'd miss the last opportunity to be in the dressing room with these guys before they retired. So I drove back and Damien Martyn came into the dressing room as well.

It made me realise how huge the opportunity was that I'd missed. From a sentimental point of view, I'd missed a chance to play with these guys for the last time and that probably was one of the saddest parts of it all. I was unbelievably lucky to have come through when I did with those guys around.

I got back to playing after the Ashes Tests were finished; at the start of the Australia–England one-dayers, I played a Shield game for Queensland and got through fine. But even then I was still running in to bowl and not thinking at all about where I was bowling the ball; I was just worried about my hamstring and willing it not to go again. In fact, I was absolutely shitting myself.

The World Cup was coming up and I didn't want to miss another big opportunity. Naturally, that affected my bowling. My pace was still up but I didn't really know where the ball was going and, deep down, I didn't care because I was so worried about my leg. I was getting smashed everywhere by the batsmen, but if I got through a spell without straining my hammy that was a great result.

Despite my wayward bowling, the selectors showed amazing faith in me again, and picked me for the last three games of the one-day series against England. It was good timing for me because it was leading up to the World Cup. However, I wasn't opening the batting in the one-dayers any more because Matthew Hayden was back and playing well. So it was two steps forward and one step back.

But at least I was playing for Australia again and that's all I wanted to do. That said, I didn't do that well and we got beaten by the Poms in that series. The Aussie team had dominated throughout that summer and then, right at the death, lost the finals 2–0.

Then we went to New Zealand and played three one-dayers over there with a few of the big guns, like Adam Gilchrist and Glenn McGrath, being rested because they'd played so much cricket. We got beaten convincingly by the Black Caps and I was still worrying about my hamstring when I was running in to bowl. After that first game I talked to someone about it, as I was now getting phantom pains in my leg as well. I can't remember who it was, but they said, 'Look, if it's going to go, it's going to go anyway. Don't worry about it—go for it, no matter what.' From then on I started to bowl a bit better.

In the third game of the series they asked me to open the batting again. Phil Jacques had opened in the first two games and hadn't done that well. So I got the nod in Hamilton, which is a beautiful batting wicket on a really small ground. I batted well but I missed an opportunity to get my first 100. I had a run a ball when I got out lbw on 68—the ball didn't turn and I just lost concentration.

Matt Hayden went on to get 180. I had opened with him and he went on with it, but his foot was hit by one of the New Zealand bowlers and his toe was broken. That meant he was in doubt for the first game of the World Cup. Having cured my hamstring anxieties, I also got three wickets.

When we got back from New Zealand, Queensland were playing Victoria in the one-day final, and there was a bit of talk about whether the players who were in line for the World Cup should play—nobody wanted to get injured. Playing state cricket wasn't the best option for me; I was still building up my fitness and I was shitting myself I'd get injured and miss another big opportunity. I said I'd definitely prefer not to play, because I didn't want to miss the chance to play in the World Cup.

Predictably, there was a bit of an uproar in domestic cricket about all that. My old mate Jimmy Maher, the Queensland captain, came out and said that I'd hardly played any cricket over summer at all—hardly played a game—surely I should get some more game time before the World Cup. It was ridiculous, he said—they were wrapping me up in cotton wool.

That created more of a stoush than there should have been. In hindsight, he was probably right and he was just doing his job as Queensland skipper, trying to get the best eleven on the oval. But call it cotton wool if you like, I was terrified I was going to miss another big series. In any case, the controversy must have fired Jimmy up, because he scored a century and Queensland won the final against Victoria.

I had the week off before we flew to the Caribbean to start the World Cup campaign and, because Matthew Hayden was injured, I opened the batting in two practice matches. In the first, against Zimbabwe, I batted really well and got 87. But the biggest game before the World Cup was against England in the last practice match.

It wasn't something that we talked about but there was an awareness that we hadn't played all that well after the Ashes, even though we had such an amazing side. Then we lost Matty Hayden and Brett Lee ripped his ankle in New Zealand, so he was out too. On the other hand we got Shaun Tait, who is a pretty awesome replacement—one of the fastest bowlers in the world to replace one of the fastest bowlers in the world—even if Shaun was a bit erratic, at least compared to Brett.

Hanging over us was the fact that we'd lost the last two games to England in the recent one-day finals series, and then we'd lost three times in a row to New Zealand. That's five losses in a row—a situation Australia wasn't used to—so this game against England was really big.

We bowled them out for just under 200, and Shaun did most of the damage with four wickets, supported by Brad Hogg and Stuart Clark.

A score of 200 is very gettable in one-day cricket, but that can work against you if you're not careful and don't stay focused. I remember walking out to bat with Gilly and feeling a lot of pressure not to lose to the Poms again. We needed to win this—especially coming from such a strong position. As it turned out, I got 50-plus and Gilly got over 70, which built a foundation for the innings and we won with about ten overs to spare. But you could feel the excitement with every run we scored, because it was so important to turn things around. It was only a practice game, but the result was a boost for us and a blow for them. Most importantly, it was our turning point as a team.

With Adam Gilchrist, Matthew Hayden back in the side, Ricky Ponting, Michael Clarke, Andrew Symonds, Mike Hussey, me at seven, Brad Hogg, Glenn McGrath, Shaun Tait and Nathan Bracken, it was an unbelievable team really. It was Glenn's last series, but he was still bowling tremendously well. Matthew was coming back after not playing one-day cricket for a year and then the injury in New Zealand, so he was determined to make his mark. His whole attitude was that he should never have been dropped in the first place and he was still the best option to open the batting for one-day cricket as well as Test matches. Predictably, he could walk the walk as well as talk the talk.

The first matches we played in the first pool round were against Scotland and the Netherlands. Those guys had to play in a preliminary tournament to get in and that's a great thing about the World Cup; unlike the Champions Trophy, which is only between the top eight nations, here the smaller cricketing nations get their chance to qualify to play serious competitive matches against top-ranked teams. That's the only way the smaller nations can continue to improve and build. As I write, there are moves to exclude the minnows next time round but I hope they don't—everybody's entitled to at least one shot at glory.

The big game for us in the pool section was against South Africa. They were, as they always are, among the favourites; they had a very good team. They were bowling well and their batting was really, really strong too. We were playing at St Kitts, a very small ground, and we batted first.

I remember the team meeting before the game and the topic was how we were going to approach Shaun Pollock, a very skilful bowler. Matthew Hayden said, 'How am I going to play him? I'm going to take him down.' We all looked at him—he was so matter of fact, it was like he was joking. But he wasn't. 'No matter what, I'm gonna take him down,' he said. 'I'm going to walk at him to mix up his length.'

And that's exactly what he did. He got 100 off less than 70 balls. Okay, it's a small ground, but he was walking at Pollock and just smacking him over the fence. Pollock went for over ten an over and we got a really big total—nearly 380. After Matthew had led the charge, Ricky and Michael put some big totals up and the Proteas were left chasing 377.

Even so, they had 160 on the board before their first wicket fell and they were looking good. Graeme Smith and A.B. de Villiers were batting really well and took Glenn McGrath down a bit. I was fielding out on the boundary when de Villiers worked one well behind square. So I ran and dived to my right, picked it up, threw in, hit the stumps and ran A.B. out by a whisker.

There's definitely a bit of luck involved in throwing down the stumps from out on the boundary. But what was it Gary Player said? 'The more I practise, the luckier I get.' Leading up to that game I had worked at throwing at the stumps from close range, just getting the lines right; it was good that it worked from way out on the boundary too. Really from that distance you're throwing to the wicket-keeper and A.B. is a very fast runner.

That was a big turning point in the game—they were cruising and could have been 1 or 2 for 200. Shortly after, Graeme Smith retired with cramp and the collapse was on. This game was a big moment in our tournament too because if we'd lost it would have dented our confidence, moving into the serious part of the competition.

From there we went to the Sir Vivien Richards Stadium in Antigua—a new ground built with a grant from the Chinese government. They were still finishing it off when we turned up; it was a sandy ground and the grass hadn't really bedded down. In fact it was like a sandpit. We played the West Indies there and totally dominated them. Once again Matty Hayden went nuts with the bat and scored nearly 160.

As usual, I came in right towards the end, which was where my opportunities were most likely to be as an all-rounder. As a result, I had been developing my range of shots specifically for that role: slogging, hitting sixes and hitting boundaries. It's not my natural style but I knew I had to be effective, wherever I played, and if I was coming in late in an innings I had to produce the goods and get the scoreboard turning over quickly while there was time left in the game.

I worked hard at the start of that tournament, practising hitting the ball over the fence and adding the lap sweep to my repertoire. The lap sweep is where you flick the ball over your shoulder to the boundary behind you. It's not what you'd call a classic cricket shot but I knew that, if I was going to free up the big six-hitting areas, it was important to be able to have it as an option. Basically, when the bowlers start sending down yorkers to try to avoid being hit for boundaries, I go across the stumps and, using the pace of the ball, just flip it over the top. As soon as you do that and hit it behind you, it puts another doubt in the bowler's mind, disrupts the field positions and frees up other areas where you can score.

So my batting had definitely developed and for the first time I was able to consistently hit balls for six, which was a big change for me. When I started out, I couldn't just stand there and hit the ball over the fence. It had been a four-year development that started when I was about 23 and was talking to Mike Young; he was our fielding coach and he had a background in baseball. He said baseballers have everything loaded up on their back foot and, as the pitch is about to be thrown, all their body weight goes at the ball. So their front leg is up ready to go at the ball and, when they shift forward, that's where they get all their power. That made sense to me because I needed more momentum through the ball so that, even if I didn't hit it cleanly, it could still go for six. It suited me because I don't like charging or running at the ball: I feel I can't adjust quickly enough if I've misjudged it.

Soon after in the nets I started using a baseball-style swing. However, because it wasn't a cricket swing, I couldn't actually get that much elevation. So I combined the two and, by the time I got to the World Cup, I was loading up my back foot, with my front foot off the ground ready to go at the ball—but I was using a cricket swing rather than a baseball swing to hit the ball. If anything, it's a bit like a golf swing and it meant I was able to get momentum through the balls and hit them everywhere around the ground. I discovered I was even able to hit them over cover, which I had never been able to do before.

Now, with just about any delivery, I could react to the ball and potentially hit it a long way. Slogging had always been one of my big weaknesses, so I never thought I would get to a stage where I could hit sixes consistently. It wasn't that important in the early stages of my career, but at the World Cup, where I was expected to be the last man standing as the overs were running out, it was exactly what the team needed.

Against the West Indies in Antigua, I scored 33 off 26 balls. I remember hitting a lap shot off Corey Collymore and just getting it so sweetly that it went for six. I managed to hit 16 off the last over, and we scored 322, winning by 103 runs.

A big bonus for me was that it was also the first time I met Viv Richards. He's a big idol for any cricketer, especially a batsman. I remember vividly his last tour of Australia in 1988. As a man and captain of the West Indies he was, and is, a legend. I just loved the way he played. He'd take 'em on no matter what the situation of the game—his swagger, his confidence, his physical presence was something I always admired.

To meet him properly in the change room and hear him saying, 'What you did today was cool'—well, it's just awesome. Viv has an amazing aura—a presence—and when he walks into a room it's like he has a layer of lights around him. And there we were, in his stadium in his country, and you had to think life doesn't get much better than this.

LEFT, RIGHT AND CENTRE

A lot of batsmen who are naturally right-handed bat left-handed these days. I am the other way round. I write left-handed, I use a spoon left-handed and play pool left-handed—so all my fine motor skills are done with my left hand. But all my power things, like playing golf, batting and bowling, I do right-handed.

I can understand why some right-handed players bat 'southpaw'. There's the fact that the bowler has to adjust to your position because, quite simply, bowlers are more used to bowling to right-handers. One disadvantage for the left-handed bat might be having to cope with more rough from the bowlers' footmarks, because most bowlers are right-arm over the wicket. But the only way a right-arm bowler can get a left-handed batsman out lbw is if it swings back in so the ball pitches in line with the stumps. This makes life a bit easier for the left-handed batsman.

Anyway, I play right-handed and it works for me. Mitchell Johnston, by the way, is amazing. He bats and bowls left-handed, but he plays tennis right-handed. He's totally ambidextrous.

While we're on the subject of left and right, the big talking point in bowling these days is reverse swing—that's when the ball from a right-arm bowler swings in towards the wicket rather than out towards the slips. At first, conventional swing moves the ball away from the shiny side of the ball, basically due to aerodynamics, with the seam vertical throughout the flight of the ball but angled to the direction you want it to swing. But then, after a while, when the rough side of the ball is really rough, the ball can start to swing the opposite way. This tends to happen late in its journey down the wicket, making it difficult for the batsman to pick which way it's going to go. Not everyone can get reverse swing at will. You have to hold the ball exactly the right way, the delivery has to be within quite a narrow range of speed and the ball has to be in the right condition.

To get reverse swing, the rough side has to be super rough—it often has bits coming off the ball so that side is grabbing on to the air. There's a bit more technique to reverse swing. You have to change your release point, for instance. The reason I've found it easier than some other guys to reverse is because my seam has always been straight.

There's a lot of talk about humidity affecting swing—and it does—but what really gets the ball rough and ready to reverse swing is the wicket. If it's hard and abrasive, the ball gets really ripped up so it will reverse sooner. In the 2009 Boxing Day Test against Pakistan at the MCG, within ten overs the ball became totally chopped up on one side, which was perfect. You just have to hope that the shiny side doesn't get too chopped up, because then you've really got to work on it to keep everything flat and smooth so it doesn't compete with the rough side.

When you play at the Gabba in Brisbane, the wicket is not normally abrasive enough, because it's really compact and there's a dry grass cover on it. So there's no real way of roughing up the ball and it usually won't reverse at all.

At the SCG and Hobart, as well as at the MCG, the wicket can really tear the ball up and I learned how to get the ball into the right condition from Indian bowlers—on one side, super rough and chunky, with little flaps coming off the leather, and on the other side really shiny. They bowl cross-seam for the first few overs, until they can see which side is going to get more roughed up, and then—but not before—they polish the other side so the ball starts reversing by about the eighth over. And don't forget: this is with a virtually brand-new ball, which is the hardest to face, because it has the most pace and bounce off the wicket.

That's why, these days, the designated ball-polisher in the fielding team is very important and they have to know what they are doing. Part of following the Indian technique is to tell the other blokes not to shine the ball too soon. It's almost an instinctive thing for many bowlers, shining the ball while you're thinking about your next delivery. Doug Bollinger is a good example of an unconscious shiner—he does it without realising it.

I suppose I've taken it upon myself to be the one who communicates with all the guys about when to shine and when not to, because swing is a big weapon for me. I'm always looking out for an opportunity to make it reverse.

There are teams who, even when the conditions aren't suitable for roughing the ball up at all, can get it to go in reverse. It's such a potent weapon, especially on really flat wickets when the ball's soft and doing absolutely nothing and the batsmen have got their eye in. Reverse swing turns a beautiful, flat batting wicket into a minefield, with the ball going everywhere.

That's when you start wondering about ball tampering. You would think that ball tampering would be a no-no, with all the cameras around, but some players have got it down to a fine art. Some fielders have plaster casts or a tiny bit of sandpaper sticking out—even an extra long thumbnail—so when they're polishing the ball, no one can see they are also roughing up the other side. And it's impossible for the umpires to say whether damage was done by the wicket, the bat or something else. I know there are guys who tamper with the ball, but it's not the way I'm built and I know it's not the way the Aussie guys are built either. You might throw the ball to each other on the bounce a couple of times, but the umpires will soon step in if they think you're crossing the line.

And in terms of doing stuff to help the shine, lolly spit doesn't work on our Kookaburra balls. It must be the kind of leather, although spitting on them can make them shiny. The Duke ball—the one they use in England—is a different story. Sugar syrup in your saliva will give the Duke a shine you can nearly see your reflection in, regardless of how old it is. You're allowed to spit on the ball and to use your sweat but that's it. And I'm not the designated shiner, which is fine by me—I don't need to rot my teeth with lollies.

No-balls have never been an issue for me. It's something I'm very particular about. I do everything I possibly can to make sure I'm getting the best out of myself so I don't want to bowl no-balls and get a wicket disallowed. You get no-balled when the heel of your front foot is over the line, so I always start bowling with my whole foot well behind the line and then get closer to it as I loosen up.

Your heel shouldn't need to go over. I guess if you're bowling flat out and trying to break the 160 kilometres an hour barrier then every centimetre might make a slight difference, but if you're just trying to bowl a good ball and get the batsman out, it doesn't really matter that much.

The idea I always struggle with a little bit is that some part of your foot has to be behind the line, even if some lines are thicker than others. If you've got your heel on the line—but not on any of the grass behind the line—it's a no-ball. If you see on a replay that someone's got their foot beyond the line, then it's clear-cut—it's a no-ball. But when you see that the foot's touching the line, but not clearly behind it, it's going to be a lot harder for an umpire to judge. That's why umpiring is such a hard job. To be able to see someone's foot hit the line (or not) and then look up and judge an lbw or a snick, when the ball's travelling at 150 kilometres an hour, is almost impossible.

Amazingly, most umpires get it right most of the time. There are times you're so sure it's an lbw and it's so clearly out that you don't feel there's even a need to appeal. Then you see a replay and it's totally not out. I'd be a shocking umpire. An umpire has to concentrate on the deliveries and be able to handle different kinds of characters. I don't have the personality for that, especially if I was dealing with someone like me.

Sometimes my appeals can be a bit enthusiastic. People say it's 'tactical' appealing—trying to build up the pressure on the umpire to give you a wicket eventually—but with me it can be frustration and desperation. It's like, 'I've got a wicket—please be out!' When I was younger and, I suppose, angrier and more aggressive, I tended to get on the wrong side of umpires. Now, the umpires keep an eye on me but the majority of them seem to enjoy the way I play. They know I'll be in there, boots and all, but if I do get it wrong, at least it will be an honest mistake.

I have a pretty good relationship with most umpires. They know it can get a bit heated occasionally and I definitely don't mind saying a few words and having a bit of banter with players, but my relationship is different with umpires now that I appreciate what a difficult job they have. Sometimes, when I'm walking back, I might be frustrated with a decision, but you have to let it go, because you know they are good guys and they are trying their best.

It's all very well sitting at home, watching super-slow-motion replays with the 'Snickometer' and 'Hawkeye'—that makes experts of us all—but even then the technology isn't 100 per cent sure. The third umpire has taken some of the doubt out of the game, but you can't remove the human element and neither should you.

The referral system works pretty well and has actually shown that most umpires get it right most of the time (in a couple of cases *all* of the time). It has also, to be fair, exposed one or two who are not quite up to the job at the highest level. But even the batsman sometimes isn't always sure if he has nicked the ball or not. When the ball is travelling at 150 kilometres an hour and the edge is just a millimetre away as it passes, you feel it . . . but it's still not a nick and you shouldn't be out. So the referral system is a good thing—especially if it includes the 'hot spot' technology which was absent from the World Cup in India. There's too much riding on games to leave the 50–50 decisions that could turn a whole match to one man, however good he is at his job.

It's great to see a former top-class cricketer like Paul Reiffel umpiring, although he may be the last to make the switch for a while. Paul was playing just before the really big money came into cricket; you can now have a career as a player that sets you up for life. But I'm sure being able to extend his links with cricket was a welcome option and it's certainly benefited the game. It's not just the years of experience playing the game that helps him do his job, it's knowing how to handle the players and get respect from them that, say, a teacher or any other 'enthusiastic amateur' might not be given.

That said, cricket is still a 'gentlemanly' game compared with some other sports. You'd never get us ganging up and monstering the umpires like they do in soccer or baseball, or punching each other's lights out like they do in the oval-ball codes. We're not even supposed

DRINKS BREAK 9

to swear in cricket, but I think they give us a bit of leeway. Sometimes it just slips out. It's not like rugby where they pretend to be polite, calling the referee 'sir'. But if a cricket player swears at the umpire, you could get fined half your match fee, or something like that.

And, okay, you can't be sent off, like in other sports, but if a batsman abuses the umpire, it won't be long before a borderline decision comes along and up goes the finger. It's never happened to me, but you hear a lot of stories from English county cricket of how the overseas pro has got under the local umpire's skin and the first 50–50 call that comes along, it's 'See you, mate!'

A good umpire can allow great cricket to happen, but I wouldn't have their job for quids.

CHAPTER 13 **FANS WITH BATS**

Our next game in the World Cup was against Bangladesh. There's always the possibility of an upset against minnows if you play particularly badly and they play out of their skins—they usually have one or two decent batsmen in their side—but it's not a big concern. For a start, these guys are in awe of players like Glenn McGrath and Ricky Ponting. As players, they're also fans and it is a big deal for them to be able to chat to legends of the game. After a game, the majority of the opposition team would come into our change rooms and there'd be a crowd around Glenn and Ricky, asking questions and listening to whatever they had to say.

And the great thing is that those two don't mind talking to people. Most Aussie players, and those two guys in particular, are the most down-to-earth people you'll ever meet. Cricket is something they love, so they can talk about it forever. The first time I saw this was when we played Kenya; after the game, all their players came into our dressing room and there were two groups—one around Glenn and another around Ricky. They were in total awe.

Playing against the lower-ranked teams also means all the players in the top squads can get a run. For instance, I didn't play against Ireland in the Super Eights—the second phase of the tournament before the final knock-out games—so Andrew Symonds batted at three and Mike Hussey opened. As middle-order batsmen, they hadn't really been needed up to then so this was a chance to push them up the order, give them some game time and make sure they were comfortable with their games for when they were needed against the big teams.

The day before that Bangladesh game, my calf was a bit tight. I put it down to how sandy the ground was. I said to the physio at the time that every step I took my calf was super tight. He said, 'We can't really pull you out just because you've got a tight muscle—you haven't got a strain.' Then, sure enough, in about the second or third over I was running in to bowl and, as I landed on my back foot, I felt my calf go. I tried to run in again, but it wasn't good, especially when I was jumping off the sandy base, so I went off.

About that time there was a New Zealand player who strained something on that ground, so it made me feel a little bit better about myself. I was trying to see every positive I could when I kept getting injured. The team management immediately set down a deadline of three weeks, by which time I had to be fit to play or otherwise I was going to be sent home.

I got a scan done and for the next four days my calf was really sore; I was still limping around a bit and I only had 16 days to get myself to a point where I'd be able to bowl in the nets flat out. The physio tended to err on the side of caution, but I worked my butt off trying to get it right. It meant I missed two games during the World Cup—the Ireland and Sri Lanka games—and there were quite a few days in between, so those three weeks felt like three months. But it did give me time to heal.

The other issue was that the media were starting to question my overall fitness; reporters were asking me if maybe my body wasn't made for bowling and if I was thinking of giving it up. I wasn't. The previous hamstring injury hadn't been a big deal—it just took time to fix after I re-strained it and I hadn't been that scarred by my injuries at this stage. In the end everything worked out perfectly and I was able to bowl by the deadline; and because I'd played quite a bit of cricket, my batting skills hadn't dropped off at all.

Even so, I was pretty hesitant in my first game back. Nobody wants to beat us more than the Kiwis and, on their day, they're capable of giving anyone in the world a fright, as they did with us when Adam Gilchrist went for one run off two balls. My contribution, coming in at seven, was 65 not out off 32 balls, including four sixes and four fours. Matthew Hayden got another 100 and Ricky got 60-plus. We had a really good total (about 260) when I came in and it was one of those days you dream of—everything I tried to do came off unbelievably well. I played a lap sweep for four and it felt like every time I wanted a boundary it went for six. My 65 took our final total to something close to 350. To finish my innings off, I hit a six over cover which I'd previously found very hard to do.

I'd been sprinting between wickets, which made the physio super nervous. There was still a good chance I would strain my calf again, because I was really pushing it, but when it came time to bowl I got through five overs and burgled a wicket as the Kiwis collapsed for 133 and lost by 215 runs. I survived, which was the most important thing, as the next game was the semi-final against South Africa. I'd snuck in just in the nick of time, otherwise I would have been on a plane heading back home.

The semi-final was an extraordinary day. We played unbelievably well as a team and had them 3 for 0 at one point. Glenn McGrath and Nathan Bracken just bowled so well and we got all their best batsmen out within the first five or six overs. They were shot ducks. South Africa obviously had their game plans but they had been perennial under-achievers in big tournaments. They hadn't made it through to the final stage at the previous World Cup, in 2003, and I think they had it in their minds that this was their big chance to put things right. It went wrong for them, but very right for us.

I had built it up in my mind as the kind of game where the best players should stand up—and I wanted to be one such player. Ironically I only put a lot more pressure on myself and so I under-performed. When I came on to bowl, I was over the top emotionally because I wanted to do so well. I didn't bowl well, compared to how I had played previously. I wanted it to be a defining moment in my career, but you can't do that. It doesn't matter how important a game is, the skill set is still the same. The reason the best players do well in the big games is because they are the best players—they've got great skills. They do the basics better than most, and under pressure stick to them no matter what. Thankfully, the collapse of the South Africans meant my lapse didn't matter.

Getting to the World Cup final was something that I'd dreamt of. Four years previously, I'd been close to getting into the tournament but got injured so this time it was important to me in many ways. I'd played a much bigger part in the group in the lead-up to this and, from a sentimental point of view, this was going to be the last game Glenn McGrath would play for Australia. All of that made it very special. Throughout the World Cup I made an effort to spend time with Glenn, because I'd missed the opportunity to play a lot of Test cricket with him. He is such a lovely guy and his stature in the game is amazing, yet he seems unaffected by it. At heart, he's still a country guy and loves the simple things in life.

His late wife, Jane, was sick at that time and it meant she didn't come over for the World Cup. So just about every night I'd go to dinner with him and just talk to him about whatever came to mind. Our friendship really grew throughout that period. When I had the injury, he told me about letters they had received from cancer survivors—their experiences and the power of the mind to turn things around.

He told me he imagines there are these little men in your body who are always there ready to work for you on your deficiencies—if you've got an injury or illness—and what you need to do is get all the little men together and channel them into the area. Your mind is such a powerful organ that, if you can imagine it happening, there's a good chance it will happen. We only use a small percentage of our brain—maybe that other part is what some people can tap into, which gives them exceptional powers.

I remember going to bed the night after Glenn told me that, visualising all these microscopic men and channelling them down to my calf. It might not have made any difference, but just to hear that from someone who had experienced what Glenn had been through alongside Jane, and still somehow be at his best, it was worth trying. The World Cup was a really special time in my life for a number of reasons, but getting to know Glenn was one of the most significant.

The build-up to the final was phenomenal. I thought about what I did last game, how I didn't perform as well as I wanted to; I'd allowed the importance I placed on the game to be an added pressure, and I didn't need that. The final was against Sri Lanka at Kensington Oval, Barbados. We had our game plan, but the first glitch came when the match was shortened to 38 overs a side because of rain. In that situation, you can't afford to be cautious because the Duckworth–Lewis calculations can come into play (as they kind of did) and you don't want to leave yourself short.

In any case, Gilly more than took care of all that when he started smacking everyone and everything out of the ground.

Fernando and Vaas were the biggest victims of his masterblaster performance, but even Murali couldn't keep him quiet. Every run we scored and every boundary was a celebration. He really put on a show.

Having been on the receiving end of that kind of batting, I can tell you it's no fun. When I started in the Indian Premier League, I got belted every time I bowled. In the end you've just got to find a way of not getting hit, but occasionally, no matter what you do, it doesn't make any difference. You hope a guy's going to mishit one sooner or later; but sometimes, on their day, they don't and they can hit you everywhere. The best you can do is give them an easy single to get them off strike so you can bowl to the other guy, who's probably not smacking them as much. It's a big mental challenge and you need to have some different options if the one you're using isn't working. But your 'Plan B' has to be very effective; it can't just be something you haven't done or haven't tried, otherwise you will continue to get smashed. And when you start going for 10 an over, you might just start praying for something to change.

So Gilly was going berserk and he got 149. I was promoted to four to make the most of the last three overs, and they wanted someone to go in and hit boundaries and try to take down their strike bowler, Malinga. He can be a threat because he always bowls very good yorkers and his change of pace is very hard to pick because of the way he releases the ball. I thought I could use my lap sweep to get him off his line. As I discovered, it's not a good option to try a lap sweep to a reversing yorker.

I only got three runs, but it was a learning experience. I also dropped a catch at third man and I was pretty down for a while, but I bowled okay. The game was just about over and they were well behind; Jayawardene was hanging in there when I got him out lbw with a beauty.

Sadly, the way the match finished was a bit of a debacle.

Initially they called it off because of bad light and we thought we'd won, so we started celebrating. And then, after a little while, they said actually the game can't finish like that—the rules are, if the game stops because of bad light, you have to come back tomorrow and complete the overs. We're like, 'WHAT!?! Come back for a few overs?' Then the captains agreed to finish the last few overs with us bowling spin, so no one got hurt in the dark. Sri Lanka had no chance of getting the 70 runs they needed off the last 20 balls and someone could have been hurt if Glenn or Shaun Tait had been bowling.

It was a bit of a farce in the end. We bowled spinners from both ends and they blocked the balls back. It was super dark. I was out on the square-leg boundary—with the Sri Lanka batsmen wearing their blue outfits, I could hardly see them. Unless it came straight to you on the ground, you had no idea where the ball was. After it was all over, they checked the rules and realised that they could have just ended the game and used the Duckworth–Lewis Method, without the pantomime of us playing in the dark. But there was no dispute over who won—even the Sri Lankans said we deserved to win, because we had outplayed them.

I walked around the ground after we were presented with the trophy and Ricky said, 'You missed out four years ago. Now, good for you, you've been able to be a part of it. You deserve it!'

CHAPTER 14 **TURNING POINT**

When I got back from the Caribbean, at the end of April 2007, I was on a high, having realised one of my major dreams as a cricketer—to be a part of a World Cup win. We then had about four months off, during which there was no cricket at all. I was living at Lee's mum and dad's house in Sydney and getting very well looked after. This was the longest break I'd had for a while and for about a month I just enjoyed myself. I was still playing for Queensland but during the off-season I had eight weeks full-on training with the New South Wales Cricket conditioning guy. By the end, I was the strongest in both my upper body and legs that I had ever been.

The Australian domestic off-season coincided with an unusually quiet time for us internationally, with the next tour after the break to be the Twenty20 World Cup in South Africa in September. Anyone who hadn't been playing county cricket in England would have been a bit rusty so we had a training camp in Brisbane leading up to it. Sure enough, I strained my other hammy bowling. As before, it was only a very minor strain that didn't really show up much on a scan, so I stayed back in Brisbane to get into the Brisbane Lions' hyperbaric chamber at the Gabba and do everything I could to get it to heal as quickly as possible. I didn't realise it at the time but this was the biggest stroke of luck in my career, because that's where I met Victor Popov for the first time.

Victor was looking after the hyperbaric chamber, which is a kind of pressure tank that forces greater amounts of oxygen into your body. The higher concentration of oxygen in your blood supports and speeds up the body's natural healing process and major sports teams all over the world use them. I had my chamber session and, as I do, I chatted to Victor about the various issues I had, to try to get a different perspective.

Getting advice from outside cricket is tricky. If you work in cricket, then you stay in cricket, and it's sometimes hard to get ideas and opinions from elsewhere. Very few people from other sports come into cricket, which can be a good or bad thing, but I wanted to hear a different point of view.

Victor had never had anything to do with cricketers as athletes. But he had covered four Tour de France cycle races and I was intrigued by that. I wanted to learn as much as I could about recovery, even though I knew playing cricket is nothing compared to what elite cyclists put their bodies through. Sitting on a bike for six hours a day, 20-odd days on the trot, and racing up mountains some people would struggle to walk up puts the human body under extreme stress, and Victor was an expert on this.

He realised that I was keen to learn everything I could and improve as an athlete, as well as to find a way of avoiding constant injuries. He had a quick look at me, but he didn't want to do too much, as he didn't want to encroach on Cricket Australia's medical staff's territory. However, he made some suggestions and, talking to him about the work he'd done with various footballers to get them from injury to playing footy again, I sensed he might have some answers for me. I had three sessions with Victor and the hyperbaric chamber before I went over to South Africa.

My first game back was against Sri Lanka. I took one wicket, but in my third over I felt my hamstring go again. It was only a minor strain but I already knew what would happen if I tried to push through the injury—a three-week strain could turn into a three-month lay-off. This was killing me. It seemed the stronger I got, the more injury-prone I became. It didn't make any sense to me at all.

Our medical staff were talking to me about the injuries I was getting, how frequently they occurred and when they occurred—always at the wrong times. They had various theories, but whatever the cause was, there was nothing they could do about it. I told them I'd had enough. The only decision they'd left me was to stop bowling, because that was when I was getting injured. I told them the only person I was working with when I got back to Australia was Victor. Hopefully he'd have time to spend with me to try to get me right. And then I flew home.

Cricket Australia were surprisingly relaxed about me going outside the system to get treatment. I think it was because he had no answers that Alex, the Aussie physio, was prepared to say, 'Okay, go and do what you need to do.' Initially Cricket Australia paid for it, because it was an injury and they pay for any medical bills for injuries. Like most sports, if you go outside their programs for prevention and maintenance, you're expected to pay for it yourself.

I knew Victor was my last hope to try to be an all-rounder. I hadn't talked to him since those chats in Brisbane, but I knew I had to work with him, otherwise I had no hope—no hope at all. Luckily, his wife was just about to have a baby and he was working at his practice full-time, so he had all the time that was needed—which turned out to be a lot—to start from scratch and develop a completely new training regime for me. We had to find out what my deficiencies were—and they turned out to be things I and the Cricket Australia physios and medics hadn't really considered.

Part of Victor's philosophy is that everything relies on the balance of your pelvis—if that's out of alignment and has become 'blocked', then it creates problems just about everywhere. Whether it's your lower body, your limbs or your upper body—everything relates back to your pelvis. In all my years playing cricket, no one had ever checked that. He said we needed to first loosen my pelvis by physio and manipulation, and then I had to start doing Pilates to make sure my pelvis stayed a lot more stable and would be less likely to go out of alignment and block again. So that's when my Pilates started, and I've done it religiously ever since.

All the weights I'd been doing, which had been a huge part of my training previously, stopped. Victor said the most important thing to focus on was Pilates, and then making sure my balance and pelvis was right. Then we could try to find out other reasons why I was straining my muscles.

Because of my history with stress fractures in my back, the immediate thought was that I had some nerve issues in my lower limbs. When bones are healing in your lower back, this can cause friction and tension in the nerve pathways that go from your back all the way down to your lower limbs. We investigated that. I started getting an epidural injection of cortisone; it goes down to the lower limbs and reduces nervous tension in the legs, which makes an enormous difference to my hamstring length.

I used to get a cortisone injection every six months after I started seeing Victor, but I've been able to stay on track for longer now and my body has grown with me; now it's used to doing what it needs to be doing. I would only get another injection now if things started to go slightly wrong and I felt more tightness in my calf. The danger sign for me is when my right calf gets generally tight for no apparent reason.

My running technique was another big part of the problem. Because I would over-stride as I ran in to bowl, I was loading up my hamstrings a lot more than I should. I had to learn how to run more efficiently, so I wasn't over-striding and was keeping my feet underneath me. I worked with the fitness guy at the Cricket Academy for about eight weeks to improve my running technique. It's still a work in progress, but it's so much better than it was.

I also went to see Michael Artmann, the naturopath and doctor; a very unconventional but lovely man, up in the Gold Coast hinterland. He checks everything—your body, deficiencies, including whether you're low in minerals, and your genetic make-up. He's got this crazy machine that tests whether you're allergic to things like wheat, for instance—you hold this metal cylinder with this bit of wire out of the top of it; if the wire starts moving one way you're okay, but if it moves the other way you're deficient in something.

When I first saw it, I thought it was rubbish and was looking for the hidden camera. But Victor had taken a number of athletes to Michael and a couple of them had serious issues that Victor didn't tell him about—Michael picked up every single one of them and a couple more with this machine.

So, after we went through all that, Michael said, 'Okay, you look like you're really intense; everything looks tight and acidic, and an acidic environment encourages growth of the bad stuff in your body. The answer is to get the pH levels within your body as normal as possible; if you have a high acidity, you've got to get some alkali—like bicarbonate of soda—into you to counteract the acid.' That was something he was really strong on.

As I've mentioned before, I have Gilbert's syndrome. It's hereditary and it's not a huge deal; but it means that, if I get tired or run down or dehydrated, I get yellow eyes. It's a form of jaundice and, when I was young, the whites of my eyes—but not my skin—would go a bit yellow. Since I've seen Michael and he's given me some naturopathic tablets to settle my liver down, it's not so obvious. Otherwise he was trying to do everything he could to get my body in balance.

The next step—and a huge part of my 'rebuilding'—was to look at my training and place some limits on it. No matter what the session was, I did exactly what Victor said I had to do, regardless of how different it was to what I had been doing. He set down a program which, in an ideal world, would have meant two hard weeks of playing, training and everything like that, then one week of doing hardly anything. If there was a game in that 'rest' week, everything around the game needed to be totally wound back. He said that even if you feel like your game is not where it needs to be and you want to do some more, you can't—it's just the way it has to be. I had to stick to my new regime for as long as necessary, to make sure that I was going into each game fresh and not fatigued, which would reduce my chance of getting injured.

Of course, the rest periods were totally against my instincts. I remember a couple of times when I wanted to get into the gym or do some extra bowling, but reminded myself that this was supposed to be a recovery week. However, once I had decided to go with Victor, I put full faith in what he was saying, even though he said it was going to be at least an 18-month process. It would take that long to get my body to be more resilient. He also warned me there would be some hiccups along the way. That's just the way it was and I couldn't lose faith when it happened. I just had to keep doing what I was doing and it would come right.

Between Pilates and a doctor who used a metal cylinder and a wire to diagnose injury, I could have been forgiven, I reckon, for thinking this was all a bit New Age and weird. But then conventional sports medicine had nothing to tell me except to give up bowling. And I guess that's when my obsessive nature kicked in to help me. Once I decided to go with Victor, I wasn't going to stop until I'd given his theories a really thorough go.

If I was struggling physically, emotionally I was in an even worse place. Having been living at Lee's parents' place in Sydney, and being very well looked after, when I came back from South Africa I went back to Brisbane, because that's where Victor was based. I stayed on my own in a friend's apartment in South Bank. I couldn't go down to Sydney because I had to do everything that Victor was saying, and that was hard too. I had to commit to doing whatever Victor told me, even though there was no guarantee it was going to work.

I was also getting nailed in the media about being injured all the time. The constant story was that I was going to have to give up bowling. Also, I couldn't handle anyone asking me about my injuries, because it had been so relentless over three or four years. It was an easy conversation starter for anyone who hadn't seen me for a while. The first question anyone asked was: How's your shoulder? How's your body? How's your hammy? What is it this time? I was getting more recognised, too, so I'd go down to the shops and all anyone would ask me about was my injuries.

You don't want to be rude and there was a lot of sympathy there, but I didn't want to talk about my injuries all the time—with strangers, my family or anyone—it was bad enough having to deal with them myself. In the end I couldn't handle it and I didn't go out of my apartment for about three weeks, apart from seeing Victor.

Lee could only come up from Sydney for a couple of days at a time because she was working full-time. I cried quite a bit. I felt like I was just about at the end of it, especially as an all-rounder. I was 26 and it felt like I was never going to realise my dreams. The very start of my relationship with Lee was about the toughest time I had with injuries. My problem was that I couldn't consider my life a success unless I succeeded at cricket.

There's no doubt that during the first couple of years that Lee and I were together our life was pretty up and down. Lee, with her experience as a reporter with Fox Sports and other sportspeople that she knew, could understand it more than most people. But I was hard to be around at times. I recall saying to her that I couldn't make her happy as long as I was unhappy and maybe we should take a break. But she could see I was suffering and hung in there. So it was tough for Lee to only have a few days now and then to snap me out of it. In the end, though, what we went through in those first couple of years seriously strengthened our relationship and gave us an even tighter bond.

I knew that so many other people in the world have a life that's 50,000 times harder than I've ever had. But I was in a spiral and, when you're like that, the only thing that matters is what's going on in your own life. The people who counted had no answers and the man in whom I had put my faith was telling me to forget everything I had ever known about training. But Victor was my lifeline, even though I was still a long way off seeing any real improvement.

Through that period the way for me to escape worrying about getting back from injury was my guitar. I couldn't handle going out of my apartment and I didn't want to see my family. It was my music and my guitar that got me to a place where I didn't have to think about what was going on in my cricket career.

I bought an amazing Gibson Les Paul '59 re-issue, which is the holy grail of electric guitars, and just played that for hours and hours. I was learning more blues, Eric Clapton stuff, and that was the way for me to escape. I know it seems like a bit of a cliché—the sad lonely boy in his room with only his guitar for company—but every challenge is a gift and I'd like to think that those hours of practice not only kept me sane but made me a much better guitarist. And when you're playing blues—with all that emotion and intensity—it's like a therapy session in itself.

Sooner or later I was going to have to come out of my cave and be a cricketer again. So I played a grade game as my first match back from my hamstring injury. I was only batting at that stage, but I got a 100 straight up. The media manager for Queensland had organised an interview in the lunch break—it was the only time the media could be there. They wanted me to do a quick interview, to say I was back playing and how was I enjoying myself, that sort of thing, which was fine by me.

Then I heard that Ray Phillips, the Queensland chairman of selectors, had complained about this, saying what I did was wrong and that players shouldn't disrespect the grade game by giving interviews halfway through. I rang him to explain, and said that this was what was arranged. I didn't care if I did it in my lunchtime—it wasn't going to affect the way I played. In any case, I scored a century—so what was the problem? He then said I should have come along to a Queensland game; my team-mates were there to support me and I wasn't showing I was there with my team—I was just looking after myself. I'm thinking, 'Here we go again. This is just a re-run of all the crap I got for going to Tasmania.' I explained the position I was in—I wasn't ready for that yet and I was really struggling with what was going on. 'You wouldn't understand because you've never been through what I'm going through,' I said and asked him to give me a bit of leeway.

He said I was being selfish, so I hung up. When I got off the phone, I was probably as low as I've ever felt. I got really upset—people just don't understand it, unless they've gone through it themselves. It was a sad time in my life.

Phillips had always been friendly to me in the past, I suppose because I'd come back to play for Queensland, and he'd always gone out of his way to be nice to me. But that was the end of that. After our confrontation, when I was back and playing regularly it never seemed to have affected his selection decisions. And if I did well he would come up to me and say, 'Well done.' I'd just say thanks and be polite. I never ever pulled him aside and gave it to him or anything like that. But I've never forgotten that kick in the guts when I was at my lowest ebb. Everyone else in the teams I've played for has been very understanding. They knew how hard I trained and how I did everything to the nth degree, and they'd also seen at close quarters what I could do as well.

What I believe now is that I have to do what's right for me. If that means that Victor and I have to break down a few barriers, so be it. There were a few people getting their egos out of joint about my treatment and the way I look after my body, but I'm the one who has to live with the consequences of my decisions.

When I did get back to playing, the initial results were, if anything, negative. My pace was definitely down a bit, for a number of reasons, but mostly because I was really conscious of my technique when I was running in to bowl. I exaggerated my movements slightly, to imprint them onto my muscle memory, and when I first started I must have looked like a bit of a goose. I was running in with really short steps; but that was what I had to do to get it right and I hoped that over time it would just become more natural. Also, whenever you come back from injury you're always rusty, no matter what, especially after a longer lay-off. It was a really long process. Apart from that century in the grade match, it took me a couple of games to score some runs.

Anyway, after I got back into the Queensland team I started to gradually build up my bowling. I was still seeing Victor every day before play and at night too. He was so kind to let me into his house—I saw his daughter when she was four days old—and his wife would cook me dinner.

His treatment was basically to loosen up my pelvis and to provide general maintenance, and it would take 45 minutes to an hour. Eventually I got to a point where I was bowling up to ten overs; then I gradually built it up to 15 overs in a day, although with no long spells. I said to Jimmy Maher, the Queensland captain, 'This is all I can do. No matter what, I can only bowl three spells throughout the day to allow my body to build up; I can't go flat out and get myself injured again.' He was fine with that and let me develop at my own speed.

But in January 2008, when I was playing in Hobart, I stupidly bowled 17 overs in the first innings. Then, in the second innings, I was bowling a couple of overs near the end of the game and I strained my hamstring again; I had to come off the field halfway through my fourth over. I thought, here I go again, and the newspapers certainly agreed, with headlines like 'Injury-Prone Watson Breaks Down Again'.

Victor was in Adelaide for the Tour Down Under cycle race, so I flew there and he said the good news is, because of where your body is at now, it's not going to take that long to get over it. He was right. It was a much quicker recovery and it only took me about a week and half to get back to batting, and then another week and I was bowling again. This confirmed what Victor had said about there being some hiccups along the way until my body became more resilient. But the underlying problems that had caused me so much grief seemed to be under control and I actually dared to hope the worst of my injury issues were behind me and I could get on with playing cricket.

READY, STEADY, GO . . .

I've got a very basic routine when I go out to bat—the same one I've had since I was a kid. It gets me settled, focused and in the right frame of mind. I play three practice drives; I do a squat, just to get my legs going; then I have a look around at the light, to get my eyes adjusted. I mark centre, I glance around the field and pick my gaps which, in the end, doesn't make much difference, because I have to play each ball on its merits.

Some batsmen can pick a gap and find it off just about any ball: Darren Lehmann was one, Brian Lara another. The guys who can do whatever they want, regardless of the ball, really manipulate the fields. I try not to premeditate too much, because that's when I've more chance of getting out. Dad always told me not to look at the fielders but look at the gaps, because that's where you've got to hit it. So I look at the gaps in the field. Then I do a hamstring stretch, and then I'm ready to go.

For whatever reason, because of the way I bat, if I don't adjust my back pad, my bat swing comes down and hits it each time, clipping it on the way through. If the ball swings in late and I've got to adjust, this would mean that, through clipping my back pad, my bat speed would be a fraction slow and I could get out. The noise of my bat clipping the pad could even make the umpire think I've nicked it. So turning my back pad around slightly has become part of my routine for every ball I face.

Then, as the bowler is running in, my thinking changes from time to time depending on where I'm at. If I'm hitting the ball really well, or if I've been batting for quite a while, then my thoughts are about taking him on or trying to take him down. It's also about watching the ball and clearing my mind—in the end, if my mind is a little bit clouded then I'm not batting on instinct, and batting on instinct is when I'm at my best.

Getting a duck is a big deal to a lot of batsmen—and even more to the press and fans—but the difference between zero and one is just one. It doesn't worry me whether I get a duck, or just four or five—it's still a low score and it's still crap! When I was younger, if I got a duck I thought, 'I can't even get one run—I must be really bad.' Now it doesn't bother me any more than any other low score—it just means I haven't concentrated hard enough or it's just not my day.

But every player is different. Michael Clarke will nearly run himself out to get off nought. He hates being on zero. It's the same with Kevin Pietersen—he hates it too. As a bowler, if you know that about a batsman, you're looking for a run-out rather than, say, a catch. They don't really force the big shot; they force running between wickets more than anything. They'll block it because they're nervous, but they'll take a half chance—and that's when you have to be ready to pounce.

CHAPTER 15 **INDIAN SUMMER**

In early 2008 I was playing for Queensland. I was back to bowling nearly flat out and I was happy with my batting. Throughout the domestic Twenty20 competition, I bowled really well—I didn't get hit for too many runs and picked up a couple of wickets in just about every game. I got a couple of 50s and, in the last game against Tasmania, I got 69 off about 35 balls.

As it happened, that's when the Indian Premier League was just getting started and the player auctions were straight after our own Twenty20s. Basically the teams bid for the best players and the winning bid was your payment if you played all the games. Like any other auction, if you're Flavour of the Month you have more chance of getting picked up for a good price. Some guys got huge money—Andrew Symonds got $1.35 million per year for three years from Deccan Chargers.

You didn't have to take what was offered—there was a base price, below which you would not play—but then it's just like a house auction, with teams competing for the players they want most. But the base prices were pretty good; even $50,000 or $100,000 is a crazy amount for six weeks and just about everyone wanted to be involved anyway.

Matthew Hayden and Ricky Ponting should have been right

at the top of the list, but their names came out of the hat when many of the teams were out of cash and were just waiting for one specific player to come up. They didn't get paid much at all compared to some less prominent players, like Cameron White and David Hussey, so it was a bit of a lottery as well as an auction. But the average price at auction was just under $500,000, which is very good money in anyone's language.

I didn't go in the first auction. I wanted to but I heard that Lalit Modi, the IPL commissioner who was running the show, just about hand-picked who was going to be in the auction, and supposedly he said they didn't want me because I was 'injury prone'. But then the owners of the Rajasthan Royals started to strategically pick players who weren't necessarily the highest profile. They worked out all these different statistics to try to build the best all-round team. Shane Warne was the captain and they also took into consideration what he wanted, because they trusted his judgement. And because Warnie liked me and he'd seen what I could do, he was keen to get me to play for Rajasthan.

My manager at that stage was heavily involved with the Kings XI, which is the franchise based in Mohali, Punjab, and he was trying to get me to go there. Tom Moody and Brett Lee were also trying to get me to join them there. In the end, because there was enough interest in unsigned players, there was a second auction, which had a much smaller amount of money on the table.

But again it was a bit of a lottery—if your name came out of the hat first, you would probably go for the most money. I sort of came out midway—I just got the minimum which was $125,000 to play for the Royals for seven weeks. No matter how much I got paid, I just wanted to be a part of something that was so new but also as close as you could get to playing international cricket without actually playing for Australia.

By this stage I'd got back into my cricket. Even though I'd had that little hiccup along the way, I'd healed much quicker than before and was making real progress. As soon as Queensland's season finished, I went straight over to India. Victor didn't come over for the IPL, but the Royals had an Aussie guy called John Gloster who used to be the Indian cricket team's physio. I didn't know much about him, but I hoped Victor and John would communicate to make sure they were on the same wavelength.

This was always going to be a big test of where I was at physically. Over a period of six weeks we would play 15 or 16 Twenty20 games if we made the finals. And even though they only go for three hours, they are super intense. You've got to be going flat out from the start, otherwise you're going to get found out very quickly.

It was amazing to have Warne's guidance there and to see him working at close quarters, captaining and coaching—and that was where my bowling mindset really started to change. As an all-rounder, I had previously seen my role as being to try not to get hit for runs and to tie up an end. The guys at the other end were supposed to go harder and really try to take the wickets—that sort of thing. But Warnie's thinking was, well, what's the point of bowling if you're not trying to take a wicket? That totally changed my thinking about what I was doing.

He'd come up to me and say, 'How are you going to get this guy out? Do you think we can get him out this way? Okay, we'll set the field like this.' Initially I thought that was a bit too aggressive, but it gave me a much better plan. Instead of running in and just hoping I could tie up an end, I was running in and hoping I could get the batsman out with this ball. In fact it's not as crazy as it sounds. It means you're concentrating more and, if you really concentrate on where you want to bowl, if you get your line or your length slightly wrong, you've got immediate feedback to help you adjust the next ball you bowl. I bowled in quite a few games and my pace was back up towards 140 kilometres an hour.

I remember the first game we played against Delhi, to a packed house. We batted first and I was like a deer in the headlights to begin with. I couldn't hear anything because it was so noisy, but I played a couple of good shots, got three fours and was on about 20 off 15 balls. Then there was a bit of a mix-up and I ran myself out. As a team we had a horrible start and only got 129.

When it was our turn to bowl, I told Warnie that I find the best way to loosen up is to bowl a slower ball, just to find my feet at the crease, and then to change up because they are not really expecting it. He said he didn't think that was a good idea, but he let me do it my way and Sehwag smacked my first two balls for boundaries. Then Warnie came up to me. 'What's all this about?' he said. 'Okay, this is how we are going to get him out. Get the ball to come back in to the stumps, because he doesn't like that. He likes freeing his hands—make sure the ball comes back in.'

Sure enough when I tried that I got him out . . . because the ball came back in. It was our only wicket and, believe it or not, my awful bowling economy of 7.75 was the best of the bunch. They scored 133 for one wicket and won by nine wickets with five overs to spare. Embarrassing.

To be fair, our side didn't have any really big stars who were still playing for their national team—in particular, we didn't have any big Indian stars. But even though Warnie had retired from Australian cricket, he was still bowling beautifully. Graeme Smith didn't take part in the first game, because he was playing for South Africa, and it was a couple more games before he came into the team. He made a big difference when he did. He's a very gifted leader and had changed a lot compared to when he first started. Originally he was very intense and trying to be somebody that he wasn't: 'I'm the captain and everyone should do what I say.' But that's not his personality. He's actually a big teddy bear—he's a very chilled-out, nice guy.

After that first game everyone was saying we were going to struggle, judging by the way we were beaten so badly. The next game was against the Kings XI from Mohali; Brett Lee was playing for them along with my Queensland team-mate James Hopes. Yuvraj Singh, something of a short-form specialist, was their captain. I didn't bowl that well—I'm not even sure if I got any wickets. But when I later went out to bat, we were chasing 170 and it turned out to be my day. It just came together unbelievably well—it seemed like every time I hit the ball it flew over the boundary for a six. I ended up getting 75 off about 40 balls. We won by six wickets with two overs to go.

That win was the start of the Royals' rise to the top and the first step in my IPL career. The Royals won the tournament that first year and I ended up getting four Man of the Match awards over the tournament—one of them in the semi-final against Delhi, when I top-scored with 50-odd runs and took three wickets for ten from three overs. The Indian people were so absorbed by the IPL that it was even hurting the Bollywood movie industry: cinemas that were normally full were half-empty because everyone was at home watching the cricket.

Indian fans really started to embrace the way I was playing. When I, a foreigner in Wankhede Stadium in Mumbai, was batting against Delhi, the whole crowd started chanting my name. It was phenomenal to be there, in that atmosphere, compared to where I'd been six months earlier. Everything was working—I didn't have any niggly injuries, I was able to go 100 per cent for every single run and now the crowd was chanting my name. Incredible!

The IPL tournament was the biggest extravaganza that had ever happened in world cricket, because there'd never been that much money in cricket before. It was a big party—a huge celebration of cricket. Out in the field, everyone was competitive, but you never went over the top because it was all about enjoying the occasion. You were able to play with other internationals whom you usually played against. I also got to know the Indian culture a lot more, because we are an Indian team. Apart from the cricket, it was an amazing all-round life experience.

It was also a perfect step towards my recovery. That tournament was the first time I had got through an extended period of cricket without any injury. On top of all that, we recovered from our disastrous start to win the tournament with virtually the last ball. Lee was there so she could experience it with me first-hand. For her to be with me, and to share my success at the end of such a long and painful journey, was very special. After winning the final I was so emotional anyway, and, given that I had been a second-choice draft, I warned Lee that I didn't know how I was going to handle it if I was chosen as the Player of the Tournament. Well, I didn't handle it. It meant so much, I couldn't hold back the tears.

In the past, every time I got a major breakthrough I'd been knocked down before I could build on it. At last I had my rewards, and then some. I rang Victor on the bus on the way home and I broke down crying again. It wasn't just that moment—it was all the emotional energy inside me that had been building up for months. I rang Mum and Dad, and the same thing happened.

I had come such a long way. When I first went to India, I flew on the same plane as Warnie and nobody noticed me at all, just him. At the end of the IPL, when I arrived at the airport in Mumbai and got my bags out of the taxi, I had about 50 people standing around me taking photos. The crowd was getting deeper and deeper—it was outrageous. I remember Lee said, 'What is going on here? This is unbelievable.' I told her that this was a really good thing—it meant I was doing really well—so I had to embrace it while I could. After it was all over, we went to the Maldives for a few days to let it soak in.

My next stop was supposed to be Hampshire to play Twenty20 cricket for them, and I thought I'd had the perfect preparation. While I had been playing in the IPL, Australia had been playing Test matches in the West Indies; but when they moved on to the one-dayers, Matthew Hayden was sent home, having strained his Achilles tendon. They needed an opening batsman. Lee and I had only been in the Maldives for a couple of days when I got a call in our room telling me to fly to the West Indies to join the one-day squad.

With everything that had just happened, it felt like things were finally turning in my favour. Dare I believe? I didn't have time to even think about that—I needed to pack my bags and get on with the next phase of rebuilding my career.

CHAPTER 16 DREADLOCK HOLIDAY

When I got to the West Indies in June 2008, I discovered I would be playing in one Twenty20 to start with and then five one-dayers. The Twenty20 started fairly well and I batted and bowled okay, but we got flogged. This was a surprise to a lot of people because Australian cricket was still very strong—it was only a year since we had won the World Cup and the West Indies were in a bit of a decline as a cricketing country.

Having spent the past couple of months in the IPL, I could see ours wasn't a specialist Twenty20 team. It was, in essence, a one-day team and the match was being used purely as a warm-up to the one-day series. A lot of the West Indian guys had played in the IPL, so they had their skills up to the mark. As a result, we were found out pretty quickly.

To be fair, Australia hadn't been taking Twenty20 cricket very seriously up to this point—we tended to have TV events involving celebrity guest players from other sports or actual cricketers talking to the TV audience. After the IPL, everyone realised this was a serious format, a crowd pleaser and a real money-spinner.

Our coach, Tim Nielsen, wanted to sit down with me and go through what I'd learnt in India. Very few, if any, Australian officials had seen it played at a competitive level for an extended period, so they hadn't been able to develop game plans or appreciate the different skills required. Even when I came back to Queensland, the guys there wanted me to talk to everyone about Twenty20 cricket, to try to get a handle on it.

West Indian crowds are lively to begin with, but Twenty20 takes them to a new level. It helped, of course, that they won the game and that it was in Barbados, which is one of the more populous islands. Otherwise, throughout that five-match one-day series the crowds weren't all that good, not like they would be during the Twenty20 World Cup in 2010, when the crowds there were amazing.

They do love their cricket in the West Indies and they are really chilled-out, cool people. Cricket brings all the islands together, and everyone walking down the street knows and loves cricket. Even though the West Indies teams of recent years haven't been putting on much of a show for their followers, not consistently anyway, they still love it—mostly thanks to the amazing team they had through the seventies and eighties. But many of their biggest and best athletes now aren't playing cricket at all. They're playing basketball, because there's more money and opportunities in it, and it's an uncomplicated game you can play on a street corner—all you need is a basketball and a hoop. With cricket only eleven people can represent all the islands of the West Indies at any one time; with basketball you can go to college in the United States, get an education, and maybe even get a shot at the millions in the NBA.

It had been a year and half since I had opened the batting in one-day cricket. Mark Waugh was probably the first Australian that I can remember batting out of his normal spot—about number four or five—to open in one-dayers. They said they thought he would be perfect to take on the new ball—and it worked. Since then, they've always looked for someone who could take on the attack and score as quickly as they can in the first ten to 15 overs.

I would have thought my Twenty20 success probably helped me but, when I got picked again to replace Matthew Hayden, one thing the selectors said was my IPL form hadn't really had a bearing on me getting picked—it was more that I had opened the batting before. They said the IPL didn't really count, but deep down I think it played a big part in why I got picked.

I got a quick start in my first game and I think I made about 30. The second game I went for a duck on the third ball and, even worse, I got hit on my big toe and broke it. Having spent so much time out injured, I was not going to let it stop me from playing. I took the pain-killers I needed to get through that day and bowled with a broken toe.

Pain-killers can only do so much. Even running caused me grief but, because it was the big toe on my front foot, this was worse. When you're bracing at the crease, you jam your front foot into the toe of your shoe every single time. I got through that game, but not with much success. I then got an X-ray; but we were in Grenada and the technology isn't crash hot there, so it didn't show a fracture. But it wasn't going to stop me from playing the series anyway and in the next game I got injections to make sure that I didn't feel it too much. I still felt it, but it didn't really matter.

In the third game in Grenada we were batting second and chasing about 220. Ricky kept saying to me the whole day while we were bowling: 'This is your day to get your first 100.' I thought I've got time to do it; we're only chasing 220, so I can take my time a bit more. Sure enough, I got my first one-day 100 in my third game back opening the batting.

The relief and the joy and the emotion that came out of me when I got that 100 was intense, but it was more of a celebration of the fact that I could even get into a position to score 100. I remember going to bed that night and I was so excited I hardly slept. I kept saying to myself, 'I can't believe it . . . How good is this?'

I can't exactly remember how many runs I scored for the whole series in the end, but I didn't score many big totals after that. There was a game in St Kitts when we got 282 all up, but the West Indies were flying. Chris Gayle was in and he was on more than 90 and they were looking as though they were going to get it easily. I was bowling with my broken toe and, because I was trying to compensate for not being able to put my foot down as hard as usual, I strained my side as well. So I was the walking wounded—I could bowl but my pace was right down and I had no power through the crease at all.

Given the sort of wickets over there, one way you can get away with it is changing your pace by bowling off-cutters and leg-cutters. The wickets tend to be a bit slower, and the ball grips a little so you can make it harder for the batsman to really take you down. I realised that was the only way I was going to not get belted.

Towards the end they were only two wickets down and needed only 50 runs or thereabouts. When I got Chris out for 92, they dug in, losing Dwayne Bravo on 247; but they were still on course. Then, after 270, it all went pear-shaped for them, losing Findlay and Chanderpaul in quick succession. Suddenly I was bowling the last over of the game; they just needed eight to win. But I got it right—they only got six singles and we won out of nowhere by a run.

From the West Indies' point of view, it really hurts when the game's there to win and there's no way in the world that you should lose it, but you do. It sometimes happens if wickets start to fall and you haven't got guys in there who have the technique or mental application to stop the rot and slow the bowling side's momentum. You need to make sure you play your percentages and shift the momentum back in your direction. The problem is that you have negative thoughts, because the momentum has changed drastically—from cruising to a win to worrying that, if we lose a couple of wickets, we could lose the game. The trick is to get rid of any negative thoughts and try to concentrate on the required skills.

If I find myself in the middle of a batting collapse, I try to rid myself of those thoughts and just worry about watching the ball. I'm also a bit more conservative, initially. You can't really go and blaze away because that means you have more of a chance of making a mistake early and continuing that downward spiral. It's more a mental challenge than a technical one.

So in one game I had success with the bat and got my first 100; and then, in the next one, I played a bigger role with the ball in our win. After the final one-dayer—which we won easily to take the series 5–0—I had a couple of weeks at home and it was a time to reflect on where I was in my career.

That level of success was something I'd always hoped and dreamed that I'd achieve. To see it come true was worth every single moment of the dark days of the previous year. The point is, I suppose, I wasn't really injury-free—I had a broken toe and a strained side—but I was able to play through that because of all the work I'd done with Victor and because of my mindset, which was to keep going, no matter what. I'd squandered so many opportunities in the past with injuries, I wasn't going to lose this opportunity for anything.

IN THE NETS

There's a set order for practising in the nets and it starts with the opening batsmen taking on your team's best bowlers. But as you go down the batting order, eventually your own bowlers have had enough and you face the part-time spinners in the team or some young guys from the host club state or country, keen to sling a few down at the Aussie batsmen.

One of the best things about opening the batting is that you are able to keep things consistent—coming off facing your own bowlers to facing the other team's isn't as much of a leap as coming in to bat after practising against a couple of grade bowlers. And since you are always guaranteed a hit in a game—because you are opening—you find it easier to maintain your form.

There's often a bit of edge when you're an all-rounder and the other bowlers are coming at you. Mitch Johnson and I have had a long-running battle in the nets—but in a good way. Mitch bowls very fast anyway and has hit me a lot. In fact, sometimes he doesn't really like bowling to me in the nets because he's scared of dragging one down too much and hurting me.

Likewise, I've gone from loving batting in the nets to being a lot less keen. During the last Ashes series in England, I was coming back from a niggling injury and the only way I could get some batting practice was to face our guys in the nets. But the nets in England then were pretty rough—they were never that well prepared and they often produced a bad bounce.

At least three or four times in the net sessions I would get hit in the ribs or hand. Since then I've been a little less keen on net practice. I don't wear a forearm guard in the game—I don't feel I need it—but I do in the nets because I don't really know where the ball's going to go, especially when I'm facing our quick bowlers. Any day I get through the nets without getting hurt is a good day.

CHAPTER 17 **BACK HOME**

Back from the West Indies in mid-2008, I was still playing for Queensland. But Lee and I had bought a house in Cronulla in Sydney so I was living between there and my friend's apartment in Brisbane, and I was renting out my apartment on the Gold Coast. I absolutely love Sydney as a city and I like Cronulla, not just because that's where Lee and her family are. It has everything I enjoy about the Gold Coast, but there you're less than an hour away from one of the best cities in the world. So my heart was in Sydney, because of Lee and because it provided me with the lifestyle I loved.

For another year and a bit I tried to balance playing for Australia, which was sort of on and off, fulfil my obligations to Queensland cricket and have a personal life too. To complicate things even further, my medical team was up in Brisbane as well, so I tried to spend as much time as I could up there to make sure my body was okay.

During the three or four weeks between the West Indies and the next international series, which was three one-dayers against Bangladesh in Darwin, my broken toe had healed and I was beginning to run freely again. But coming back from that injury, I must have been subconsciously favouring that foot and

I slightly strained my calf, which put the Bangladesh series in jeopardy. On top of that, straight after the Bangladesh one-day series there was to be a Test tour to India.

At this time Andrew Symonds had a meltdown. Roy is a brilliant player and a larger-than-life character, but he could be a bit of a loose cannon. When people first realised he might have a drinking problem, it was swept under the carpet. Sadly, that's how a lot of issues—especially in relation to alcohol—are dealt with in Australian sport. There's an old-school mentality of having a few beers with your mates after a game which is fine. But binge drinking and all that goes with it doesn't quite gel with being highly paid professional athletes and, significantly, with the media pressure on our generation of sportspeople.

When everybody has a mobile phone and every phone is a camera and people can't wait to get their pictures and videos on YouTube or the social networks, there's a lot less privacy and a lot more scrutiny. Simply put, you can't get away with what they used to back in the old days. With Roy, 2005 in England was a turning point and I was a much bigger part of that than I ever wanted to be.

We were in Cardiff during the one-day series against England and Bangladesh, and it was my birthday; we had been told the team for the match the next day—I wasn't in it, and neither was Brett Lee nor Brad Haddin, so we said we would have a few beers together. A few other guys who were playing came out at the beginning of the evening. Before a game you might go out for dinner, and you might go to a bar and have one or two beers to be sociable, but you're expected to be sober and back in your room by about midnight. However, my birthday was a whale of a night for the non-players.

Cardiff is a very dangerous place, but in a good way. It's a fun city, with one street that has some pretty cool bars and clubs. Brad, Brett and I knew we weren't playing the next day so we had a few more drinks than normal, but at one point we realised Roy was staying out with us, later than anyone else. To be honest, we shouldn't really have been pushing the boat out, because there's always a chance that you could be called in at the last minute if someone broke down in the warm-up, or something unexpected happened. But Roy was in the team!

Next morning, I remember getting on the bus at 8.30 am to go to the game and Roy was sitting up the front of the bus, looking like he'd just woken up after a massive night. He couldn't really talk—he was fluffing his words and blowing bubbles a bit. He had bags under his eyes and when I looked at him, he told me he was really pissed. I just burst out laughing and said, 'You idiot.' Brett and Brad and I were talking about what a cool night it had been; when we got to the ground, we started to warm up, even though we were a bit hung over. We were in no fit state to play, but then we weren't supposed to be playing.

Roy was a different story—he was supposed to be playing. He started warming up, did a couple of exercises, tried to balance himself against a wheelie bin and knocked it over. People started to realise something wasn't right. I was standing next to Brad and we both said this was not good. We should have been ready to play if required. That's when I thought, 'Shit, if Roy can't play, I'm the next choice as all-rounder and the previous night I was the Birthday Boy.' I wasn't really in the best condition myself.

Ricky knew something was up, so he went to John Buchanan and asked him if Roy was pissed. The coach said he didn't think so, but Ricky knew we'd gone out for a few drinks for my birthday. So he came over and asked me and Brad, 'Was Roy out with you last night?' We looked at each other and shrugged. There was no point denying it. Ricky walked off, spewing, as you would be. I thought, 'Oh no, this is going to be a long day.' Ricky walked up to Roy and said, 'Did you go out last night?' Roy said yes. Ricky asked him how many beers he'd had and Roy said 'a couple'. Ricky said: 'Bullshit—you're pissed and you're not playing today.'

John Buchanan and Ricky talked about who was going to play, because it was late notice and there was no selector on tour. Strictly speaking, as the other all-rounder in the team, I could have got the nod. But Simon Katich was there and he was the next specialist batsman in line, so they picked him. The next game I replaced Simon so, looking back on it, there was a good chance I might have been asked to step in against Bangladesh; I dodged a bullet there.

I remember that day like it was yesterday. We were sitting on the balcony outside the dressing rooms; Roy could barely stay awake because he had been out all night, but Ricky and the team hierarchy made him stay and watch the game. To make matters worse, conflicting messages were sent out about why he had pulled out—one report said he had the flu; another said he was a bit stiff from the previous game—so the media jumped all over it.

Someone in the crowd yelled out: 'Andrew Symonds was out with us last night . . . we saw him at 2.30 am walking down the street.' And then it all blew up. I remember the camera panning onto Roy and he was clearly having trouble staying awake. To compound matters, we lost the game to Bangladesh; all in all it was a horrific day and I was in the thick of it, even though I wasn't playing.

We had a huge meeting afterwards, because it was such an embarrassment. John Buchanan was trying to find out what had gone on—some people were saying one thing, others were saying something different, usually standing up for their mates; overall it was a bad situation. I knew I had made a mistake; but I wasn't paying for it, because I wasn't on the team sheet. I don't want to make excuses; I stuffed up as well and I will never make that mistake again.

Roy was suspended for a couple of games and they were even talking about sending him home. Typical of him though was that, when he did come back into the side, he took five wickets against Bangladesh, and then scored over 70 against England in the next match and 42 not out against Bangladesh in the one after that. You can see why the team management persevered with him—he was a champion, no question.

The next year he made 160 in a Test against India at the SCG. He was phenomenally talented and a player you always loved watching in any form of the game—Test cricket, one-day cricket or Twenty20. His power, his physical presence—he's a big guy, 6 foot 3—his stature at the crease and what he can do are all intimidating.

Roy was actually born in England, in Birmingham, and early on he could have played for them because he'd done so well in county cricket. At the age of 20, playing for Gloucester, he hit 16 sixes in the first innings (which was a world record) and 20 for the match (which was another). He could have played for the England team of that time, but he wanted to play for Australia which, back then, was much harder to do.

If the Cardiff debacle had been Roy's only lapse, everything would have been okay. But the fact is there had been a number of minor issues, like being late for the bus because he slept in and that sort of thing. And I know this goes against the whole blokey culture of sport, but if somebody, somewhere had paid any attention to the warning signs and dealt with the issues when they first became apparent, his career with the Australian team could have lasted a lot longer than it did.

Cricket is in a strange position because the social side has always been a big part of the game. But that comes from a time before cricketers were highly paid professional athletes. I enjoy a drink and a night out as much as anyone; but you have to be really stupid not to know that alcohol carries a lot of risks, and in so many ways. When you are drunk, it changes your behaviour and the choices you make; drink affects your fitness and it can even make you more injury prone. All of those things individually and collectively can come back to bite you on the bum.

I knew there were statistics out there that alcohol could contribute to injuries so, when I was trying to get back to full fitness, I didn't drink for over a year. I didn't touch a drop, because I knew that's how it had to be. It was a personal decision because of my physical condition, not because of anything else—I needed to give myself every single opportunity and not create any issues for my body. If alcohol was a potential danger, then it was out.

That was my choice for me and I'm not saying it should apply to anyone else. But someone should have said to Roy: 'Look, the only time you get yourself into trouble is when you're drinking, so it's one or the other. If you want to play for Australia, you need to stop drinking while you're under contract. Meanwhile, let us give you the support you need to help you to achieve that.' Sadly there were a few more incidents before they got to that point.

Back in August 2008, three years after the Cardiff incident, Roy was dropped for missing a compulsory team meeting before our one-day series against Bangladesh in Darwin. He'd gone out fishing on his boat (which he'd had towed up there) with his mates. Meanwhile everyone was asking, 'Where's Roy?' People were desperately trying to ring him, because we knew he'd be in the shit again, but no one knew where he was or what was going on. Then he turned up in the evening, not knowing we'd had a team meeting. He said, 'What's going on? What have I missed? I didn't know there was a meeting.' But he was sent home anyway.

I had missed the first game with my calf strain and they said that, with Roy now unavailable for the Test series, I had to be fit to play the second one. There was an opportunity to play Test cricket in India coming up, so I had to get right for this game. Somehow I got through the next two games without really doing much; but it was more a case of doing my share without aggravating my calf and then hopefully getting an opportunity to play in India, where there might be a chance to bat at six.

That was the next planned step in my career—to get back into playing Test cricket—and I got the nod. I was once again opening batsman in one-day cricket and back in the Test side as a number six batsman. But I didn't have a great series with the bat in India.

I did get 78 in the second Test in Mohali though, in really testing conditions. The ball was reversing when I went in to bat and we were in a fair bit of trouble at that stage. Apart from the reverse swing, Harbhajan Singh was turning the ball a lot and it was a big challenge for me. I batted very patiently—so differently from how I bat now, when I usually go out there and really take on the opposition and back myself. I was still finding my feet and I was a lot more defensive. In any case we were beaten fairly convincingly and I missed out on an opportunity to get my first Test century. The rest of the series I didn't do much. In truth, my batting still had a bit of development to go.

But on the flip side of that, my bowling really did come on. I was bowling 17 or 18 overs in an innings, which hadn't happened for a long time, and doing pretty well. I didn't get a large number of wickets, but I was getting the ball to reverse, because of the way I bowled, while other bowlers weren't having much joy.

Reverse swing is really a bit to do with luck, to be totally honest—how you're built and how you bowl and how you release the ball—but with some guys their natural action makes it easier to reverse the ball, while with others not so much. With

Mitch Johnston, for instance, it's not really a natural thing for him to swing or reverse the ball, but he bowls consistently over 145 kilometres an hour throughout the day, so each person has different strengths.

Of the other bowlers, Brett Lee had just come back from having time off due to his broken marriage and he was still below his best, because he had spent a few months trying to get his personal life in order. Stuart Clark had an elbow injury and went home after the second or third Test, while Peter Siddle only played one game; so it was left to Mitch, me and Brett to do what we could. Having played in the IPL helped me a bit—but not that much. The ball doesn't reverse in Twenty20, but I knew India and I knew the grounds from playing there. I was definitely more comfortable in these surroundings, because it was where they'd seen what I could really do.

Australia still hadn't seen the best of me and that was what I longed for. I knew the majority of people thought I was over-rated and soft, so I always had that negative press and negative energy in Australia, and I hadn't been able to turn that around. To be honest, I felt a lot more appreciated for my cricket skills in India than I did in Australia.

The third Test was memorable for all the wrong reasons. I enjoy a bit of banter on the field, challenging the other side, especially when I'm bowling. Not so much when I bat, but I'm still competitive—if someone has a go at me, I'm going to go back at them. That's how I play and that's one of the great things about being an all-rounder—if someone sticks it to you when you're batting, you've got a chance to get back at them when you're bowling.

Now, India's opening batsman Gautam Gambhir doesn't mind a stoush. Even in the IPL he always seems to be looking for a fight. You just need to glance in his direction and he'll go, 'Watcha looking at?' There was a bit of sledging throughout the whole of the first day, during which they were batting. Then he thumped me with his elbow as he was taking a run.

There can't be any physical contact on the cricket field, apart from accidentally, if you're running between wickets and you can't help it, but this was clearly intentional. I was shocked and turned round and said, 'Hey, you crossed the line there, mate!' Well, maybe not those exact words. 'You're going to be in trouble now!'

Well, the official line was that I had overreacted and I got charged with bringing the game into disrepute. He actually claimed he hadn't heard what I said; when he said that, I thought I was going to get off—which I felt I should because I hadn't done anything wrong, apart from being competitive and saying a few words to him during the day. But, in the end they said that whatever I'd said was enough to tip him over the edge, so I was fined. The only consolation was that he got banned for the next match.

On Indian TV that night they ran footage of the incident, but they didn't show him elbowing me—all they showed was him running past me and then me reacting. They missed out the critical moment! I wish our media was as supportive.

The fourth Test was a complete disaster for just about everyone—except maybe Jason Krejza, who got the world record for the number of wickets taken on a Test debut (12), something even the great Shane Warne hadn't done.

The Indians were playing some amazing cricket, batting really well while their bowlers were unbelievable in those conditions. It seemed like Ishant Sharma hardly bowled a bad ball in any match. Zaheer Khan seemed capable of taking a wicket with just about any ball. Harbhajan Singh was bowling really nicely; Anil Kumble was doing okay; Amit Mishra bowled well for the whole series and got a five-for, bowling leg spin on debut in Mohali. We knew we had to be at our absolute best to even be able to compete, let alone try to win the game. Unfortunately, something that happened leading into that game meant that we effectively played with nine players.

We had three days in between the Delhi test, which was a draw—not a bad result in India—and the final match in Nagpur. At 1–0 down, we needed to win this Test to tie the series and retain the Border–Gavaskar Trophy. After the Delhi Test, four or five guys had a night out but something they ate gave them a bad case of Delhi belly.

To make matters worse, the group that got sick included two of our senior guys—Michael Clarke and Brett Lee. When we got to Nagpur the next day, just about all of them went down, crook as dogs. What caused it? Ice in your drinks will do it or a salad you think is bound to be okay because you're in a posh hotel or restaurant that claims all its water is purified and all food preparation is super hygienic. Brett was the worst; it was touch and go whether he would be able to play at all. He said he was all right but in the end he really wasn't. He bowled a few overs on the first day but he had to go off and get fluids into him. Michael was like a shadow on the field and however hard he tried—and he did—he couldn't give us much. I was on the point of being pushed up the order to bat in front of him because he was really struggling.

It was hard for us to go into such a big game with two senior players down. We were a newer generation of the team and it would have been a huge achievement to win in India. With only nine fit players, against a team of India's calibre, in India, we shouldn't have stood a chance. Even so, we had India on the ropes at one point. They were 6 for 166 when Tendulkar was run out on 12.

But then the game got away from us. The whole business of the sick players was swamped by accusations that Ricky had chosen the wrong tactics for the wrong reasons.

The truth never got out. Why was our senior strike bowler barely given 30 overs? Because he was struggling with serious dehydration, that's why.

CHAPTER 18 GOING BACK

I knew that when I came back to Australia all the talk would be about Andrew Symonds and whether he was going to be picked for the next Test, which would be against New Zealand in Brisbane. I accepted that he deserved to get straight back in because of the success he'd had in Test cricket over the previous two years. But I bowled a bit faster than him and I could provide a little bit more with the ball, so it wasn't as cut and dried as that; but I knew I hadn't done enough with the bat to nail down the number-six slot.

It was November 2008 and, when I got back to Australia, Greg Chappell pulled me aside and said, 'Look, mate, tell me to go away if you want to, but I'm going to be honest with you. If you keep doing what you're doing, you'll be an okay Test player—you'll do okay. But if you want to be a really successful Test batsman, you've got to make a few adjustments.'

I was very taken aback by that initially. I felt I was in a pretty good place with my batting—or getting there—so this was quite confronting, especially to hear it from a legend like Greg. But I was listening to what he had to say. Greg had been in India for the first part of the Test series, when Tim Nielsen got him over to work as an interim coach with us. Greg had coached India for a few years and he knew their players very well, so that was an added advantage. And to be able to talk about cricket with someone of his stature and knowledge of the game was brilliant.

It took me a while to get on his wavelength, his philosophy of the most successful way of batting. He has an amazing cricket brain; he has done a lot of research on the best batsmen in the world, the guys who have averaged over 50 in Test cricket throughout history, to see if there was something they had in common. He thought there had to be something they all did that contributed to them being so good; it couldn't just be they were naturally talented.

So Greg analysed all the film and TV footage and pictures he could find, and he discovered that they were all in pretty much the same position when the ball was released. He showed me footage to prove his point, although it wasn't until a little later, when I had a stress fracture in my back and time to consider all this, that I totally understood what he was talking about. But that's another story.

Both Roy and I were in the first Test against New Zealand as we didn't play a spinner and, as if to prove Greg's point, I only scored a one and a five. Andrew did better (but not much) with a couple of scores in the 20s. However, I took some wickets so I did make a contribution to the win. After that match I was told by the selectors that I wasn't going to be playing in the second Test in Adelaide—they were going to play a spinner (rather than four quicks), which was what they should have been doing anyway. They said they didn't want to take me along for the ride as I needed to keep playing cricket. Also, I needed to score more runs—that was a big issue for them and I needed to get my batting going again.

That really annoyed me. Why couldn't I just be twelfth man? Why should I have to go back and play more cricket, when I'd played a lot already? They said it was a case of horses for courses and they were picking players depending on what ground the matches were being played at. I was really disappointed, especially with the whole 'horses for courses' thing. I did a newspaper interview and got myself into a bit of trouble when I said that, no matter what the conditions are, the best players are going to adapt. The only way to get better and be able to adapt to all conditions is if you play in all conditions.

That didn't go down too well. It got a few people, including some of the selectors, offside. Nothing was said officially, but one of the selectors came and told me the chairman wasn't very happy with what I'd said. I stayed in Brisbane to play for Queensland against South Australia and I was still working with Victor. He hadn't been in India, so when I was there I'd wake up at 6.30 every morning to get half an hour's treatment from Alex Kountouris the physio, to make sure my body felt right every time I went out to play or train. I'd also go in the pool every morning for 20 minutes to warm up. But that meant I didn't get as much sleep as I really needed and I was always tired. During the day, waiting to bat, I'd sit there and fall asleep, have a little power nap, just to compensate.

So as soon as I got home, I worked with Victor intensively. I'd see him before and after the games and he'd do all he could to make sure everything was in alignment.

In the game at the Gabba I got 19 and 81 (one way to get 100!) and Lee Carseldine—who was an inspiration to me because of the way he'd fought back from a terrible back injury—got 150 in our first innings. The big difference for me as a bowler was that, in the Test set-up, I was the fourth of the four quicks but, playing Sheffield Shield, I was one of the main bowlers; it all came good for me in South Australia's first innings, when I got seven wickets for 69 off 21 overs—my best bowling figures in my career.

I wasn't swinging the ball but I bowled a really good pace and had good control over my length. The wicket had a little bit in it too, which helped. Then in the second innings I had to bowl more overs than I really wanted to, or was used to bowling, and my back started to get sore. This was not great; my back hadn't hurt at all throughout India and I'd bowled a lot more overs than I had previously. When I saw Victor, he said I was a bit blocked in my pelvis but it was only one game—it should be okay.

I then played a one-day game for Queensland. I remember running in to bowl and my back was starting to get really sore. I didn't have as much power as I'd had, and the pain was starting to get really sharp and never really went away. I was seriously worried. Straight after that game I was supposed to fly to India to play in the inaugural Champions League, an international Twenty20 cricket competition between domestic teams from Australia, India, England, South Africa, Sri Lanka, New Zealand and the West Indies.

However, just before we were about to leave, there were those horrendous terrorist attacks on the hotels and bars in Mumbai on 26 November. One of the places they hit was the Leopold Café on Colaba Causeway in South Mumbai, which features in the book *Shantaram*. Lee and I had gone there and had lunch after the IPL final because of the book. The Leopold Café was one of the first places to be attacked when terrorists opened fire. At least ten people, including some foreigners, were killed; many more were injured. So they pulled the pin on the Champions League just as we were about to go.

After the two Tests against New Zealand, the next series was to be against South Africa. The first Test was in Perth, and I went over there as twelfth man for the game. But when I was bowling in the nets, my back was killing me; I got through five overs but I was getting worried, because it was really starting to affect my pace and energy behind the ball. Alex and the medical staff were trying to get me through it.

The second Test was in Melbourne on Boxing Day and we had a training session on Christmas Eve. I was running in to bowl and I couldn't handle it any more—it was absolutely killing me every ball I bowled. So I went and got an MRI scan. Normally for a back stress you'd get a CT and bone scan to see if there were any hot spots in your back; but because I'd had so many bone scans, they thought it might be a good idea to not expose my body to any more radiation and so they did an MRI instead. It didn't show anything. They thought it might just be a facet joint that was inflamed, so they injected it to see if it would settle down.

On Christmas Day I was okay. My back was still really sore, but I wasn't ruled out yet. I was twelfth man again and I didn't bowl; but during the Test match Brett Lee broke down with a stress fracture in his foot, so I had to field. It was a disastrous day at the MCG; J.P. Duminy got over 150 and Dale Steyn got over 70 in a big lower-order partnership. Although I didn't bowl, I fielded for the whole day, but my back was sore and I couldn't run that well. So they did a bone scan to see if there was anything there: the bone scan showed a hot spot and the CT scan showed a fracture. I knew exactly what that meant—a long time without bowling.

You might think I would have been shattered, but I put my problem down to that one game when I'd played well, when I'd bowled more overs in a concentrated spell than I had throughout the Indian tour. It usually takes more than one game to get stress fractures but, because of my build-up that year and my workload in India, it just took that one spike in my number of overs to cause a problem. But mentally I was okay. The success I had at the IPL and my first century in one-day cricket were keeping me going.

Ironically, once again my own misfortune coincided with someone else's. The second Test would turn out to be Andrew Symonds' last for Australia. He hurt his knee in that game and needed an operation, so they drafted in Andrew McDonald from Victoria to be the all-rounder. I'm 100 per cent sure that, if I'd been fit, I would have played in the Sydney Test and gone on to be the all-rounder in the subsequent series in South Africa. But, like I said, I now had some real success behind me even if it was in other forms of the game so I wasn't too shattered.

As usual, I tried to make the best of it. I had six weeks of not doing much except letting my back heal; so, apart from going back and forth to see Victor I spent that time in Sydney, for the first time in my life doing things I really wanted to do, like going to see some bands that I hadn't had the chance to before because I'd been away. I saw British rock legend Jeff Beck at the Enmore Theatre and also Diesel—I've always loved his music—and ended up meeting Jimmy Barnes and getting to know him. So at least through this period I got a fix of music—the thing I love most when I'm away from cricket.

I also needed to get my head around what I was going to do after cricket. Realistically, if the worst came to the worst in terms of injuries, it could all end very abruptly. So I started talking to my management about it. I knew that, even if I wasn't going to play for Australia for a while, the IPL was going to be there, and that would keep me going until I hopefully got another opportunity with Australia. But that also meant I had to be fit.

One thing I realised: whatever happens, I want to do something in music, although I'm still working out exactly what that is. I would love to play in a band. Whether it's just a garage band—and we just play songs in a room amongst ourselves, or at a tiny gig in front of three people—it's something I want to do.

Jason Krejza has been a huge inspiration to me as a musician, singer and guitarist, and he reminds me how big a part luck plays in cricket. Jason plays for Tasmania and is a very skilful spin bowler. In his first Test, the fourth match in our tour of India, he took eight wickets in the first innings and was named Man of the Match despite Australia's defeat. Jason was then dropped for the first Test against New Zealand in Brisbane because they thought the pitch would suit seamers. He injured his ankle before the second Test in Adelaide, but played his first Test in Australia against South Africa in Perth. He took 1 for 209 and was dropped from the squad in favour of Nathan Hauritz. The idea was for him to go back to Tassie and 'refine his craft'; but Jason would have felt confused by this hot-and-cold treatment and it took him until this year to get back into the one-day squad for the World Cup, when he had a couple of good games and a couple that were okay.

I just wonder how good Jason would be if he'd spent the last two years being nurtured and coached in the squad. Anyway, I owe him a debt of gratitude for introducing me to some great music.

We have talked about forming a band when we finish with cricket, maybe with Julian Huxley, another mate who I got to know through Brett Lee. Julian is a Super-14 rugby player who had a brain tumour that they discovered after he had a fit on the field during a game. But he had surgery and radiation treatment and, incredibly, played for the Melbourne Rebels Super Rugby team this year. He's an amazing guy; he plays guitar and sings and loves the same sort of music as I do: Guns & Roses and Eric Clapton. It could work . . . we'll just have to take turns with rhythm guitar, lead and vocals.

I have played a couple of times in public; my biggest gig was playing with Jimmy Barnes at a charity dinner for the Steve Waugh Foundation, which raises money for kids who've got rare diseases. A couple of weeks earlier, Brett had introduced me to Jimmy and we realised we'd all be at this function. Brett, I think it was, joked that we could all perform together. Jimmy, who is one of the most open and generous souls on the planet, said sure, that would be great. I thought no more about it but, at lunchtime on the day of the event, Brett rings me up and says, 'Are you still keen to play tonight with Jimmy?' I said, 'I don't know his songs that well.' I liked 'Flame Trees' but I didn't know it off by heart. He said Jimmy would like us to get up there and play with him.

So I sat in my music room, downloaded the chords from the internet, and tried to learn it as quickly as I could. We had to get there early to do a sound check with Jimmy's band, which was awesome. And that night became my first gig. It was an incredible night. There was a fabulous dinner; Jimmy was there, Human Nature sang, plus there was an enormous orchestra. There was even a circus performance—all in the famous Hordern Pavilion.

I have played cricket in front of massive crowds all over the world, but I was *so* nervous. I got up there and we played 'Khe Sahn' and 'Flame Trees'—I got a couple of chords wrong but, when you've got other guitars there as well, you can get away with the odd mistake. It was such an amazing thrill—similar in a way to the thrill of going out to bat in front of a stadium crowd. That was the sort of buzz I got and that's why I want to do it again. That rush from the heightened anxiety, I think, is what I'm always looking for.

The only other gig that I've done was in Hampshire in 2010, after the Ashes Tests and before the one-dayers. Brett and I were having a quiet dinner with the Hampshire chairman and good friend, Rod Bransgrove, and we got the guitars out. Rod's got a few guitars and loves his music as well, so we played some tunes and he kept saying Brett and I should play a quick set at Hampshire's pre-ODI dinner the next night. I said, 'Oh I don't know about that...' We were at training the next day and Rod said it would be good if we played—people would love it. Brett said he didn't want to sing, but I was confident enough with my singing so I said I would do the vocals.

We played two songs in front of the Hampshire guests—'The Drugs Don't Work' by The Verve and 'Don't Look Back in Anger' by Oasis. They hadn't known this was going to happen and it was something a bit different. Halfway through the second song Brett blew a string and it was getting in his way. So I ripped the string out of his guitar and he played on with no G string. It was a rush.

Getting back to that six weeks I had off in Sydney, as soon as I started training my plan was that, once my back had healed a bit, I would bat only. So, at the end of the six weeks I returned to Brisbane, partly because I was working with Victor but also because I wanted to return to the Queensland set-up, to make sure I had them on side. It was about eight weeks after I got injured before I was in the side again. But again whenever I've been injured I've always thought things happen for a reason. Then I ask myself what it is that I should be doing to justify the injury. This time it was working intensively with Greg Chappell to help me understand what he was talking about regarding my batting and then to practise it over and over again so that it became second nature and hard-wired into my muscle memory by the time I started playing again.

My two weeks with Greg were phenomenal. His theory was that the best batsmen in history, as the ball was being released, would all have their front foot slightly in the air. All their weight was on their back foot ready to go forward at the ball. He showed me all these still pictures of batsmen at the point when the bowler is about to release the ball. Each in their own slightly different way were in the same position. Once I saw that, I understood where I needed to get to and I knew I could do that.

This is an echo of the baseball swing theory of shifting your weight from your back foot to your front foot as you swing, in a way, but Greg's method was based on a more conventional cricket stroke. When I am slogging, baseball style, I have my front foot in the air, but I am deep in the crease and all my weight is loaded up on my back foot. Greg's theory was a less extreme version of that. I worked with Greg and after our sessions I listened to his stories about when he was playing for Australia. I'd read all the biographies anyway but to hear these stories, about Botham and that generation of cricketers, from the horse's mouth was awesome.

My first game back with the Bulls was against Victoria at the MCG in March 2009 and it was the best I'd ever batted in my life. Technically I was more confident playing shots that I hadn't played as well before. It was just a slightly different way of hitting the ball, but I ended up getting 130 and batted through until near the end of the innings. Greg's advice had added a whole new dimension—especially to my four-day and Test batting.

My one concern was that the new pre-movement would commit me to an aggressive shot. But your instincts take over. If they bowl a good ball, you defend it right at the last moment. My first instinct used to be to defend, whereas now, because of my stance and the way I am batting, my first instinct is to attack. If it isn't there to attack, then I'll defend it or let it go at the last moment.

And that's how my batting has progressed to where it's at now. I'm at my best when defence is my last resort, and a good example of that was my second innings of the final Ashes Test in Sydney in 2011—I was 38 off 40 balls with a strike rate of 95. And then I was run out.

After that Queensland match in 2009, I got a call from Greg Chappell. He hadn't seen my innings because it was down at Melbourne, but I talked him through it and he was delighted for me. It was unbelievable that what we had worked through came together so quickly. And that was when my progress as a batsman really started taking off.

THE MEDIA

As a player you have a love–hate relationship with the press—you love them when they say positive things, but hate them when they have a go at you, especially if you think it's unfair. I remember, during the week of my first Test in Sydney, Peter Roebuck wrote a nice article on me in the *Sydney Morning Herald,* talking positively about my potential as an all-rounder. He's changed over time and he's not backward in coming forward with his thoughts, but I try not to take press reports too much to heart.

But the most disappointing thing about the media is that a majority of people believe what they read. No doubt that's how I was as a young kid as well and, if that's your only source of information, you'll take it as gospel. If it's in the paper, it's got to be true. But once you get involved, you read things that are extremely harsh, or over the top or plain wrong.

But it doesn't matter to the journalist whether it's right or wrong, he or she doesn't have to cop the consequences. The only person for whom the story has consequences is the person who's being written about and their friends and family. There are people out there I know who take it all with a grain of salt, but that's only a few people. The rest say, 'Well, they obviously know what's going on—no smoke without fire.'

That definitely has been the most disappointing aspect for me because I have occasionally felt some articles about me were over-the-top and harsh. People were writing me off and saying I was completely overrated and soft as I was getting injured all the time; the average cricket fan was agreeing with them, because that was all the information they were getting. Even when Ricky, Glenn McGrath and Warnie came out in support of me, this was still at the time when I hadn't totally showed what I could do and the press were relentless. That was the hardest thing for me to get my head around but, looking back, I realise they had a point. The public had only seen glimpses of what I could do so in the end it was fair enough.

Often there's one player that the media are swarming over. One of the harshest attacks I've seen was against Matthew Hayden—he got absolutely smashed and battered by the media just before he retired. You could see it really affected the way he played towards the end. The media guys who were nailing him were disregarding all the amazing things he'd done previously, they were so determined to get rid of him. When the media pressure gets that intense, it affects anyone, no matter who you are.

I remember talking to Graeme Smith of South Africa about it after the series. He was absolutely blown away by what had happened during that summer. He said the media were being totally disrespectful of what Hayden had achieved. They were personal attacks, and the guys who were writing them completely overlooked what he'd done for Australian cricket. Sure, talk about how he should maybe move on if he's not scoring that many runs. But it shouldn't be so personal.

CHAPTER 19 **BAT OUT OF HELL**

With my batting getting better, I realised I needed to get my bowling up to speed and thought I might get it going in the five one-dayers against Pakistan in Dubai and Abu Dhabi in March and April 2009 (held in the United Arab Emirates because it wasn't safe to tour Pakistan). I tried to gradually work up my bowling speed, but my back was still a bit angry; then, just as I was about to bowl in my first game, I strained my groin because my action had changed, compensating for my back and trying to make sure my technique was safe.

Victor wasn't over there and, significantly, neither was Alex Kountouris, the Australian team physio, who was having that tour off. So they had a stand-in physio, who had no idea what I had been doing or where I was at, which really annoyed me. I need to have someone with me who was on the same wavelength—Alex had got me through India and was able to keep me going when Victor couldn't be around.

I had planned to bowl a few overs in the one-off Twenty20 against Pakistan at the end of the tour. But when I came off after batting, my groin was really tight and it got worse when I tried to bowl warm-ups before the Pakistan innings. I ended up not bowling and then missed out on the IPL for two weeks, which was a big hit financially as well. Most importantly, it meant my push for selection in the Ashes squad was going to be more difficult. Disturbingly, there was an asterisk beside my name when the Ashes squad was announced: '*subject to fitness'. It felt like a beacon over my name to keep people talking about my injuries rather than my selection.

On the upside, that series in the Emirates was the first time I was picked for Australia purely for my batting, which I thought was going to take a lot longer to achieve. I was the second-highest scorer of runs throughout that series and I got my second one-day century there. But I was disappointed with the way things had worked out. I knew with the right maintenance this injury wouldn't have occurred, or at least there'd have been less chance of it happening.

At that stage, I didn't have much long-term financial security. Cricket Australia contracts change from year to year. Fair's fair—no matter what, they offer very good money. But they can vary greatly from one year to the next, and you can go from being very well paid to considerably less so. What if you buy a house and then you get injured? Or they change their minds about you and put you down the list, where you just scrape in and get the base contract? Even if Cricket Australia give you a three-year contract, you still can go from being ranked number three to being ranked number 25—and that's a huge difference in the amount that you get paid. You could theoretically go from $1.5 million to $200,000 (based on the 2010–11 figures). Then you think, 'Next year I might not even get a contract, so I might have to sell this house.' Sure, it can happen to anyone who has a mortgage, and you can make more in match payments, if you play, but it's not the kind of pressure anyone needs in their lives.

Rajasthan in the IPL were good to me. They said: 'You've done so well for us that, if you sign an extra year on your contract, we will re-sign it for a much higher amount.' It was very good money and offered me the kind of financial security that I was looking for; Rajasthan locked me into an amount I got as long as I played for them in the IPL. If I'd been injured in the lead-up to the season or if my form had been bad playing for Australia, it didn't matter: as long as I played, I got paid the agreed rate. However, because of my groin injury, I couldn't play so I missed out on those payments.

These injuries were costing me serious money. I decided it was too big a risk to leave my health and fitness in the hands of other people because I was the one who suffered the consequences. That's when I decided it was a priority to get Victor on tour with me, even if I had to pay for his services myself. Hiring a top medical professional full-time is a big financial commitment. Victor's one of the best at what he does in Australia, so he doesn't come cheap. No matter how much he likes helping me out, he's got his family and commitments too, not to mention a heap of other potential opportunities.

My finances were in pretty good shape and, if worst came to the worst, I would have to sell the place I was living in and downsize. People sell or mortgage their homes to invest in a business; well, I was prepared to do that, if need be—to invest in myself. I knew deep down what I could achieve, just from my good form in the IPL and the one-dayers, and I knew that, if I was fit and strong, I could do it at Test level.

It was a big decision; Lee and I talked it over and decided that, even if it didn't work out, at least we'd know, when I finished my career, that I'd given myself every possible chance to have a really good crack at cricket at the highest level. I wasn't going to die wondering.

Roughly, I was going to have to earn $300,000 a year, before tax, just to put Victor on the payroll. So I went to Cricket Australia with my contract in hand and they obviously weren't expecting it. I asked if there was any chance that they would be able to help me out. Victor would be open to working with Alex, if needed, so they'd have another guy on tour. Even if they could help pay some of his accommodation, or just part of his fee, it would be great. And there was an upside for them—they'd get the services of one of the best sports physios in Australia, so I would be subsidising them in a way.

But it was no go. They said it wouldn't be setting a good precedent. If they said yes to this, then other players might want to bring along their own physio, or their own coach, and expect Cricket Australia to subsidise it. So I made the only decision I could—to pay for him myself.

They didn't like that very much either—they thought it wouldn't be good for the team dynamic. But I said that the only person who was really affected by this was me: 'If it all goes wrong, you guys will only need to find someone else to do what I think I can do,' I told them. 'I'm the only one who has to live with the consequences of this decision, and I'm going to do it.'

I got Victor over for the Twenty20 World Cup in England in June, 2009. It was the first time I had bowled for a while and I got belted. Because we got knocked out of the contest in the first round, we had a two-week training camp. They wanted us to do a training drill in a circuit—you do an exercise and then run to the next station, stopping dead while moving to your left. I did that and felt my quad go, and I knew what it meant straightaway—I was going to miss another opportunity to get into the Ashes team.

While all this was going on, the final curtain had come down on Andrew Symonds' career. Roy loves his rugby league and he loves Queensland, so he went and watched the first State of Origin match on TV with a few of the guys. Because of the time difference with the UK, it all finished up around 10 am and everyone else went back to the hotel; but he stayed on to have a few more beers to celebrate Queensland's win. In the afternoon we had fitness testing scheduled and Roy rocked up at about 3 pm, having been in the pub all day. He was mumbling and not looking all that sober, so the physio said, 'Get out of here, you're not doing this, you're pissed.'

Ricky Ponting had supported Roy the whole way, backing him to be the fifteenth man in the World Cup squad in 2003 and helping him significantly to get where he was as a cricketer. And even though he was furious after the Cardiff incident, Punter had backed him through 2005, talking him through it and trying to get him back on the rails. But enough was enough.

We had the English Professional Cricketers' Association dinner that night and Roy had been told not to drink, but he just kept going. It is really sad to see anyone, but especially such a talented sportsman, in that place. Cricket Australia ripped up his contract; but he went on to play for Gloucester in England and in the Twenty20 for Queensland and, of course, for the Deccan Chargers in the IPL. It's not over even now—in January 2011 he got a tidy $850,000-a-year contract to play in the IPL again.

With Roy now gone for good, I felt the only way I could get in was to bat at six, as Marcus North was also providing another bowling option. But this new injury put all those thoughts on the back burner and I know Victor, who was based in Monaco and working with me in between his Tour de France commitments, was just as frustrated as I was.

Management were checking on me twice a day, asking if I was going to be all right as a spare batsman for the first Test. It was going to be pushing it to be fit, even just as a batsman alone with all the running between wickets. In the end there was no chance of me playing, but they didn't call another batsman into the squad. They had Andrew McDonald, another all-rounder, although they couldn't see how he could replace anyone within the team apart from the spinner if they decided to go with an all-pace bowling attack.

I realised some of the other guys in the team were starting to get frustrated with me because I had another injury. Even my good mate Brett Lee said, 'Why don't you just inject it and get on with it?' Brett has had his share of injuries but they were almost always fractures or bone spurs on his ankles, that kind of thing. He'd never had soft-tissue injuries that kept him out of games and, like most people, he didn't quite get it that, by playing on with painkillers, I would definitely make it worse and turn a two-week injury into a two-month problem.

So I missed the opportunity for that first Ashes Test (which we should have won but ended up drawing when we couldn't get that last wicket). I was fit to play as an all-rounder in the second Test at Lord's, but there were only a couple of days in between the Tests and no tour matches in which I could push for selection, so I missed out again. That was the Test we lost, where Freddie got a five-for in the second innings.

Worryingly for Phil Hughes, he didn't get any runs in either Test match. After a spectacular start to his Test career in South Africa—a century in both innings of only his second Test in Durban the previous year—the England bowlers seemed to have worked him out. He got out to short balls each time in the tour matches to Steve Harmison, a very good bowler who gets unbelievable bounce when he's at his best. And Freddie worked him over in the first two Tests.

After the second Test there was a tour match in Northampton. Ricky sat out that game, but I was fit and ready to go so I batted at number three in his place. Phil Hughes got out twice to short balls again, this time from a tall medium-pacer called David Wigley and in the first innings for only ten runs. He seemed to be really quite spooked by this guy's bowling. It was only 130 kilometres an hour at best, but Phil was ducking balls he shouldn't; even when he got a 50 in the second innings, he fell to a medium-pace ball that was short.

In contrast, I felt very comfortable right away, hitting 84 off 96 balls. The track was pretty good and every time I got near loose balls I was putting them away. I think I got 20 off one over, all from loose balls. I wasn't slogging; my technique felt great and I was seeing the ball unbelievably well. I knew I could bat like that in Twenty20 and one-dayers; but to do that in a longer game was something else again. It wasn't a conscious effort; it was the way my game had evolved.

The selectors and Ricky watched me and, I assume, saw how Phil was struggling; but I still didn't have any sense that anything was really going to change. I should have, though. During the first Test, Stuart Clark and I didn't play. We were sitting there and he said, 'I reckon you could open the batting at some stage during this series. The England bowlers could really give Phil a good working over so keep your mind open because I reckon that could happen.' I thought that was a funny thing to say about a guy who got 100-plus in each innings in his second Test, and in South Africa, too.

But he must have sensed something was up. When we got to Birmingham, before the third Test, Ricky texted me and asked if I was free for coffee. We sat in the bar and Punter said, 'Phil Hughes isn't going that great at the moment. Obviously he knows how to score runs like he has throughout his career. But they are looking at maybe dropping him and you opening. What d'you think about that?'

I was rapt, obviously; but I had to remind myself that my previous experience of opening in the longer form was absolutely dreadful. I'd opened three times for Queensland when an opportunity came up in the Australian side with Justin Langer's retirement. I told Queensland I wanted to open, so I could be considered for Justin's slot. They said, 'Do what you want, but we don't think it's right for the team.'

They were right. In four innings I got three ducks then a 14 although my batting had improved a lot since then. Ricky said, 'The way you're batting, you could take them on.' At training the next day Jamie Cox, one of the selectors, came up to me. 'You're going to be opening,' he said. 'There's no one else really to do it. Mike Hussey might, but we don't really want to use him there. We know where your game's at; and we really believe you have the technique to be able to do it.'

CHAPTER 20 **RIGHT SAID FREDDIE**

Going to that third Ashes Test in Birmingham as an opener, the one bowler that I was most anxious about facing was Freddie Flintoff. He'd played the second Test and his knee was giving him grief, but he was always going to play the third Test. I hadn't really played against him much. I faced him in the World XI, when he really worked me over, but I hadn't even confronted him in one-day cricket because I hadn't opened the batting against England. I'd seen how he bowled at Lord's, and he had it over everyone really; he bowled fast, lots of bounce and very few loose balls—always in your face. I thought he was really going to test me out, especially with a brand-new ball.

Apart from Freddie, I knew what to expect. I'd faced Jimmy Anderson a few times leading up to the World Cup, when Matt Hayden was injured, so I felt comfortable enough playing him. His pace isn't frightening and there's no extra bounce. You just have to watch the ball.

I remember the first day when we got to the ground, it had been raining and the outfield was very wet. We won the toss and batted—but not until 5 pm when the rain cleared. Simon Katich asked, 'Do you want to face the first ball or do you want me to?' I thought, 'If I'm going to open, I've got to be prepared to take the first ball on.' On the other hand, the last time I opened I got out in the first over . . . twice! But I knew I had to do it, even though it was the most anxious I'd ever been going in to bat.

I had no idea what to expect. I knew Freddie was going to work me over, because that's what I would do in a similar situation. But Jimmy Anderson bowled to me first; I let a couple go and then I got a single. Okay, that was a relief. Then I got down the other end and next over I was facing Freddie and I thought, 'Oh, what's going to happen here?'

He was bowling a good pace, without really swinging it to begin with, and he was a bit back of a length. I faced him for a couple of overs and the more I played him the more comfortable I felt against him. And even though he started swinging the ball, I was able to take him on, be aggressive and put it back on him if he bowled a loose one. Once I settled down I was backing myself and it seemed to work, putting the pressure back on the bowlers. Simon and I got to 85 in 19 overs; I got my 50 in fairly quick time and I was 60-something not out by stumps.

I went to bed that night thinking, 'Jeez, that's a good start—hopefully I can keep that going in the morning . . . keep taking them on.' It wasn't meant to be—I was out first ball the next day. But the most important thing was knowing I could go out there and not try to hit every ball for six, but be consistently aggressive. And it worked. They bowled well to me, but I was able to get some really good shots away and prove to myself I could do this at Test level. I knew I had to concentrate hard every ball, especially with Freddie, firstly because he could hurt me and secondly because he could get me out. But I knew if I really locked onto every ball, I could do well.

The second innings started off in similar fashion. It was just before Freddie went off because his knee was almost gone, but he was still giving it everything he had. I remember him steaming in and he bowled an unbelievable spell—his pace was very good and he hardly bowled me a bad ball. Maybe he bowled one on my pads but, apart from that, he gave me nothing at all. It was his last go, really, before his knee was too sore.

He bowled one ball that was a bit shorter, one of those awkward lengths, and it hit me right in the forearm. Sometimes a hit like that can break your arm; but other times you get lucky and it just gets you in the right spot so it doesn't hurt. I don't wear a forearm protector—I prefer to trust my instincts. So when Freddie hit me on the arm, being competitive and aggressive, I just looked at him as if to say, 'That didn't hurt—you'll have to do better to hurt me.'

Jimmy Anderson is someone who has always got on my nerves, the way he bowls and the way he is—arrogant, as if you shouldn't even be out there trying to compete with him. And when you do he looks astonished, as if to say, 'What do you think you're doing, hitting me for a boundary?' So for the first couple of overs I started getting into him when I was batting. I said something like, 'You think you're so good now, mate? You've got a few wickets, have you? So you think you're too good now, do you?' But he'd talk back to me a bit, because he had Freddie as his saviour and protector.

After the second Test, according to all the reports, that's exactly what the team management felt we needed: someone to go in and not get intimidated, to put it back on them and be aggressive with their body language, and even put it back on them verbally as well. That's how Matthew Hayden played when he opened. He was aggressive, and that's why he was such a major force in the game. He would get up in their faces and into a scrap from the first ball—that was his philosophy. Ironically, he's such a chilled-out bloke off the field; but once he crosses that boundary rope, look out! That's what they call 'white line fever'.

I got two 50s in that game and it's just as well because the

CENTURION: Celebrating my first one-day international ton at St George's, Grenada.

ONE OF THE BOYS: The fourth one-day international against the West Indies in 2008. They needed eight off my last over to win—we restricted them to six.

JOB DONE: Hitting a six to score the winning runs as well as bring up my century in the 2009 ICC Champions Trophy Final against New Zealand in South Africa.

AT LAST: I finally get my first Test century—after several near misses—at the MCG against Pakistan in December 2009.

BLISS: Lee and me on our beautiful wedding day.

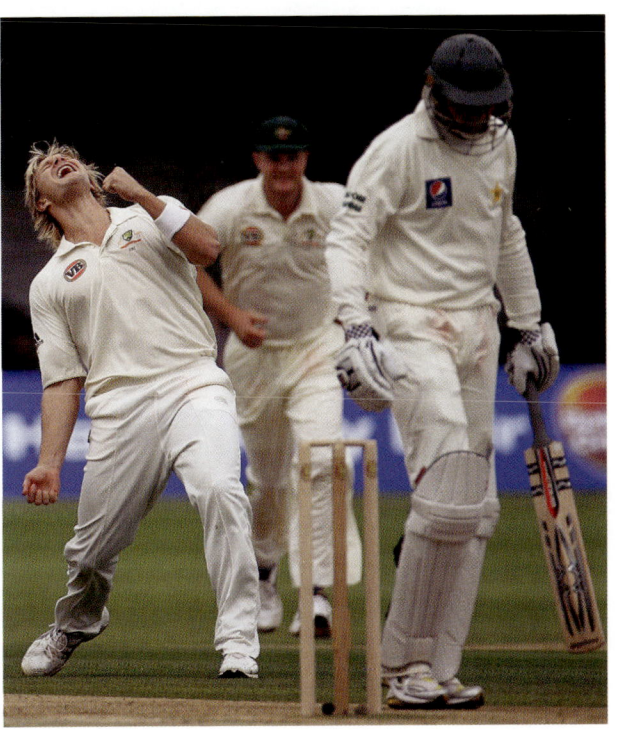

ON THE BOARD: Celebrating my five-wicket haul against Pakistan at Lord's in 2010. Danish Kaneria was the batsman.

TURNAROUND: Winning the first one-day international against England at the MCG after our Ashes disaster of 2010–11.

KEEPING IT REAL: Up in my home town of Ipswich, hoping to raise a few spirits after the devastating floods of early 2011.

SOMETHING IN THE AIR: Back to business—in the one-day internationals against England I get Ian Bell out, caught and bowled, at the SCG.

LIFESAVER: Celebrating my first Allan Border Medal in 2010 with Victor Popov, the man who rescued my career as an all-rounder.

AT THE DOUBLE: With Allan Border as he presents me with the medal that bears his name—my second in two years.

SLOGGED: Hitting a six against New Zealand is a bright spot in a generally disappointing World Cup campaign in India, 2011.

HAPPY CHAPS: Cricket Australia announces Michael Clarke as the new national captain at the SCG and me as his loyal sidekick.

ON OUR WAY: Helping the 'new' Australian team run up a 3–0 one-day international clean sweep in Bangladesh, 2011.

FAMILY DAY OUT: Spending some quality time with our dogs, Bobbi and Clappo.

media were going nuts. 'What's happened to Phil Hughes? What the hell are they doing putting this guy Watson in as an opener?' The media saw it as a sign that the team management were panicking. From our point of view, the Poms were targeting Phil and we needed to shore up the top order. It worked out well for me, because no one expected me to perform at all. I had nothing to lose; I had no pressure. Okay, I was nervous because I didn't know what to expect and my previous experiences of opening had been awful. But everyone was expecting me to fail. If I did, then that's the way it was supposed to happen. But if I did well—it was a perfect scenario to go into. In the end it was an amazing opportunity, and one that some players never get in their entire careers.

That's why I believe luck has such a big part to play in your career. I was lucky, not just because I got that opportunity but because I got it when I was batting better than I ever had in my life. With Greg's help I had developed my technique to be able to take on some of the best bowlers in the world with the new ball. Mentally I was confident; physically I was fit; technically I was prepared, and there was no pressure on me because no one had any expectations.

On the downside, my bowling was shocking. I was still very nervous about letting rip, because I thought I might get the dreaded stress fractures back again, even though I had Victor there and he was working on me non-stop. When we got to the one-dayers, I bowled more and I gradually got a bit better, although my back was sore occasionally.

My batting started to go off during the one-dayers. After a 95 against the England Lions and 60-odd up in Scotland, in the serious stuff against England my scores were 10, 34, 7, 36, 4 and 0. But the worrying thing was that I was getting out lbw every time—going back to a ball that I should have gone forward to. That started to play on my mind a bit; the England bowlers knew it and, just about every time they got it right, they got me out.

So again it was two steps forward and one back. This was the first time in my career that I'd had a prolonged period of games against the same opposition and I was getting out the same way. It was embarrassing. They were laughing at me every time they got me out in the end.

We went from England straight to the Champions Trophy in South Africa. I worked on a couple of things technically with Tim Nielsen and thought I'd sorted out the problem before the first game against the West Indies. I never got a chance to find out—I got a first-ball duck against Kemar Roach. I hadn't seen this guy before and thought his first ball was going to be a wide. It was an absolute thunderbolt and I was clean bowled by a 150 kilometre an hour inswinging yorker. I bowled okay, and Ricky and Mitch Johnson both got into the 70s, so it turned out all right and we won pretty easily.

The next game was against India in Pretoria. I felt I started a bit better, but I ended up getting out in the first over for another duck. That didn't do my confidence any good. But the amazing thing about batting is that when you work on something technical, all of a sudden things start to click and you can go from thinking you can't score a single run to feeling like you're back in the groove. It's incredible. One match you're dying, feeling like you've lost it completely—you can't even show your other shots off because you keep getting out—then you get into the nets and you start to feel okay again. And you think. 'Yes, I'm back!'

Playing against Pakistan I started to feel confident again, but we only just scraped through. We had to tie or win to get through to the semis, but we nearly screwed it up. We were cruising, but then we lost a bunch of wickets really quickly. In the end it was our last men in, Brett Lee and Peter Siddle, who got us into the semi-final against England.

Compared to the Champions Trophy team that I'd played with in 2006, the side had changed immensely. We didn't have Gilchrist, McGrath, Martyn, Symonds or Hayden anymore. We had an almost totally new young side, so no one was expecting us to do that well. There was me, Ricky and Tim Paine; Michael Clarke was injured, so he'd gone home; Cameron White was batting four, Callum Ferguson batted five, Mike Hussey was in at six, then James Hopes, who bowled with Nathan Hauritz, Peter Siddle, Mitch Johnson, Brett Lee and me.

It was basically a raw team, and getting into the semi against England was a huge achievement. But we'd beaten them in England 6–1 just a few weeks before, so we knew we had the upper hand against them, even though they'd beaten us in the Ashes.

We bowled first and did really well. I went as well as I ever had in one-day cricket with 2 for 35 off just under nine overs and we restricted them to 257. Tim Paine briefly joined me at the top of the order, but his only score was one boundary off four balls. Then Ricky and I batted through the rest of the innings—I got 136 off 132 balls with seven sixes and ten fours and Ricky got 111 off 115 balls, including 12 fours and a six. Ultimately, we rolled them with nine wickets and eight overs to spare.

The final was against New Zealand, who are often capable of stringing a few results together and always raise their game against Australia. They are one of those teams who are always better than the combined talent of their individual players. They do punch above their weight; they don't have many people there who play cricket—most of their best athletes play rugby union—but we always know that, if we have an off day, they can beat us. And this was the final of a major tournament, which meant anything could happen.

One of New Zealand's best players is their then captain, Daniel Vettori, who is a world-class left-arm finger spinner, but he didn't pull up well from their semi-final against Pakistan and that was a huge blow for them. To make matters worse, their acting skipper and opening bat, Brendon McCullum, was out for a duck in the first over. Brett Lee and Peter Siddle really took it to them and we contained them to just over 200.

When they bowled, although Vettori was out, they did have Shane Bond, who had previously been banned from international cricket for playing in the unofficial ICL Twenty20 competition in India. But when he got out of his ICL contract, they brought him back in. When he's at his best, Shane is one of the finest bowlers in the world. He is fast—up into the 150s—and swings the ball into the stumps, which is quite different from most blokes, who either bowl straight or swing the ball away. He was backed up by Kyle Mills, a tall and skilful medium-fast right-hander, who is another bowling threat.

Despite the low target, we had a fair bit of trouble to start with. We hardly scored a run in the first 15 overs and lost Tim Paine early on to Shane Bond; then Kyle Mills got Ricky for only one. Shane was bowling incredibly well and, to be honest, he could have got me out with any ball. It was down to me and Cameron White, with a bit of help from Mike Hussey and James Hopes at the end. I knew there was a lot of responsibility on me to bat through the innings; I was desperate to win this for us—we were a new team and this would be a big achievement, bigger even than the 2007 World Cup or the Champions Trophy in 2006, for me anyway, because those wins were achieved with a long-established and very successful team.

This team was pretty new, so it felt like we were starting afresh and still winning when it counted. I got 105 not out and Cameron batted beautifully for 60-plus. At the end of the forty-fifth over, I was on 93 and James Hopes came up to me and said, 'Make sure you get your 100.' I said, 'I don't care—you score the runs if you get the chance. I don't care if I get 100 or not—it doesn't matter as long as we win.' But he said, 'Go for it if you get the chance.'

Jeetan Patel, who bowls right-arm off-breaks, was up. First ball of the over, I slog-swept him for six. That was me on 99 and the scores were level—we just needed a single to win. So I went for it again and smashed it into the stands over long-on. That felt great, of course, but a bigger achievement than hitting the winning runs was to score back-to-back centuries in the semi-final and final of a big tournament. I also got Man of the Match awards for those two games.

The ICC was trying to raise the profile of the Champions Trophy, so they had put the prize money up to an amazing $2 million for the winning team. If you got Man of the Match, you got a beautiful IWC Schaffhausen Swiss watch, worth about $8000. When they gave me the first one, they asked what I wanted engraved on it—I told them the date, the semi-final, how many I scored. But in the final, after I got a second one, I said, 'Do you mind if I don't get it engraved? I would really like to get a new guitar—something that makes sure I will always remember achieving something this special.' So I ended up buying an Eric Clapton 'Blackie' signature Fender Stratocaster guitar in exchange for the watch. I've still got that one watch from the semi-final, but out of the final I got an amazing guitar that I love to play. That was my reward to myself for one of the most special times in my life and I remember it every time I play that guitar (which is as often as I can).

The sense of achievement for us as a group was phenomenal. We had a brilliant night of celebration and we only had a couple of hours sleep before Ricky and I had to do media in the morning. Ricky got the Player of the Series and the Golden Bat for the most runs in the tournament. We met up for lunch with a whole group of guys who were still there because a couple of them had to fly over to India for the Champions League. We had a great day, lunch and a few wines—after all we'd each won about $140,000, and it was probably five or six hours before we had to jump up and get on the plane.

On the flight home I realised I was happier in myself than I had ever been. I'd started playing Test cricket and made a good fist of it. I'd opened for Australia and was doing all right. My body was holding up; I'd done well on the international stage and played a big part in a major trophy win for Australia.

I thought my life couldn't get any better—then I realised it could. This was a perfect time to think about getting married. Lee had stuck by me through thick and thin and I was ready to find out if she would marry me.

CHAPTER 21 **LAST MAN STANDING**

Lee had been with me in England throughout the Ashes series, but she'd had to go back to Sydney to work for Fox Sports during our one-dayers there. She watched a lot of it whenever she could, though, and had to report on it as well.

After the Champions Trophy I only had a week off at home before I was due to go to India for seven one-dayers. I had to work quickly. So I hired a yacht, we anchored in a bay for the night and the skipper made himself scarce. We had a romantic dinner and I proposed. Thank God she said yes—I'd have been tempted to jump overboard if she hadn't. Seriously, this was an amazing time in my life.

My one regret on the cricket front was that my success wasn't happening in Australia. The die-hard cricket fans knew what I was doing, but the Australian public—and sections of the press—hadn't seen the best of me yet. However, we were already looking forward to the Australian summer so I could only hope I could keep things going. Before then there was the small matter of a tour to India.

Once again it was a shame that it all happened overseas, but I did okay despite having an injury. Alex, our main physio, didn't go because he had spent 14 weeks away from home without seeing his family, which was really hard for him. Unfortunately I developed a bit of a glute problem—I was able to bat and run but I didn't have heaps of power through the crease, so it meant my bowling was slightly off. In the first game I didn't get any runs and when I bowled, even in the second-last over in the game, when they had no chance of winning, I couldn't execute my yorkers and produced a horrific over.

I ended up going for 20 and they only needed nine off the last over. Thank our lucky stars we had Peter Siddle. First he sent Harbhajan Singh back to the pavilion, clean bowled, then he kept the tail-enders to five runs. We won by four, but my bowling had almost blown it.

Over the following two games, Ricky looked after me. I only bowled five overs in the next one—but then that might have been because I was leaking runs—and none in the third one. However, we lost both of them and suddenly we were 2–1 down and it was time for me to shape up or ship out. Thankfully, Victor came over to India, wove his magic, and got me back to being able to bowl flat out within a week.

In game four I didn't quite get my 50, but I did take the last three wickets and we won by 24 runs. I was back firing on all cylinders. I got Man of the Match and the game turned the series around for us. On the other hand, we were gradually being crippled by injuries. Peter Siddle had to go home because of early signs of stress fractures; Ben Hilfenhaus had a sore knee; Tim Paine broke his finger; Brett Lee hurt his elbow and had to go home too. It was a disaster. We had different people flying in and out on a daily basis.

But I was very lucky to have Victor there to get my body back on track with massage and manipulation. He knows my body so well because he's the one who made it what it is through all the advice he's given me. He normally finds a chain that's involved in whatever the problem is. With most physios I've seen, if it's, say, a shoulder problem, they will work on the shoulder. With Victor, he's looking to see where the problem starts and it may be a different part of the body entirely. He finds the chain and works on every part of it. That's one aspect where he differs from so many people.

He also knows how to spend time on an injury. When I hurt my leg in England, he spent two hours on an area just above my knee, using really slow massage to try to get the fluid out. A regular sports physio would probably really get into it for 15 minutes and that's it. With Victor it would be painstakingly slow as he dispersed the swelling and it was amazing how you could have a full range of movement once he was done. Of course, he had the time to do that because he was only there for me.

So it was 2–2 with India going into game five, and my batting was really starting to come together. In this match I was pushing towards my hundred and my opening partner, Shaun Marsh, was heading for his 50 when I top-edged Harbhajan to mid-wicket and was caught on 93. He was happy—I'd caught-and-bowled him in the previous match. Shaun then took up the challenge and got 100-plus on our way to 4 for 350.

The thing about being an all-rounder in one-day cricket is that, when we bat first, if it's hot and I score runs, it means I'm out there too long to be able to then turn around and bowl ten overs. Quite simply, you are physically drained after batting and you need to have some recovery time. So at times as an all-rounder, when your side bats first, it does play on your mind when you get to 50 or 60. You start to get a bit tired—especially when it's hot and humid—and you realise that, if you're still there in the forty-fifth over, there's no way you can operate as a strike bowler. You think, 'I'm going to only get two or three overs, and then I'll be well and truly cooked.'

That's what happened in this game. I was saying to myself,

'Whether I get a hundred or not, I need to get on with this. I can't fluff around.' So I tried to hit a six and got out; but I'd made 90-plus off 80-odd balls, including nine fours and three sixes, and I'd got my 50 off 26 balls. It was one of those days when everything you do comes off beautifully—almost.

I was glad to be walking off in the twenty-fifth over. 'Good start,' I thought. As soon as I was in the change room, it was straight into the ice bath to get my core temperature down in a hurry, mainly to stop sweating so I didn't get any more dehydrated. Then you're trying to get enough fluid in to re-hydrate and eating bananas and trying to get some energy into you as well. I've cramped up quite a bit in the past and it's awful because, as soon as you start to cramp, you just get worse. Now you can take these soluble electrolyte tablets that you put in water—and they have been the only thing that has stopped me cramping. Normally once you start cramping you need to rest and get fluids into you to stop the cramps getting worse. But these drinks have been brilliant because they can fix it immediately, even during the game.

By the way, when I had thought 'Good start' I never thought 'Job done'. You have to take Indian determination into account. They fell only four runs short, thanks to a magnificent 175 by Tendulkar. I got three wickets, including Harbhajan again, but they only needed eight off the last over, with one wicket left, and I was last up to bowl. I managed to restrict them to singles on the first two balls and then Graham Manou, our stand-in wicket-keeper, missed a run-out on the third. They tried to get two runs off the fourth ball and Nathan Hauritz hit the stumps with a direct throw. The umpire went upstairs to make sure, but it was all over. We were ahead 3–2 with two to play.

The sixth game was in Guwahati, way up in Assam, in the north-east between Bangladesh and Bhutan, the foothills of the Himalayas. There's no mobile-phone reception there and hardly any internet—just enough to send through a couple of messages to say you're alive and that's it. We had a really early start—about 8.30 am—because the sun goes down early there. We won the toss and bowled India out for 170 with a couple of overs to spare. I got two wickets and Dougie Bollinger got a five-for. I got 49 off the bat and we chased them down without too many dramas in less than 40 overs.

That was it—we were 4–2 up with one to play. The team hierarchy gave me and Mitch the last game off and we flew home to get an extra couple of days' rest before the Australian summer started. As it turned out, the final match was a wash-out anyway—rained off without a ball being bowled.

Despite my ordinary start, I ended up getting Player of the Series, which capped off a very good northern summer. I'd gone from getting two successive centuries and Man of the Match awards in the semi and final of the Champions Trophy to Player of the Series in the Indian tour. More to the point, we had won a series in India even though we were not only a team in transition but we'd been decimated by injuries.

The other big thing for me was that my investment in Victor over those few months had really paid off. That was reinforced when I saw a newspaper headline that said: 'He's the last man standing.' It actually had nothing to do with me, but it resonated with me and made me realise how far I had come physically. Winning the Champions Trophy paid for having Victor in England. But more than that, everything was beginning to turn around for me as a professional cricketer.

Coming back from India for the upcoming Test series with the West Indies and then Pakistan, there was a question over whether or not I would stay on as opening bat. I was thinking it might be easier if I did bat down the order, especially if I wanted to bowl as much as I had been doing. But the only way that was going to happen was if Mike Hussey opened the batting. I heard later on that the selectors had suggested this as a possibility—Mike would open the batting and I would bat at number five.

Going into the first game against the West Indies at the Gabba, I sensed that some people were wanting me to fail. Nobody in Australia had seen what I was capable of and there was a lot of negativity about me as an opener. I remember thinking about this even when Jerome Taylor was running in to bowl. Despite the fact I'd grown up in Queensland and this had been my original home ground, some of the comments people made as I was walking out to bat were pretty negative. My mind definitely wasn't where it should have been and I got out in the third over. As it turned out, we scored 480, rattled through them and enforced the follow-on; I didn't have to bat again, although I did take a few wickets and a couple of catches.

There was much talk about whether I was ready to open, whether I was a makeshift opener just doing the job till they could find a proper one. That was partly because all I'd done on Australian soil was during the World XI game, and that had been five years ago in 2005. That negativity weighed on my mind. Maybe it was a good idea to bat down the order. Even going into the second Test in Adelaide, I was still thinking about it. But I decided I couldn't worry about what people thought, or if they wanted me to fail; I just had to concentrate on each ball and let my skills take over.

The wicket in Adelaide was absolutely beautiful. In the Windies' first innings, I bowled pretty well. The ball was reversing and I got a couple of wickets, so that gave me more confidence. Then, about halfway through the second day, we began to bat and I was 96 at stumps. That night, watching TV, was the first time I ever saw myself on the highlights of a day's play in Australia. It was amazing to think, 'That's me up there, playing for my country, batting like that at the Adelaide

Oval.' I was thinking people might see that and realise I did have enough shots and the game to be an opener.

Unfortunately the next day it didn't work out—I was thinking so hard about how good it would be for me to get my first Test century that I didn't even get through the first over!

Sulieman Benn, their spinner, bowled the first over and, on about the second or third delivery, he dragged down a shorter ball. I thought 'You little beauty!' but it was an arm ball and skidded through. I wasn't quick enough to get to it and I was bowled. I was so close. I have to admit I let the occasion of possibly getting my first century get the better of me; but deep down I still had the satisfaction of showing I could open and get runs on the board.

The other thing I had to adjust to was bowling my share and then getting ready to bat. But Ricky was looking after me. When there are a couple of wickets to go, unless he needs me to get someone out, he won't bowl me—making sure I'm as fresh as possible going into the next innings. When the innings is over, I have to run off and change out of my bowling shoes; because I wear compression tights—athletic leggings that increase blood circulation and oxygen flow to your muscles—under my whites, I've got to totally change my outfit before I even get padded up. So it's a rush.

The West Indies batted well in Adelaide and we drew the match, so there was a chance for them to draw the series if they won in Perth. We batted first and it was another one of those days where everything you do comes off. Chris Gayle dropped me at first slip before I got to double figures; after that, I thought, 'What's the point of just trying to defend?' The wicket was doing a little bit, but I thought, 'Be aggressive—the bowlers are good enough to get me out if I'm just defending, so I'm going to take 'em on.' Simon Katich and I scored pretty quickly after that, well over 100 in the first session. When I got to 89, I thought it would be nice to get 100 this time—but then I got a ball from Kemar Roach that was too good!

My concentration wasn't lacking—I was doing everything the same as I had previously been doing—but he got the ball to seam away a little bit and I was caught behind. Good on him for getting the better of me—sometimes the bowler bowls a ball that you can't do much about. When that happens, I don't get upset—it was just too good a ball. Okay, I didn't get my century, but I was so thankful that I was able to bat as well as I did on an initially challenging wicket in Perth.

We declared at 8 for 520 and then I bowled really well into the wind, which helps the ball to reverse—more air flowing against the rough side of the ball means I can get it to move a bit more against the breeze than I can downwind. We ended up winning the game with 50 runs to spare. It was a pretty good win and a very fiery match—sadly, that match will probably be remembered for a couple of altercations. The first was between Sulieman Benn, Brad Haddin and Mitch Johnson—push came to shove; bats were pointed; and Benn was banned, while Brad and Mitch were fined.

The second incident was between me and Chris Gayle, and ended up with me getting a fine. Worse than that, I was really annoyed that people didn't know both sides of the story. It all started when Kemar Roach hit Ricky in the arm and hurt him so badly he ended up not being able to bat on for the first time in his career, for the simple reason that he couldn't hold onto his bat. So Gayle starts saying 'Your skipper is soft' and that sort of thing. He said it to me when I was batting the second time and then when we were bowling in their second innings. Ricky knew about it and Gayle said it to his face: 'Yes, you're soft.' Obviously Ricky wasn't happy about that—none of us were— he was our Captain Courageous. You can never accuse Ricky Ponting of cowardice, because it's just not true.

Then, when I was fielding at midwicket and Gayle was at the non-striker's end, I said to him, 'What you said about Ricky—how can you talk with your record?'

'Oh, I can't wait for you to come in and bowl. I'm going to take you down,' he said.

'Is that right?'

'Oh yes, you wait . . .'

So I came on about two overs later, still steaming about this. I had two thoughts in my mind: firstly, I want to get this guy out; and secondly, I don't want to get pumped for six. As it was, I got him out first ball and I'm embarrassed to watch it now. I carried on like an absolute goose.

It was relief as much as anything. In the first innings he'd got 100 off 70 balls and taken everyone down; this time it could have gone either way. He's an unbelievably talented batsman when he gets going, so I knew he could hurt me and the team with another aggressive innings. On the other hand, I've probably got him out more than any other batsman I've bowled to throughout my career. Deep down, he knows that as well. So my reaction was raw emotion; but in the end I carried on too much and it didn't look good at all.

When I look at replays now, it's embarrassing to see how over the top I was. I started off fine; but it was how long I did it for that was so bad. However, you learn from your mistakes—you've just got to control your reactions, because you don't want to get into trouble, which I did.

It all blew up in the media—as you'd expect—but I unintentionally added fuel to the fire.

At the time, I was annoyed that people didn't know the whole story and pissed off at the way the media wrote it up—it was wholly and solely about me, and no one was asking why I overreacted like that. Nobody asked what was going on between me and Chris.

That's where I made my first mistake. At the time, Ricky and the media guys talked to me about it and asked me how I wanted to handle it. I said I felt like no one knew the full story and I wanted to get it out there. I had some people saying I should tell them—that it's not a bad thing to tell the whole story. But one of my major mentors, who knows the media better than anyone, was saying I should just say, 'Yes I've totally stuffed up—it was an error and it can't happen again.' He said, 'If you talk and try to explain, you give it oxygen and it could go crazy.'

I should have listened but instead I tried to tell people that there was a reason I had overreacted, that Chris had baited me. However, I didn't tell them the whole story—all the stuff about Ricky—and it looked like I was saying 'He made me do it . . .'

Instead of putting the record straight, I looked stupid and the press coverage just got worse. After that, for the next couple of days I thought, 'I don't want to put up with this because it's full-on.' I was under the microscope and I was being nailed left, right and centre as a complete idiot. I definitely learnt from it. I know if a situation like that arose again, I would deal with it very differently.

I was pretty down then. I told myself, 'I'm going to totally change my play. I'm not going to sledge or be over-aggressive. I'm not going to push myself to the limit, because I don't even want to come close to having anything like that happen again.'

I remember Ricky asked me how I was travelling and I said, 'I'm struggling because I feel there's no point in being super-competitive. I don't want this to happen again and to get nailed.' He said, 'In the end you know where the line is—you know you stepped over it. Learn from it and move on. You're at your best when you are in a contest on the field.'

You can't control what people think of you, whether they think you are a dickhead or whatever. What I want in the end is for people to appreciate what I can do. But then, once I get into a game, those thoughts are switched off and my competitiveness is switched on. I know I've just got to walk that fine line.

In the final wash-up, we beat the West Indies by 30-odd runs and then moved on to the MCG for the Boxing Day Test against Pakistan. In the first innings there, for the third time in three matches, I found myself looking at the possibility of getting my first Test century.

Strangely, having come close twice in the two previous matches, I didn't feel any added pressure. For me it was more the excitement of scoring runs. Apart from all the hoo-ha over the Gayle incident, I couldn't have been happier. I never dreamed I was going to be an opening batsman, especially in Test cricket, or to bat in the top order other than by going from number six to five and so on. So my maiden Test century was something built up in the media, but it wasn't such a big deal for me. I was just loving the opportunity to score runs in Australia in a Test match.

What *was* a big deal for me was playing in a Boxing Day Test at the MCG. This isn't just a big part of the cricket calendar, this is part of our sporting DNA, like the Melbourne Cup and the footy grand finals. There is no cricket stadium in the world like the MCG, especially when it's full. This is where heroes have walked and legends have been created and, if you are going to score a Test century, this is probably where you want to do it. This is the stuff you dream about and act out when you're a kid playing in your backyard. So was there extra pressure? Maybe just a bit.

When my first century did come, in the second innings of this Test, it was a big relief partly because I lost my wicket in the 90s again, in the first innings. This time, in the 90s, the ball was reversing a bit and the Pakistanis had set a field with just about everyone on the off side, then bowled really wide, which made it very hard to score.

I'd been going along really well until then. But now, even if I hit a really good shot, I'd get a single—and that's if I could even reach it. At the other end I was running out of partners. Simon Katich went for 2, Ricky went for 12, Mike Hussey 4, Michael Clarke 37, Marcus North 8, Brad Haddin 0; but then Mitch Johnson came in and stuck around. Meanwhile my wheels were spinning and I was on 98 when we went to lunch.

Sometimes a break can cause you to lose concentration and in the end it was a stroke of luck that got me through. I got a single and I was sitting on 99 when I tried to hit Amir to the boundary with a square drive. The ball was up in the air and went straight to Rauf, one of their big, clumsy fast bowlers, but he dived and luckily dropped it. We took the run—I finally got my maiden Test century, and unfortunately Rauf never played for Pakistan again although I don't think that had much to do with his fielding.

But getting that ton wasn't the be-all and end-all either. It didn't mean that if I didn't get a Test century I would be a failure. Deep down the most important thing for me is hoping that, when I finish my career, people in Australia appreciate the way I played. Instead, all I'd had up to then was 'This bloke breaks down', 'He's soft', 'He's weak', 'He can't play', 'He can't bat', 'His bowling's not great'—and that's how it'd been throughout my career.

Even just falling short of centuries in the previous two games and the first innings were being looked at negatively in some quarters.

So it was an amazing feeling to get my 100 and the recognition that brings from ordinary cricket fans. It was great to have people stopping me in the street saying, 'Congratulations—you were brilliant to watch!' If I'd been caught on 99, maybe that wouldn't have happened. But I got my first 100 and it really blew me away.

The media obviously helped along the way to build it up and I had to work for it. Whatever I had felt before—about getting a century being less important than consistently scoring runs—went out the window in that moment. To have everyone there to celebrate with me, even though it wasn't a really big crowd, was a special moment. Mum and Dad came to the dressing room after the game to see my name on the board—they get it up that quickly. It was very special for all of us. Even on the way back to their hotel, some fans recognised them and congratulated them. For the first time ever, I felt appreciated by the majority of Australian cricket fans.

RENT-A-QUOTES

One of the saddest sights in modern cricket is the old pro who earns a crust slagging off current players. A player like me, whose career has had more false starts than Linford Christie, has to get used to criticism. Most of it has some validity, but probably the person who really annoyed me the most was Jeff Thomson. It wasn't so much to do with my list of injuries—it was just his general opinion of what I was like as a player.

More than that, it was where and when he chose to do it—right on my own doorstep in Ipswich, when I was maybe 22, just starting out. Jeff was doing a guest-speaking gig at the Ipswich Jets Rugby League club, and someone asked him what he thought about Shane Watson. He absolutely gave it to me.

He said something along the lines of, 'His batting is not up to scratch at all and he's bowling just to get the batsman in. He's not an all-rounder's arsehole . . .' Now he's entitled to his opinion, but I thought that was extremely harsh, especially in my home town. He must have known that people in the cricket community, friends of my mum and dad, would be there. It wasn't the first time, either. And he's done that to a number of players.

I was ropable and I wanted to stick it back to him in the media. But Dennis Lillee, Rod Marsh and Greg Chappell said that, away from all this, I'd actually get along with him—he's a nice guy. But that's how he works; that's how he does his guest-speaking gigs, and he's extremely crude. I've heard a number of times that, when he does a gig at a formal dinner, because of the language he uses, some people just walk out. Nowadays, with the things I've been able to achieve in my career, he can't say too much.

Actually, I heard recently that Jeff had said he can be wrong—'like I was about Shane Watson'. It takes courage to admit you're wrong but surely these former professionals understand better than most how hard it is to be successful. Things happen on the cricket field—you don't mean to get out or bowl a bad ball! It's just the way it is. These commentators at times are so quick to judge and often the way they say it is really over the top.

And then you get people like Neil Harvey saying how good it was when he was playing and how bad it is now—he always comes out and nails everyone. The same with Jeff Thomson and Geoff Lawson—they never have anything positive to say.

The guys who do have positive things to say end up not getting any airtime. Steve Waugh, for example, tends to give a balanced opinion and he's been very supportive every time he's been asked about me, especially when I was struggling with injuries. But in the end the media don't want to hear that. I heard Dennis Lillee lost his newspaper column because he wasn't controversial enough.

Then the guys who do stick the boot in wonder why the current players don't want to have anything to do with them. Jeff Thomson has burned so many of the current players with his comments that none of them will talk to him. Surely that's not a good feeling for an ex-player who has achieved the things he has in the game.

Ex-players making a buck as commentators and after-dinner speakers at your expense is one thing, but criticism really stings when it comes from a current team-mate. Once, when I was coming back from injury, Andrew Symonds, who replaced me, was asked what would be the best thing for me—how was I going to be able to get back? And he said something like, 'No one's got any confidence in him and in his body. The best way I think for him to get back playing is for him to spend a year in first-class cricket getting his body hardened up and doing what he needs to do.'

Thanks, Roy. My injuries had given this guy an opportunity to play Test cricket. But anyway, he was his own worst enemy.

It's good that ex-players can have a life in cricket after their playing days are over. Like Dennis Lillee, they can take their skills to new generations with their coaching clinics. David Boon is now an international match referee and Greg Chappell is heavily involved with the national

DRINKS BREAK 13

team. Others become commentators, where their knowledge of the game adds valuable insight.

But if you can only earn a crust slagging off fellow professionals to entertain people in a club somewhere, it looks a bit sad.

CHAPTER 22 **BEST OF ENEMIES**

We were on another high as we beat Pakistan in early 2010. After my 'will he ever do it?' century in Melbourne, I scored another 97 in the second innings in Sydney and we won the series 3–0. Then we beat them 5–0 in one-dayers, plus a Twenty20. And we beat the West Indies 5–0 in one-dayers and 2–0 in the Twenty20s. Okay, both these teams had their problems but it felt good to have a successful summer in Australia.

The day after the final Twenty20 against the Windies, we flew to Wellington where we had another Twenty20 the next day against New Zealand. I didn't mind the workload; this was the first time I'd got through a full summer without injury, although they did give me a couple of games off during the one-day series against Pakistan, just to rest up a bit.

In New Zealand I was shocked at how aggressive the fans were, but I suppose that's what it must be like when other countries come to Australia. Come to think of it, we get abuse from our own supporters on the boundary, so I can only guess what it's like for visiting teams. But in New Zealand, the crowd was so aggressive it was like they wanted to kill you.

I didn't help myself there either, because in the Twenty20 I had a run-in with James Franklin. He's a bits-and-pieces all-rounder who can get on my nerves. When I was bowling to him, I didn't execute my bouncer exactly right and he hit me for a big six; because of that I started to give it to him a bit. We won pretty easily in the end, but the crowd really got stuck into me.

Then we played a one-dayer in Hamilton and it was disgraceful how ugly the crowd was. I was standing at the boundary, hearing every kind of abuse under the sun. One muppet shouts at me: 'Your mum gave me clap!' My mum was actually there so I said to him, 'If you've an issue with it, why don't you go up and talk to her—she's sitting up in the stand.' That shut him down pretty quickly.

Sometimes, depending on where my head's at, I go back at hecklers in the crowd with a bit of banter and try to win them over, especially in England. But the Kiwis were super aggressive.

Throughout that series I got a few 40s; I was batting really well but I kept strangling myself and getting out before 50. My bowling was still going okay too. But then, in the second-last one-dayer, I tried to play a pull-shot off Shane Bond and the ball hit me in the back of the hip. Later on, when I was batting in the nets leading up to the Test match, I went to play a pull shot and I just about collapsed. I sent an SOS to Victor to fly over and I ended up missing a Test match. That was the first Test I'd missed for a while through injury. Luckily it was fairly minor and Victor fixed it within a week.

It's safe to say I get injured more than most players and that's because I try to do way too much . . . or I used to. Previously, when I got a niggle, I would keep going and it would turn into an injury which would mean that I would miss some games. The difference now is that, with some of the injuries or niggles I get, I can play through them. When I get a minor tweak, at worst it means I might not be able to bowl for a couple of games till it settles down. But now that I've been able to score runs pretty consistently, I can get picked in the team for batting alone and that's taken a lot of pressure off, knowing I can still play for Australia whether or not I can bowl.

But I love being an all-rounder and that's the role I relish most in the team. As a cricketer you don't always have success, even when you're playing well, because of the way things can pan out in any game. You can get a really good ball when you're batting or a not so good decision when you're bowling, then, if you miss out a few times in a row, the media gets on your case. That negativity can build up and if batting is all you do, you've got no relief from it.

During the 2010 series against Pakistan in England, the conditions were really tough to bat in and I didn't score many runs but, because I was also bowling, I was able to play a big part in the games and get my best bowling figures ever—a five-for and a six-for. As an all rounder, you're never totally reliant on one skill or the other; and when they both come off you feel you're invincible.

If a batsman misses out during a game, that's all they've got—apart from in the field, they can't make that much of a difference to the result. And vice versa, if a bowler is slightly off and gets hit, without batting well they can't make up those lost runs and have an impact on the game. Also, with the IPL being such a lucrative competition, I am a lot more valuable as an all-rounder—two players for the price of one, if you like. So I'd be crazy if I gave up my bowling before I absolutely had to: I wouldn't be as valuable to the team, whether I was scoring runs or not, and I wouldn't be making the most of what I can do.

In the end the New Zealand tour was a bit of an anti-climax for me. I was consistent, but I wasn't really all that good. As soon as the second Test match finished, I flew straight to Chennai and two days later I was playing in the IPL for the Rajasthan Royals. I think I was physically exhausted by then without being really conscious of it and I got smashed every time I bowled.

However, my batting was very good, even in the first game—we were chasing around 240 and I got 60 off 24 balls with four sixes and four fours. I really took Muralitharan down and hit him for three sixes in an over. We only missed out by 20 or so runs.

It was great for me to be able to come in and continue where my first IPL had left off. It's such an important tournament, allowing you to show your skills in India. Everyone loves their cricket so much and it's awesome to be in a country where a billion people have the same passion for the game as I do. If you do really well in India, you could potentially set yourself up for life with the IPL contracts and endorsements.

In the second game I think I got 50-something off 28 balls, but my bowling let me down again. Warnie, as captain, was talking to me about where I was at and how I was going. My pace was down a bit because of how much I was playing and I just couldn't do what I did when I was 24 years old. I don't like failing, so for the next couple of games I charged in harder, put more energy behind the ball and bowled much better. I opened the bowling against Mumbai, which was a game we had to win, and got three wickets in my first couple of overs.

Throughout that IPL, I was batting at three or four, depending on the situation of the game. I really wanted to open, but the batting order had been settled before I got there and they were happy with the openers. I had to adjust my thinking. If I came in at three or four it meant we had already lost a couple of wickets and, if I failed, the team was in trouble. That made me realise one of the reasons I love opening—you don't have as many constraints on your play. You don't want to get out, obviously; but my mindset is if you do, there's another seven or eight batsmen there to take up the slack. So I feel like I'm batting with plenty of back-up and this is when my mind is free to let my talent go.

When you're batting three or four in Twenty20 and you've

lost a few early wickets, you're supposed to score ten an over without getting out. That's a big ask and requires a different mindset. I said to Warnie that, if there's an opportunity, I really want to open, and finally I did in the last game. I think I ended up getting out quite early, but only after I top-scored with 44 off about 26 balls. That proved to me that opening the batting now really suits me.

The IPL was very disappointing for us—we ended up coming second-last. We lost the last couple of games that we needed to win to make it to the semis. Everyone realised we were just missing a couple of world-class players. Every single side we were playing against had four top-quality overseas players as well as three or four top-drawer Indian players. We had Yusuf Pathan, an Indian player who once hit 100 off 37 balls, but that was it. He only got one score throughout the whole tournament. He was our main Indian player and he had one good game out of 14.

The first year of the IPL we were so lucky—the overseas guys played out of their skins and the young Indian guys stepped up as well, which was how we won the tournament. In 2010 we had me and Warnie—and he was 41 years old and in the side after not playing any cricket for a year. I replaced Shaun Tait and then we had a few guys like Adam Voges and Aaron Finch—good players, but not yet world-class performers—and Michael Lumb, an English guy who'd played in the 2010 Twenty20 World Cup the previous year.

I think they got the balance of the team slightly wrong, but they know where they made their mistakes. Personally, I performed pretty well with the bat, more so than with the ball, and they must have been happy because they retained me for the 2011 season.

Straight after the IPL we went to the Twenty20 World Cup in the West Indies and our first game was against Pakistan. They are a very talented team and we hadn't performed well at all in the last Twenty20 World Cup, losing both our opening matches disastrously, so the pressure was on. We also had a new captain in the West Indies—Michael Clarke was in charge.

We got off to a good start against Pakistan at Gros Islet in St Lucia. I made more than 80 off less than 50 balls and David Hussey batted beautifully and got 50 off around 25 balls. I didn't bowl so well, though. Being the medium-quick in a bunch of fast bowlers means you are the one they are really going to target—and, boy, did they go after me. But we won and it was a very important game that enabled us to get our confidence up at the start of the tournament.

Next we played India in Barbados, which was a very big game because all their players play in the IPL, so they've got a lot more experience at Twenty20 pressure situations. I ended up getting about 50 off 20 balls although my bowling was still getting belted. I got two more decent scores, but then it didn't really go my way with the bat for the rest of the tournament. In the semi-final against Pakistan we were chasing 190, a big score in Twenty20, and I got off to a good start, but then I smashed one straight down to long on and was caught on 16. Dave Warner had already gone for a third-ball duck, while Brad Haddin went for 25, Michael Clarke for 17 and Dave Hussey for 13. Thankfully Cameron White and, even more so, Mike Hussey steadied the ship.

We needed 34 off the last two overs and Mike got 16. Then, in the final over, needing 18, he hit a four and three sixes and we won by three wickets with only a ball to spare. We probably shouldn't have made it, but suddenly we were in the final. It was unbelievable, really.

The thing about Michael Clarke was that, as the then vice-captain of the Test and one-day sides, he was the obvious choice to skipper the Twenty20 side. But he'd never played in the

IPL, always passing it up because of his workload and, to be brutally honest, because he's not a natural Twenty20 batsman. You've got be able to hit sixes and fours out of nowhere. And, supremely talented though Michael is, that's just not his style (as he pretty much conceded this year when he stepped down from the Twenty20 team). The best Twenty20 batsmen are the ones who can quickly work their way into a match, rotate the strike, hit boundaries and, when they need to really go, they are able to get 25 off an over. Michael is probably a bit too technically correct a player for Twenty20.

Okay, we were in the final, but that was down to Mr Cricket—Mike Hussey. We deserved to be there but Twenty20 requires such fine skills—if you're slightly out, whether you're batting or bowling, you get found out straightaway. If you get lucky, you might get away with it for a while. But if you're slightly off, you won't be able to score anywhere near as quickly as you need to, because you'll be mishitting balls that you should be hitting for four or six, and you're likely to get out cheaply. In bowling, if you're slightly out, you can get absolutely smashed for 20 an over, which is far from ideal.

In the very first IPL, we lost the first game badly and one of our owners told us we needed to win the next game. Then, as we progressed, each match became more pressured till we got to the semi-final. Michael Clarke, Mitch Johnson and Brad Haddin are all fine players, but at this stage—going into a final—they had never really played a Twenty20 tournament where there was something really riding on it. Apart from the semi-final, they'd never experienced that type of pressure.

Anyway, we were facing the old enemy, England, in the final; but there was a bit of a distraction just before it. We hadn't been home for four months and, even then, we'd only had a week and a half at home after New Zealand and the IPL. After we made the final we were told that we were going to have to stay around for another two days after it to get a flight home. It was no big deal really but it caused a lot of irritation. I wasn't going to wait. I had a wedding to organise—it was only two weeks away—and we were moving into a new house, so I got my sister to book me on the first flight home after the final, whatever kind of seat she could find.

We got absolutely thumped in the final. I scored two and then leaked 42 runs in three overs. We lost by seven wickets with three overs to spare. There's no question everybody was a bit distracted by the confusion over flights home to Australia. But my life was changing in so many ways and I really needed to be home ASAP.

CHAPTER 23 **LEE AND ME**

As I said before, Lee and I had been through the toughest times together. Our relationship was tested to breaking point before it really got going—and we survived. There were times when we talked about how it wasn't working, and it was wholly and solely because of what I was going through and how I was handling it—or not handling it, to be precise.

It toughened us both up as a couple; it got a lot of the crap out of the way early. That's one thing about Lee—because she's so young and for four years been a female in the male-dominated environment of *Fox Sports News*, she's had to be tough. She's very mature and she's got her eyes open, which means she's been able to handle different things that have happened in our lives as a couple.

I was 22 when I started going out with my former fiancée, Kym, who's from Sydney, and I learnt a lot from that part of my life, so I was able to make a much better go of my relationship with Lee. I'd found new ways to have fun—like my music and surfing—and so I made sure I embraced and enjoyed every single day that I wasn't playing cricket.

In the end, for Lee and me one of the most important issues, especially at the start of our relationship, was privacy—and we did everything we possibly could to keep super private. Of course, it's all very well to say that, but it doesn't mean much if the media don't really respect your privacy—at the start of our relationship, the media were all over us, trying to get us to talk about it.

I said to Lee, 'If we don't encourage it, by just not talking at all, hopefully within a couple of weeks it will die down.' And that's exactly what happened. Sometimes we would get photographed, but that was only occasionally. We are so happy with the way we handled it, because now we have got lots of privacy and I am glad that, given our careers, we do have a personal life away from the public.

When we started planning our wedding, initially there was a bit of media interest but then, as it got closer, it began to grow legs. In the end we tried to keep it as low-profile as we possibly could. For some people there's money to be made from the women's mags—selling them your story and that sort of thing—but that's not for us.

We are lucky to be well paid and we don't want to sell our souls. That's just about what it feels like if you sell yourself to the media. That's a bell you can't un-ring—it's open slather on every single part of your life. Some people who sell their stories are very wealthy already and don't actually need the money—what's an extra $100,000 or $200,000 if you're already a multi-millionaire? How much is enough? That's not going to make a big impact on their life financially, so why would they throw their privacy away? In fact, a lot of the time it's probably not for the money—it's more that they feel insecure and need the attention.

With us both working in the sports entertainment business, if you like, we do have some obligations to the general public, so it then becomes a question of balance and boundaries. If someone asks me whether Lee has been a support to me throughout my career, I'm going to say, 'Of course, she's been brilliant.' But I'll keep it fairly general. I'm prepared to talk about it a little bit because people do want to know about us.

And then, with Lee's job, there's been a number of times when things were happening to me—with injuries or performance or controversies—and *Fox Sports News* were all over her to get an exclusive with me. But in the end they understood it was hard for both of us, her reading the news about me, especially when I was getting injured all the time. She got used to the situation fairly quickly but her workmates took a bit longer to adjust.

Television news can be pretty tough although Lee doesn't have that hard-nosed, foot-in-the-door journalistic mentality, which is why she's enjoying her life now she's doing more presenting on TV shows.

Being away from home a lot and for long periods can be hard for both of us, but we spend time together on tour as much as we can. Cricketers aren't like rock stars, with women throwing themselves at you. It's there but you have to go looking for it. However, if you are known you do stand out from the crowd a little more.

It was something that I struggled with when I started playing first-class cricket. I'd go out and get talking to a girl and, when she asked me what I did, I'd make something up. I felt that, as soon as I said I was a cricketer or a sportsman, they'd stereotype me. When I met someone new, I wanted to meet them on my own terms and not be pigeon-holed immediately about what type of person I am before we even got to know each other.

It can be difficult for some partners, particularly if there are insecurities individually or in the relationship. Then there can be relentless questions: Who were you out with? . . . Where did you go? etc. etc. It's really important, when you're away so much, to have someone who is not only content with how you are in your relationship but is confident enough in themselves. We cherish what we've got, and do appreciate the privacy that we have.

CHAPTER 24 **WEDDING BELL BLUES**

Don't get me wrong, I understand that being well known is a two-way street, even for sportsmen and women. We are part of the entertainment industry and, if you are in a position where people want a piece of you, then you are probably lucky enough to be making a decent living out of it. The IPL is a perfect example of where your cricketing ability is only part of it—your ability to put bums on seats, because of your personality as much as how well you play, can be a big factor in how much you get paid.

The trouble with being well known is you can't turn it on and off. Weddings, especially, seem to bring out the worst in the media. Lee and I wanted ours to be a family affair and—even though she is a TV personality in her own right—we decided not to sell our wedding pictures to any magazine. There were a few offers; but basically we put the message out that we weren't interested in the money and we'd appreciate it if everyone would just let us have our wedding day without any interruptions or intrusions.

Lee and I are both a bit old-fashioned and very family orientated. My dad was my best man and Lee's mum, Vicki, was her matron of honour—you don't get much more family than that.

We stayed at Pretty Beach House and the wedding and reception were at Bells at Killcare, on the New South Wales Central Coast at the end of May 2010. We'd planned to have the reception outdoors but it poured with rain—which worked out beautifully as two women's magazines sent helicopters to film the event. The rain meant we had to have it indoors so the choppers didn't see much, but a few paparazzi got in somehow and were able to take photographs of Lee and some of our guests.

But rain aside, it was an amazing day. Lee, her mum and the wedding planner had everything under control. All I had to do was organise the music—I got Diesel, who's both a hero and a friend, to do the honours.

Because we hadn't 'sold our souls', we didn't have to put any restrictions on our guests. However, when they arrived, we gave them a letter to thank them for coming and telling them they were free to take pictures for their own purposes but we'd prefer people not to put their snaps on Facebook or Twitter because that's when they get out and the media can use them.

That was another reason we didn't sell our story. I've been to a wedding where the couple had sold their story and that meant none of their guests could have a camera there. They didn't want anyone to take photos because, if they got to a rival magazine, they wouldn't get paid. But we wanted our family and friends to be able to take as many pictures as they liked—our guests were part of the celebrations and should be able to have their memories too.

Afterwards, some papers started complaining that they didn't get a photo. I guess they were the ones that didn't get the paparazzi shots. They confronted Lee at the airport on her way to Brisbane for some filming in between the wedding and the honeymoon, and grumbled that they weren't included. A few threatened to follow us around all the way up to Hamilton Island, where we were going to have our honeymoon, and they were going to hound us to get photos. However, they would let things go if we released a photo of the wedding.

It wasn't what we wanted but, after talking to our managers, we decided the best thing was to release one photo to the media, just to get them off our backs. That was fine, but we wanted to make sure that everyone knew that we weren't getting paid for it. They had no details of the wedding and we were able to keep our privacy . . . we thought.

Woman's Day came out the next week with a big spread on the wedding and the amount of information they had was horrendous. They knew everything, including our vows and every little thing that had happened. We'd had all the catering and event staff sign confidentiality agreements, but one of them had chanced her arm and taken the goss-mag dollar. We eventually got pretty compelling evidence about who had done this. It was an inside job for sure—but there's a difference between knowing it and proving it, and sometimes you just have to move on. We didn't worry about it in the end. We were happy; we were married; and we'd had an amazing weekend.

Then, just when everything seemed perfect, I got another niggle. I'd managed to squeeze the wedding and honeymoon into a three-week break we had before a tour of Britain and Ireland. But as I started training and playing again my knee inexplicably flared up. The big difference from previous injuries was that I didn't miss any cricket this time. Even if I did have this problem, I was still able to bat through the one-dayers against England, although without making a big score.

We got found out as a team in England and they beat us very easily for the first three games. We batted first in all three matches, but simply didn't get enough runs. Our scores were mostly adequate—267, 239 and 212—but that's not enough on those grounds.

However, there was a bright spot for me in the very first

game. I met Ian Botham at a Hampshire function just before the one-dayers against England. During a long chat about his life, his charity work and his injuries, I asked him, as a hypothetical, how he would bowl to Kevin Pietersen to get him out. He said he'd set a straighter field, with a catcher at cover, and he'd try to get the ball to swing up and away a bit. K.P. hits the ball on the up and on the move and, if it swings, it'll go to a short cover. If it doesn't swing and holds its line, you get him out lbw.

I didn't really swing the ball at that stage, but I was talking to one of the greatest competitors who ever took a wicket; so I decided that, if I bowled to Kevin at any point in the series, I was going to set my field like this and hope to get him out that way—or along those lines anyway.

So I suggested this to Ricky when he brought me on to bowl against Kevin in the first match and he said, 'Okay, let's give it a go.' Within an over of me starting to bowl to K.P. with that field setting, Ricky caught him driving off the splice of his bat. Okay, Ricky was at gully, not short cover, but it was pretty cool to be able to do something that Ian Botham had suggested and get one of England's better batsmen out.

Shaun Tait came in for the fourth and fifth matches and gave us a lot more firepower, while everything came together on the batting side of things. It was brilliant to be able to win the last two games. We played very well; not only did we avoid a 5–0 whitewash, we struck a bit of a psychological blow leading up to the Ashes a few months later. We knew that, if we were at our best, we could beat them.

The next big challenge was the Spirit of Cricket Tests against Pakistan. It's a tragedy that Pakistan cannot play at home. It takes away the advantage any home team has and that is what all professional cricketers crave—to play a rival on their turf and, hopefully, beat them. It doesn't get any better than that. But after the attack on the Sri Lankan team in Lahore in March

2009, no one was in a hurry to play in Pakistan and that isn't likely to change until the security situation is resolved.

So we were playing Pakistan in two Test matches in England. The first match was at Lord's and the crowd, considering it was a neutral venue, was surprisingly good. It wasn't absolutely packed but there were good numbers there—a few Aussies, a few Pakistan supporters in the outers, a few neutrals and a fair number of members throughout that Test. It was a real contest even though neither of us was the home team. It was certainly more comfortable for us to be playing in England.

It was the first Test match I'd played at Lord's and, as I've said earlier, it's the ultimate ground in every sense. There's a sense of awe as you look out from the balcony and think, 'This is where it all started, this is where everything kicked off.' And every last detail about the place lives up to that sense of occasion and importance.

We were so well looked after. The lunches are phenomenal; it's like a restaurant, with a choice of five or six mains and four or five desserts, so you have to be very careful or you could pig out and put on some extra kilos. You also get your own towel with the date of the Test and the opponents, and with 'MCC' embroidered on it. Everything is total class.

I'd heard before about the feeling as you walk through the Long Room on your way to or from the pitch. All the members are there and they just part to let you through, clapping on the way in and saying bad luck if you get out. It's an amazing place to play.

On the first day, there were perfect bowling conditions: the ball was seaming around quite a bit and swinging a lot. Unfortunately we were put in to bat and they got us out pretty quickly for 253. But the next day, when we were bowling, it was overcast. After not getting any runs, I knew conditions were perfect for me to bowl and suddenly it all came together.

Throughout the time I had off from bowling, because of my knee, I had been able to sit back and think; my bowling wasn't going to plan and every time I bowled I was getting targeted and batsmen were taking me down. I wasn't enjoying getting smashed around and I thought I had to do something different, because what I was doing was just not working.

One thing I know is that a big weapon in England is swing. So in the nets leading up to the Test match, I adjusted my grip, giving me a better chance of swinging the ball. It worked. I remember going home after that practice session and saying to Lee that it was the best I'd ever bowled—I was swinging the ball both ways. I had total control over what I was doing; my pace was good and, anyway, you don't need to be super fast when you're swinging the ball.

When I started to swing the ball on that second day, some of the guys in the Australian team were surprised, let alone the Pakistanis. The Aussies knew I was not normally a big swinger of the ball so they spotted something was a bit different. Everything just worked. The ball was swinging quite a bit and the slope at Lord's helps you out as well. Sometimes a normal ball, even if it's not swinging, will go down the slope, whichever end you're bowling from. Next ball, for some reason, it won't go down the slope; it will just go straight through. But if it's swinging and seaming, and you've got the slope coming into play, it brings in an extra dimension and it can be a batsman's nightmare.

As it turned out, I got three middle-order batsmen out for fairly low figures; and then, for my fourth wicket, I clean-bowled Salman Butt, one of their openers who'd been batting quite well. I suddenly thought, 'I could get a five-for here . . . at Lord's!'

Dougie Bollinger had other ideas—he wanted the last wicket too. He tempted Danish Kaneria into a huge swipe, which was sliced right over me in the slips. Of course I would have caught it if it came to me and that would have been the end of my five-for. But it went well over my head anyway and away for a four. Then there was a break for rain.

When we came back on, all the time I was running in I was thinking how close I was to getting on the honour board at Lord's. That had been a dream of mine for as long as I could remember, although I was hoping it would be for an Ashes century, if it ever happened at all. I didn't think I had a chance to get up there on the bowling board. One name I saw up there was Keith Miller—he got five wickets in both innings in one Test match in 1956, but he never got 100 at Lord's, even though he was a very good batsman as well as a tremendous bowler.

When it happened—Danish got a thick-edge to Steve Smith at third slip—I wasn't able to really take it in because I had to run straight off and put my pads on to open the batting in the second innings. I couldn't believe this was happening. But as I jogged up to get changed into my batting gear, the room attendant was already putting tape on the 'Other Test Matches—Bowling' honours board: *S.R. Watson . . . Australia (v Pakistan) . . . 5–40.* When it was properly etched on it, my name would be the first on this new board.

I got a great reception when I walked out to bat. Especially at Lord's, they appreciate good cricket. Out at the crease, conditions were still difficult and I was still thinking I can't believe this has happened—who cares about batting? I got a few runs and I bowled okay in the second innings, but I didn't get any wickets. Marcus North got 6 for 55—and became the second name on that honours board—so we won pretty easily.

At Headingley we won the toss and the wicket didn't look that bad—in fact it looked better than Lord's did on day one—so we batted. I thought that it seemed pretty dry and shouldn't do too much, but then, in the second over Mohammad Asif bowled a ball to me that seamed at right angles and I missed it by at least a couple of inches. I thought, 'Wow, where did that come from?'

Then he bowled another one that felt very similar to the first, but instead seamed back in a mile, and got me out lbw trying to drive. The balls were swinging a lot because it was overcast, but the pitch was a big seamer too and we were bowled out for 88. It was a disaster. They bowled very well, especially Mohammad Amir, the young bloke. He's a genius—probably as good as anyone in the world in those conditions—and it's a tragedy that he's had five years ripped out of his career because of the betting scandal. More on that later.

When we came out to bowl, it was like we were playing on a totally different wicket. We bowled absolute rubbish and they were flying. At the same stage that we were 88 all out, they were 2 for 130. Our bowlers couldn't get it right because everyone was trying to bowl the perfect wicket ball and they kept smacking us everywhere. However, because the conditions really suited how I bowled, I was able to get a couple of wickets in my first few overs. I was one of the few in our team who could really swing it, but also get the length right so as to be able to make the most of the conditions. Just like that day at Lord's, everything fell into place and I got 6 for 40.

In the second innings the wicket was much better to bat on; but I ended up stuffing up to a part-time bowler. They're often the hardest guys to face, because you just don't want to get out to them. You don't know what to expect—they're not 100 per cent in control of what they are doing and they're barely hitting 115 kilometres an hour—and you think, 'I can't get out to this bloke.' But, of course, I did.

We lost by three wickets. If we had bowled a bit better we'd have had a chance, but we didn't—we were out-bowled. They were too good for us on the day, but we should have kept ourselves in the game.

It was a strange series. I went into it knowing my batting was keeping me in the team and trying to keep that going while hoping to do something about my bowling. Well, I got that part right—a five-for and a six-for in successive Tests, which is something I thought I'd never do. I don't bowl 25 overs in a day like the full-time strike bowlers, so there's less opportunity to take a big haul of wickets. If I'm going to take a five or six, it's going to have to be in ten or 15 overs, which doesn't happen very often.

Lee was over in the UK at that time, and we went to Paris for a few days after the series finished—it was like a second honeymoon. Reading the English papers, I couldn't believe people were talking about how I'd performed. Some cricket writers had even started comparing me with some of the best all-rounders in the world—which, I had learned the hard way, was for them to do and me to take with a pinch of salt. But at that stage I was averaging 27 with the ball in Test cricket and anything under 30 is pretty good.

I can't see me finishing my career with figures like that, but it's nice to have been there. Coming away from that English summer, I thought, I could retire now and be happy. I've already achieved more in cricket than I ever dreamed I would. But I'm not going to retire. Having come so far has made me realise there are still things I could achieve and, like everything else in my life, I'm not giving up till I've given it all a really good crack.

THE SECOND 50

Once I'd established myself in the Australian team, cricket fans began to get frustrated by my tendency not to turn 50s into 100s. Okay, I've had a couple of big scores recently but, before that, I was getting just as frustrated myself. It was an issue even in my one-day cricket and some people said it was asking too much for me to open the batting, bowl my share and field at first slip, but I don't think it's that. I felt I had been batting really well for the last 18 months leading up to the 2011 World Cup—I was Australia's top scorer in both Tests and ODIs in 2010—but I hadn't got the big scores to really make the most of it.

Throughout the Ashes I was at the top of my game technically; I felt I was in a really good place. But then, out of nowhere, I was just getting out in random ways. I knew for me to be a really successful Test cricketer and batsman in general I needed to be able to turn 50s into centuries more consistently.

It has to be a mental thing, because it's not like it was a technical deficiency—I wasn't getting out the same way, with the same error, every time. I needed to find the perfect mental balance that I have at the start of my innings and hold on to it. It's a bit different when you first get out there as an opener and you're just worried about taking the bowlers on with a brand-new ball. Then once you get further on in the innings, your concentration starts to waver a little bit. I've talked to a number of different people about it and what you have to do is push yourself and get yourself switched back on—*really* switched back on.

That's what it all comes down to—it is a purely mental thing. To bat as well as I did in the second innings in Perth in the 2010 Ashes series, reaching 95 only to get out to an innocuous ball—there's no doubt that the excitement had got to me a little bit. But that is a natural feeling, and you've got to switch that off.

To say that I'm doing too much—opening the batting, as well as bowling and fielding at first slip—is too easy an out. No, I've just got to get better at it—and the more I do it, the better I'm going to be at really channelling my concentration. I admit that when you field at first slip, you have to be concentrating on every single ball. If a catch comes to you and you're not switched on, you've got a much bigger chance of dropping it. But I love fielding in the slips because there are no easy catches there. Some are easier than others but they are all pretty tough and very rewarding. Also it saves my body and my energy as well, because I don't have to be running around.

As far as bowling goes, I have to be concentrating then too. If I'm slightly off, I've got less chance of executing what I want to do. I can set a field and the majority of the time I will bowl to it. I'm not trying to bowl 150 kilometres an hour and my technique's very simple—not too much can go wrong with it—so I've got more chance of bowling consistently where I want to.

It's been a challenge for me to be able to concentrate with everything that I'm involved in, but I really believe I can do it all. I've just got to find some effective techniques that will allow me to get every ounce of concentration out of myself—and I will. I've always dreamt of being able to play a big role in the team and now that I'm vice-captain, this is my chance to prove that I can handle a lot of responsibilities, including batting and building big scores, bowling, fielding and now supporting Michael on and off the field. It's early days, but the 185 in Bangladesh would suggest I'm heading in the right direction.

CHAPTER 25 ALL BETS ARE OFF

Just before we left for the short tour of India in September 2010, the *News of the World* newspaper in England ran a story based on an elaborate sting involving three players from the Pakistani national team. The direct fall-out from that was bad enough—Salman Butt, Mohammad Amir and Mohammad Asif were all suspended by the Pakistan Cricket Board, accused of taking bribes to spot-fix bets on their matches. In February this year, Butt was banned from cricket for ten years and Asif for seven—pretty much ending their careers. Amir was banned for five years; at 18 years old, he can still come back but that's a tragic waste of talent all the same.

These three weren't accused of fixing matches—just creating unlikely moments in matches that punters could bet on, like a player bowling a no-ball on a specific ball in an over. When a sports agent called Mazhar Majeed was filmed, predicting exactly when the no-balls would be bowled, it was pretty much game over for the tainted trio.

Betting is illegal in India and Pakistan, so it can attract some pretty shady people. Also, predictably, all the stuff about Mark Waugh and Shane Warne giving pitch and weather reports to an Indian bookie in 1994 came up again. However, back in September 2010, there was a new story that chilled me to the bone. It was known that a couple of players had told the Australian team management about an approach from an Indian bookie after the 2009 Ashes Test at Lord's. Suddenly, the press had two names—me and Brad Haddin. That was all we needed—we were about to get on a plane for a tour of India and there was all this stuff in the press about me and Brad dobbing in an Indian bookie. It's time the true story was told.

I was in the Royal Garden Hotel in London during the 2009 Twenty20 World Cup, where we performed really badly. One morning I went up to the breakfast bar to get some cereal and a very well-built Indian guy came up and started talking to me. 'I like the way you play,' he was saying. 'I watched you during the IPL, playing for Rajasthan.' This was no big deal for me at the time. Indians love their cricket and Indian and Pakistani fans will often say hi and tell you they like you or your team or whatever. I ended up talking to him for about ten minutes, all the time just standing at the breakfast bar. He said, 'I'm very well connected here in London. I'd like to take you guys out for a drink, show you a good night.' He asked me for my number so he could call me and organise a night out. I don't like giving my number out at the best of times, so I said I didn't have an English number and left it at that. You don't want to be rude to people, most of whom are genuine fans who can sometimes get a bit carried away.

That was all fine. But after the Lord's Ashes Test, which I didn't play in, Lee and I were getting ready to go down to the bar before we went out to dinner and I had a call to my room saying one of my Indian friends would like meet me. I asked who it was. I didn't recognise the name, but I told the receptionist I was going down then anyway so whoever it was would see me as I was passing through the foyer.

Lee and I walked down and the guy from the breakfast bar

was there. He said the same thing: 'I really want to take you guys out. Whoever wants to come, I'll take you to some of the really nice spots in London. I know people and we can get into all the best places.' I said we had plans anyway, but I really appreciated it, etc. etc. He said, 'Can I get your number, and then I can call you and organise a night out?' I should have just said no, but that would have seemed rude. However, Lee then jumped in and said, 'How about you give us your number and we'll give you a call if an opportunity comes up.'

Lee got his number, but we both knew this was never going to happen. It wasn't that we were suspicious—we weren't. People can do this at times—they see you at the bar and want to shout you a drink (which I never take, for a number of reasons). But this guy was a bit more full-on—people don't usually ask you for your number—and I said as much to Lee.

I didn't think much more of it until I was talking to Brad Haddin about it later. 'Is it a big bloke?' Brad asked. 'He came up to my room during the Twenty20 World Cup. I had my bag outside my room ready for the concierge to take, so he obviously saw my name on my bag. He wanted to talk and said a similar sort of thing—he wanted to take us out for a drink.'

I said, 'It doesn't sound great does it?' And we agreed it all sounded a bit fishy. To be totally honest, I still didn't think much of the first approach and, if I hadn't talked to Brad, I would definitely have let it go. But I reported it to our team manager, Steve Bernard, and gave him the guy's number so he could maybe find out who he was. Eventually it came back that this guy was one of the bigger illegal bookies in India and he was in London to try and reel someone in. It's a bit scary, especially when you've reported him. You think: 'This guy knows who I am—I wonder if he knows I dobbed him in. He's a gangster, for God's sake!'

I forgot all about it until September 2010, when it all came out. Somebody on the inside must have leaked what had happened, with all the major details intact, and Brad and I were named.

The way this is supposed to work is that Cricket Australia reports incidents like this straightaway to the ICC Anti-Corruption and Security Unit and the only people who are supposed to know about it are the teams concerned. When I read it on the internet and saw how many details were there, I felt sick. I thought, 'How the hell does that get out in so much detail? This is supposed to be totally confidential.' And this was three weeks before we were due to fly to India. I could only hope this bookie and his people didn't come looking for us.

You always hear rumours about different things going on in different parts of the world. The Pakistani players got exposed by a British newspaper and sometimes it takes an outside body with no connections to the problem—whether it's cricket, the police or whatever—to be able to expose what's really going on.

Unexpected stuff happens in sport all the time. Cricket fans are obsessed with statistics so people are always on the lookout for unusual patterns. But does that mean every time a bowler gets a hat-trick we have to call the Anti-Corruption Unit?

Kamran Akmal was under the microscope because he dropped a few catches against us in Sydney. And it happened again during the 2011 World Cup. I know Kamran fairly well—we played together for nearly two months in Rajasthan in the first IPL and I spent a lot of time with him, got to know him and I saw how hard he trained. I found him to be a really nice guy; he worked hard and he wanted to be successful.

How hard players train is often a good gauge of how committed they are to the sport. To see him drop those catches, I definitely did not think anything of it at all. I feel like I know him pretty well and I don't think he would do anything like that. Unfortunately he had a couple of bad games; you can at times. You make one mistake and things can just spiral down. For example, in a game I played in New Zealand, I dropped one catch and then things went pear-shaped and I ended up dropping another couple. It's just one of those things—a bad day at the office. We all have them, and it was great to see Kamran cleared of any suspicion a couple of months later, although it's sad that he has since been dropped from the Pakistan team.

Spot-fixing is a very different issue from match-fixing. In spot-fixing, the players engineer events that punters bet on, but which have no real effect on the outcome of the match. So put yourself in the shoes of those Pakistani players who were busted: they are brought up in a totally different culture to us, they hardly get paid any money compared to other international players—only match payments and that's it, no contracts—and they now can't play in the IPL for political reasons, so they aren't financially able to make the most of their cricketing talents.

Say you're a young player and a senior member of the squad tells you, 'Look, I want you to bowl a no-ball in the third ball of your first over. It won't affect the outcome of the match but there's big money in it for you. What do you reckon?'

And there's also the pressure of what happens if he doesn't do it. What happens to him and his family? For the sake of a no-ball? It's easy for us to sit in judgement—none of us is facing that kind of pressure.

I'm not saying that's what happened, but Mohammad Amir was the player who bowled the no-ball, just exactly as predicted in the *News of the World* video. Amir is a hugely skilful kid who's always trying to get you out with every ball—that's how I've felt every time I've played him. He's just about the most skilful bowler that I've ever faced and he's only 19. He knows exactly what he's doing; he bowls good pace and he swings it. He still got six wickets in that innings, so three no-balls hardly affected the outcome of the game.

We'll never know the whole story. Players may have been threatened or they've done a small favour for someone once, years ago when they were young, and that's got them on the hook and they can't get off it or they'll be exposed and shamed. We're not exactly squeaky clean here in Australia, when you look at some of the very strange events in rugby league, for instance. Wherever you get sport and betting—especially illegal betting—you will get the potential for corruption. And when there's spot-betting, then you can multiply that a hundred times over.

THE ALLAN BORDER MEDAL

The Allan Border Medal is Australian cricket's equivalent of AFL's Brownlow Medal for the player of the year. Leading up to the 2010 medal I never really thought about it, especially during the summer, even though I'd had a very good season and got a few Man of the Match awards. I'd been going to the ceremony for a number of years, but mostly when I'd been injured; it was always a nice night, but it was often pretty depressing for me too. I'd see the guys for the first time in a couple of months, because I'd been away rehabbing, and it would remind me of how much cricket I had missed.

Going to the 2010 medal was very different. I knew I had a chance, especially for the one-day award, because I'd played really well in the Champions Trophy and on the India tour and I'd played some good games throughout the summer as well. And it felt great when I won the one-day award. But I thought Mitch Johnson was going to be the biggest chance for the Allan Border, because he'd won the ICC Player of the Year award, which is the ultimate award in world cricket, and especially because he'd just missed out the year before.

The way the voting works is that after every game—Test matches, one-dayers and Twenty20 as well—you get a voting card. The players, the umpires and the media all get a vote. Each of those elements is important. I remember in 2004 Damien Martyn had an unbelievable year, getting six Test centuries and Man of the Series for the Tests against India. But, partly because of how Damien was viewed by the media, Michael Clarke ended up winning the Allan Border Medal. Michael had had a very good year too but the media votes were so much higher for him that he overtook Damien in the overall votes.

When I got up for the one-day award, that was something very special. I got interviewed by Mark Nicholas, the Channel Nine presenter, but I thought there's no point in saying much; the only time I really should say anything is if I do win it.

When Allan Border read out my name for the main award, all of a sudden a wave of emotion came over me and I thought, 'I'm in trouble here.' I never thought I'd get that emotional, even though I am an emotional bloke. I didn't expect that anything so unbelievably good could happen to me. The thing that was uppermost in my mind was that I'd been so close to doing things throughout my career, but whenever I thought good things were going to happen—they'd evaporate.

I was a mess. I was struggling to get words out; there were people I really wanted to thank and I could barely remember their names. I know how much the people in my corner had been through with me—all the hours Victor had put in; all the shit Lee had to put up with; all the setbacks and heartache my family had experienced just as strongly as I had. I'm not ashamed of my tears that night. All of my frustration and relief and pride and gratitude came out in that moment.

It was very different in 2011. Getting the AB for the second year in a row was a bitter-sweet feeling. I'd just won the one-dayer and Test player awards by a couple of votes, but everyone else had been a bit hot and cold over the year whereas I had been able to perform consistently. I take no pride in that. I would rather have had a bunch of other guys pushing me all the way, because it would have meant we as a team had done a lot better. I'd love to win a third Allan Border Medal . . . this time by a single vote.

CHAPTER 26 **FOOT ON THROAT**

During the trip to India the whole question of not being able to finish off games that we should have won came up. The problem was we'd been getting ourselves into a position where we could and should have won, whether it was in one-dayers or Tests, and we weren't closing the games out.

Aussie teams in the past had become notorious for never taking their foot off the throat, as it was often put. A lot of the credit for that had gone to Steve Waugh's hard-as-nails leadership, but it's a lot easier to do when you've got Glenn McGrath and Shane Warne to come in and clean up the opposition's tail. There's no doubt the 2010 Australian team often couldn't seem to get over that line.

In the first test in Mohali, I got 126 in a total of 428; but India came back at us with 405. Then, even though we only got 192 in the second innings (I got 56 and Simon Katich got 37) we had them at 8 for 124, chasing 205. Then, disastrously, Dougie Bollinger went down with an injury and didn't bowl during the last 20 or so overs. V.V.S. Laxman, meanwhile, dug in and got them home with a 73 not out, aided and abetted by Ishant Sharma. I didn't bowl much during that game because I'd had back spasms on the morning of Day One. If Dougie had been able to bowl even a few overs, it would have given us a much better chance of getting the last two wickets.

The second Test was a similar story, with a familiar outcome. We got off to a fairly solid start (I got 57, Katto got 43, Ricky got 77 and Mike Hussey got 34). Then, on an unspectacular 4 for 198, Marcus North came in and plundered 128 runs. We were on 478 by the time the last wicket fell—a score from which you'd think you could get a draw, at least, with every chance of a win.

But then again, they had the 'Little Master', Sachin Tendulkar, who came in when India were 2 for 38. By the time he left, having scored 214 runs in a 308-run partnership with Murali Vijay, they were eight runs ahead on 486, on their way to 495.

We began our second innings after lunch on day four and all the talk was about pushing on into the final day, setting up a decent score and leaving enough time to bowl India out. We should be so lucky. By tea, we were 3 for 94. I got 32, Simon was out for 24 and Michael only scored three, but Ricky and Mike Hussey looked set to take us into the next day. It was not to be. Mike went for 20, Marcus couldn't repeat his first-innings heroics and got three and then Ricky fell on 72. By stumps we were 7 for 202, with Mitch Johnson and Nathan Hauritz at the crease.

Now, Mitch has a Test century to his name and Nathan's top score is 75, so these guys could potentially have made the tail wag. But not that day. We only lasted ten overs, leaving India a modest target of 207 and plenty of time in which to get it. Forty-five overs later, Sachin Tendulkar swept Nathan for two runs to win India the series 2–0 and himself Man of the Match and Man of the Series.

It's not often you can score 600 and 700 runs in Test matches in India, and yet feel like you've let yourselves down. But here were two opportunities to get all-too-rare results in India and two chances that had slipped through our fingers. Our batting in the second innings of both matches was poor and we paid the price.

This inability to finish our opponents off went back to the first Test in Cardiff against England in 2009, when we really should have won but were held to a draw by Jimmy Anderson and Monty Panesar hanging on for grim death. We were all over England in the first Test of that Ashes series, but we just couldn't finish them off when it mattered. All I can say is that, when you are in the thick of it, you sometimes have such a single-minded vision of how to get them out that you can't see the bigger picture of what a different tactic might do. There's no doubt that in the Indian games we never felt like we bowled that badly, but little things can fail to go your way as well.

It just takes one ball, or one miss, or one thick edge to a fielder and suddenly the picture is very different. You think the batsman's bound to play a bad shot and get out, and you mentally relax because you assume you are going to win. But you can't relax, not ever. We need to make sure we get across the finishing line before we even think about winding down, and I really believe that's been the biggest reason why we haven't been able to finish teams off.

The history of Australian cricket over the last ten years has been of us getting to a position where it looks like it's going to be quite an easy victory, and it always was—in the past. You call up the big guns for a final blast and just blow the tail-enders away. But these days we don't have players of the calibre of Warne or McGrath who are able to do that consistently. We need to change our thinking, to make sure we don't take the foot off the pedal.

We paid for it big time in the first Test in India when we lost a match we really should have won. And that would have made a huge difference—to our confidence, to the result of that Test series and, probably, in going on to the Ashes too. You need three or four people in the side who are capable of halting the other team's momentum and turning it back on them, by getting a big score and getting us out of trouble. But just recently, when we lose a wicket, there's a sense of 'uh-oh, here we go again' and we end up losing wickets consistently until the last one falls.

If it hadn't been for Mike Hussey in Brisbane and Perth, the 2010–11 Ashes series could have been a clean sweep. But there are three or four batsmen in the middle order who are supposed to do that job, and that's been one of our really big issues. We just don't get enough runs on the board, so our bowlers are under pressure to come up with the goods every single time.

It's been a huge issue within our team lately and that's the reason we had such poor results throughout India and the Ashes. I have to hold my hand up and accept my share of the blame. Unfortunately I wasn't able to convert throughout the last Ashes series every time; but then you expect the other guys in the middle to maintain whatever momentum you do have and build a partnership. Instead we just seemed to lose wickets steadily.

All of this raised questions about the captaincy, which I think were mostly unfair. Some people thought that all the debate affected our morale, but it didn't. At least, not within the team. We knew what was going on—I mean, really going on. We knew what Ricky was doing.

A lot of the spotlight was on him for the fields he set for Nathan Hauritz, especially after Shane Warne bagged Ricky on Twitter. But I knew, and everybody else in the group knew, that Nathan had total control over his fields. He was always talking to Ricky about the fields that he was setting and about how he was going to bowl to a certain batsman; what his Plan A was, and his Plan B, and what his options were. For anyone to say it was all Ricky's doing and Nathan failed because Ricky made bad decisions is absolute rubbish.

The whole question of Ricky's leadership was a furphy. His batting in India was good—he got three 70s, and would have got more if I hadn't run him out in the first Test. Throughout last summer, admittedly, he wasn't at his absolute best. The English know how big a wicket Ricky is, so they worked out a plan and, most importantly, they executed it.

So they hardly ever bowled Ricky a bad ball and took every chance that came their way. People started asking if he should step down from the captaincy and just concentrate on his batting. I know he's a brilliant batsman and, now that he no longer has the captaincy weighing on him, he has a few years at the very top left in him—look at the way Tendulkar has come back. But a lot of what Punter had to cop as captain, from the end of the India tour and throughout the Ashes, was completely unwarranted.

Personally, I thought he was doing a great job. Ricky had so much on his plate at the time; everything that went on in our team—from management issues to flight arrangements—went through him. He probably didn't need to be across so much, but he just wanted to be sure that things didn't happen that shouldn't happen. Ricky was willing to take it on but it meant he had no time for himself, no time to get away and mentally recharge.

Throughout last summer I felt there was a growing sense of panic all over the place which, to be honest, wasn't helped by Cricket Australia announcing a bigger than usual Ashes squad down at the Rocks in Sydney in November 2010. I don't know why the squad was named that early; there was still one more round of first-class games as well as the Australia A game against England to be completed. For guys who might have been under pressure, there was another week to be able to find some form.

On the flip side, the players who were in contention for a place had a chance to put some pressure on the guys already in the team.

To compound it, some selections didn't seem to make much sense: for example, dropping Nathan Hauritz when he seemed to have rediscovered his form, then bringing Xavier Doherty into the team. It was really disappointing more than anything. I know quite a few people felt the same. There was a sense of panic, as I said, and subconsciously that spread throughout the team.

CHAPTER 27 **ASHES TO ASHES**

Sometimes adversity brings teams together but if this doesn't happen quickly, any creeping sense of negativity can start to infect the players. And it's only made worse by the kind of thing that happened with Mitch Johnson.

There's no doubt that, over the previous six months, through England and India, Mitch's technique had been letting him down a little bit, even though in India we had Troy Cooley as the bowling coach on tour the whole time. Mitch was then rested from the one-dayers, along with Ricky and me, to give us a break before we kicked on into a couple of first-class matches leading up to the Ashes. When we got to the first Ashes Test it went totally wrong for Mitch. Troy and a few other people then went, 'We just need to do some work with him,' and he got dropped for the second Test.

This was a huge decision and you can assume it wasn't taken lightly; if you can avoid it, you don't take your main strike bowler out of the team to work on his technique in the middle of the biggest contest the side has faced for years.

From the team's point of view, everything we'd done since the previous Ashes in England had been geared towards getting everyone right for this first Test but it was all falling apart.

You could say this should have been sorted out when the first signs started to show in England. Whatever the problem was, it should have never got to the extent it did in the first Test.

When Mitch is bowling well, he's one of the most feared players on the planet, as he showed in his comeback in Perth. He went back there in between the second and third Tests and worked with Dennis Lillee, someone who's had a big impact on Mitch's life. Dennis picked him up from when he was a 16- or 17-year-old; he believed Mitch was a once-in-a-generation bowler and talked to Rod Marsh and got him down to the Cricket Academy, which was where he progressed. Dennis has had a lot of input into Mitch's technique and can still make a great difference to his bowling. Maybe if they had grabbed Dennis back in England or India to make sure Mitch was going right, everything would have been different.

I felt really sorry for Mitch. He's a nice, sensitive guy and things like this can affect him. For this to happen to him when all of Australia had their eyes on him was, I think, especially tough on him. And it had a knock-on effect; there's no doubt the bowling squad was wondering what was going on.

In fact, they were absolutely shitting themselves every time they went out to bowl, because bowlers are the first ones to get dropped when things go wrong and always have been. Bollinger, Siddle, Hilfenhaus and Harris (a shame he got injured because he was phenomenal) are all first-class bowlers, yet they were going into games thinking, 'If I don't bowl that well, I'm definitely gone!'

And that's exactly how it was. Hilfenhaus didn't have a great game in Brisbane—dropped for Adelaide. Dougie Bollinger didn't have a great game in Adelaide—he wasn't super fit and tired very quickly—he was gone. Mitch didn't have a great game in Brisbane—gone! Xavier Doherty had two not-so-great games—gone!

Meanwhile our batters, with a couple of exceptions, were failing throughout and nothing happened. There seemed to be no pressure on those guys, while our bowlers were in meltdown. I see both sides of it. I see the batting side of things, but then I'm also close with all the bowlers, because I'm chipping in to help those guys out as well. I'm good mates with them. I know what's going on and they just felt under siege all the time, whether it was in team meetings or out there bowling. It was like everything was stacked against them.

The Ashes series, as everyone now knows, was a disaster. Okay, England were very good—but partly because we let them be that good. They batted well and for long periods of time, but that's because we didn't take our chances in the field. We also allowed them to bowl as well as they did because it was only in Brisbane and in parts of the second innings in Perth that we kept their bowlers out there long enough to be able to test their stamina. They just had three quicks and one spinner; if we'd been able to keep them out in the field for long enough, we would have opened up any holes in their bowling squad. But we didn't, and that's to their credit and our shame.

We saw their frailties as early as Brisbane, with the big centuries Mike Hussey and Brad Haddin scored in our first innings. Then in Perth, Mike and I got through a period in our second innings that really exposed a couple of their bowlers. But apart from that, we never batted long enough to let them tire, so every time they bowled they were fresh and at the top of their game. They were also well-skilled and had good plans—but we should have pushed through their good spells and then waited for them to get tired. Collectively they were also a better side than the one we played in 2009, when we had a chance to beat them.

Jimmy Anderson was one of the bowlers who'd improved since 2009. He was always skilful when the conditions suited, but now he's got the ability to sustain pressure. More than anything, that was the key for their team. For the first couple of Tests they had Stuart Broad providing impact, and he did it very well. He didn't really get the rewards, but I thought he was the pick of their bowlers in the first two Tests.

When Jimmy wasn't bowling with the new ball, he was still able to sustain pressure, with Graeme Swann doing his job at the other end. Jimmy's ability to swing the new ball both ways is an asset. He still gets on your nerves a bit, but there's no doubt that was the Poms' plan too, to have one person who's willing to try to get under our skins and take one for the team.

On the batting side, Alastair Cook was amazing. He'd improved a lot since the last time I played him, and his powers of concentration and his technique had come a long way. He's not the most flamboyant or attractive batsman to watch—he doesn't really drive that well straight or through the covers—but he defends, cuts and pulls really well and just bats for long periods of time. For someone still quite young—he turned 26 on Christmas Day 2010—I think he's played 65 Tests and has 16 Test centuries under his belt. He's really impressive both on and off the field, and seems like a class act.

The other guy who impressed me was Tim Bresnan. As a bowler in the one-dayers in England the year before, he was always a threat if the conditions were right. He swung the ball and got a bit of bounce. Then the way he came in at Melbourne for those last two Tests, he bowled beautifully—every ball was spot-on and he was really impressive.

You have to give Andrew Strauss credit for his performance as a captain. The way he's been able to galvanise a team that was basically on its knees a couple of years ago is a huge achievement. There was so much you heard going on when, for example, Kevin Pietersen was captain—it seemed like they were all over the shop.

They'd also had a change of coach—Andy Flower from

Zimbabwe came in and was able to take different personalities and control them well within the group. Strauss must have had a big input into that. As a captain he's obviously got a great record in the Ashes but, once again, we never really tested out his tactical skills because we never put him under pressure consistently for long periods. The real test of a captain is when a good plan doesn't work—what does he do then?

Andy Flower seems like a very impressive bloke. He averaged 50 in Test cricket in over 100 Tests—so he was clearly a skilful player. I'm sure he would have brought a bit of stability; he also seems to be an extremely level-headed guy. And David Saker should be *our* bowling coach, not theirs. We should never have let him go in the first place. It's been very frustrating over the last couple of years to see some of our best coaches not coaching where they should be.

I know I'm biased—David Saker is one of my mentors as well as one of my best mates—but if he'd been offered the Cricket Academy job when Troy Cooley moved on to be the head coach at the Centre of Excellence, he would have stayed. That's all he wanted. David had done a hell of a lot with the young Victorian bowlers, so you would have thought they'd have tried harder to keep him in the system. Instead we've lost possibly the best bowling coach in Australia to the Poms and you just have to look at the Ashes result to see he's obviously making a big difference with them.

That Ashes result hurt. In the final Test at the SCG, we couldn't win back the trophy but we could at least have drawn the series . . . then we fell apart again.

I realised how disappointing we had been throughout the series and I wanted to provide some entertainment for the crowd. I mean, I'm no quitter, but needing 364 runs just to make them bat again, let alone give them something to chase, was a very hard ask.

Perth had been tremendous and got us back into the series. But then to have the absolute disaster of Melbourne, and to be bowled out in the first innings in Sydney without getting any runs, while England got so many—they made it look so easy, it was humiliating. We were so far behind in the game, I thought I'm just going to go out there and totally back myself and try to provide some entertainment for those people who have watched us playing absolute rubbish throughout the series.

Unfortunately, the entertainment turned out to be a comedy of errors more than anything. Yet again, I was involved in a run-out . . . and that's a whole other story.

RUN-OUTS

Over the summer of 2010—11 I got involved in a few run-outs. Some were my fault, some were the other guy's fault and some were just sheer bad luck. But because I was involved, I acquired a bit of an unwelcome rep.

There are different reasons why run-outs occur. There could be more of them, but often it just comes down to luck—you're a long way out and someone has a shy at the stumps; if they miss, no one thinks any more about it.

The first one in that particular string of run-outs happened when we were in India. As a group we were conscious of trying to keep rotating the strike, because that's something the Indians don't like—especially Harbhajan Singh. Ricky and I were going well, but there were a couple of times that we were both close to being run out. Finally I hit the ball off the player at bat-pad and I could see the angle it had taken; but Ricky couldn't, so he was a little bit slow taking off. Then a fielder threw it and it ricocheted off the bat-pad again, onto the stumps. Ricky was only just out, so that was really sheer bad luck. It was a shame, because India were struggling and we were scoring runs very freely.

But there is a history. Back in 2009 I was involved in a bizarre run-out with Simon Katich at the MCG, when I was on 93, still looking for my maiden century and we both found ourselves at the same end, with the video umpire having to tell us who was out. Then in Adelaide in the second Ashes Test in 2010 we were at it again, except he was the one caught short. I felt it was an easy single, but I didn't really call that loud and Simon had an Achilles problem going into that game and that's something I should have been more conscious of. Also I was thinking I might have been lbw, so I just wanted to get away from the stumps before the umpire decided it was.

Anyway, then came the two Phil Hughes run-outs during the Ashes—they were truly horrendous. The one in Melbourne, I claim full responsibility for. I had played the ball into a gap, but it closed up quicker than I thought and he was out by a little bit.

As for the one in Sydney, I took the blame for that too; but go back and look at the tape sometime. My thought was that Swann was giving Phil a bit of trouble—there was some rough outside off-stump and he didn't know which ball was going to spin and which one wasn't. Anyhow I thought it was a cruisey two—I was jogging, not even running.

So I get to the other end and check to see what Phil is doing. He's starting to run the second. Cool, so I start my second and look over to see where the ball is—as you should—which means I can't see that Phil has changed his mind and gone back. Next time I look up—we're both at the same end.

That night I had to do the media. It was a shocker—we'd had another disgraceful day where we'd just about lost the game, the series and the Ashes and I got put up to talk to the press. I knew the media was going to say something about the run-out and, sure enough, they absolutely grilled me.

But I'm not going into a media conference and hanging anyone out to dry. That's just not how I am—you've got to look after your mates. So I went in there and took full responsibility for it; unfortunately, because of what happened in Adelaide and Melbourne, they absolutely gave it to me. So in the end I copped it; but I can handle it more than Phil can, because he's still finding his feet. I wasn't going to dob him in—I'm big enough and tough enough to take it.

As for making sure it doesn't happen again I know it's one thing I have to improve. I think sometimes the problem arises when you are batting with players you don't know that well. I haven't batted much with Phil and I'm still trying to understand how he runs. You need to set a pattern so the guy at the other end knows what to expect—you can't be off like a hare one moment, and then dithering like a novice the next. And that goes for everyone, myself included.

The crowd plays a big part too. Sometimes, when they are loud, you need to use both your voice and a hand signal. But I'm not making excuses. I'm honest enough with myself to know if I've got an issue—I've been involved in more than my fair share of run-outs, no question. I've just got to be a bit more cautious, and I've got to be more conscious of who I am running with as well.

You know that some people are always going to be ready to run, like Ricky and Michael Clarke. You know that, even if it's a bit tight, they could take off and you have to be ready too, because they are going to be more aggressive running between wickets. With new players coming into the team, it's probably worth taking the time to watch what they do and have a chat. Meanwhile, I've got to concentrate a lot more to make sure there's never another stuff-up like there was in Sydney.

CHAPTER 28 **ONLY A GAME**

By the end of the first week of January 2011, it felt like Australian Test cricket was at an all-time low. We had drawn with a faltering Pakistan in England, lost one match especially that we should have won in India, and then failed to regain the Ashes against a rampant England in Australia. We were ranked fifth among the world Test nations, behind India, South Africa, Sri Lanka and England. And while our team was a mixture of old hands and new names, the England team that beat us so comprehensively in 2010 had many of the same players we had flogged four years earlier: Strauss, Bell, Collingwood, Pietersen, Cook and Anderson all came back to haunt us, bringing their newer generation of heroes like Swann, Broad, Trott and Bresnan.

For our part, we'd lost almost a whole team of legends and icons: McGrath, Warne, Hayden, Gilchrist, Martyn, Langer, Symonds and Lee were all gone from the Test arena. Of the team that beat England 5–0 in 2006–07 only three—Ponting, Clarke and Hussey—were still playing Tests (Mitch Johnson and I had been non-playing squad members).

So when we played a couple of Twenty20s against England, we were desperate to turn it around. We didn't manage it the first time, losing by a wicket, even though I did okay. In the second I only scored 17, but I took two wickets and we won by a handful of runs. It was nice to win, but it didn't dispel the gloom from the Ashes debacle. Even so, the cloud hanging over the Australian team was nothing compared to what had been darkening the skies of Queensland.

What happened in early January has been described as a 'flood of biblical proportions' and, even before the water hit Ipswich and Brisbane, it had covered an area the size of France and Germany combined. As images of despair and destruction dominated our TV screens, players on both sides gave their match fees from the first Twenty20 to a flood relief fund and even the Barmy Army chipped in with several thousand dollars.

I have to admit my mind was more on what was happening in Queensland than it was on the upcoming one-day games—especially knowing that Ipswich would be the next major town to be hit.

I even told my sister, Nicole, I didn't think I should be playing. Cricket was only a game, after all. I wanted to be back home in Ipswich, doing what I could to help. I never imagined I would see my home town totally engulfed in water. Then hearing about a young child being swept out of his mother's grasp in Marburg, half an hour away from Ipswich, was just horrendous. But Nicole told me I could do more good doing what I do best—playing cricket and taking people's minds off their problems, giving them something to cheer about. Talking to a few mates as well, they said I could lift people's spirits in some way. I didn't go into the game thinking that was my duty, but I suppose it just worked out that way.

We got the Twenty20s out of the way and I spoke on TV about the floods, then buckled down to preparing for the first of the one-dayers, thinking that, as soon as it was over, I wanted to be on a plane back to Ipswich. My family weren't directly affected, but people I knew were, so I still didn't sleep much.

However, it really put what had been a horrific Ashes series into perspective. It was not the end of a life—it wasn't as though my world had been totally turned upside down and I might have to work unbelievably hard for the rest of my life to get it back to what it was. That's what the people of flood-affected Queensland were going through.

Just before we left to go to the ground for the first one-dayer in Melbourne, I was on the phone to Tony, my manager, organising my trip up to Ipswich and making sure we had plenty of things—bats and balls and stuff—to give away to kids. It all had to be managed very quickly so it definitely did take my mind away from what I was doing. Playing all the time, everything is just about cricket. In an odd way, thinking about something else freed up my mind.

There's a theory of sport that your hands and eyes know exactly what to do—as long as you don't let your brain get in the way. Maybe I was distracted into playing better. But, to be fair, I had a few things going my way as well—I got dropped once and I mishit a few balls perfectly into the gaps.

It was one of the most special days in my life: to be able to bat through the whole innings, to chase down 294 and win that first one and get the ball rolling in our favour. It's especially good to win from a tough position, where you start off wondering if your team has what it takes. It provides more belief within the team when you do something like that—chasing down a big total under the pressure of *having* to win to set up the series.

As for my contribution, 161 not out was my highest ODI score, the fifth-highest score in Australian ODI history, and it contributed to the highest successful run chase at the MCG—these were all great achievements. Apart from that, I was glad to show that I could get past 50 and go on to score a century . . . and more.

The trip up to Ipswich, straight after the first one-dayer,

was heartbreaking. I remember driving from Brisbane and seeing this big shopping centre at Goodna with its McDonalds, and the whole place had been totally wiped out. The mayor then took me to the worst-affected areas of Ipswich and they looked like a war zone, with all these families' personal belongings stacked on the lawns outside their homes.

The thing that made the biggest impression on me was that whenever you sympathised with people who had lost everything, they'd always say, 'Oh, there's a lot worse off than me.' The human spirit is an amazing thing.

Meanwhile what any individual does to win a game off his own bat can inspire other players within the team that they can have that impact as well. Proof of that came in the second match in Hobart. We were in a little bit of trouble when Shaun Marsh stepped up, batted beautifully for 110 and gave us a total we could defend, all on his own really. Performances like that give every individual the belief that, if they have a really good day, they can win the game for Australia. Looking forward to the World Cup, it also made us realise we could win from different and difficult positions, whether it was defending a low total, like in Hobart, or chasing down 333, as we did in the sixth game in Sydney. And it has the opposite effect on the other team.

You could see this in the England camp, especially after the second Sydney match, where we chased down such a big total. That made it 5–1 in our favour and you could see them thinking, 'Jeez, no matter what we do, no matter how good we feel or how well we are playing, we can't seem to win.' You could definitely see Andrew Strauss's persona change, compared to what he was like during the Ashes. We were seeing him under pressure for the first time. We were challenging his tactics, which we didn't really do during the Ashes, for the simple reason that we didn't play well enough. So it was nice to be able to turn things around and head off to the World Cup with our memories of the Ashes pushed to the back of our minds, because we'd been able to turn things around so convincingly in the ODIs. Of course, it wasn't the Ashes—but it was a 6–1 hammering we handed out and that had to feel good.

But we didn't have much time to savour it—three days, to be exact—before we were on the plane heading for India, Sri Lanka and the World Cup.

CHAPTER 29 **A WORLD OF PAIN**

The World Cup schedule was far from hectic, although there was a fair bit of moving around between India and Sri Lanka. We had our two warm-up games—against India and South Africa in Bangalore—before we went to Ahmedabad in Gujarat, north-west India, for our first game in the tournament.

I was very disappointed to lose our warm-up game against India. I thought it was really important to win it after we were in such a strong position to do so; but we ended up collapsing in a big way, losing by 38 runs. It was never going to be easy, but those runs were definitely gettable. After our success against England, I wondered if we were slipping back.

Some of the guys said it was only a practice match and we'd take out of it what we could. We had another practice match against South Africa in a couple of days, leading up to the first game, against Zimbabwe, so we still had a chance to pull it together. But I was disappointed that we weren't able to finish off that game against a really big side. It was important to have a belief within our group that we could do it against anyone, anywhere.

The match against South Africa was, in the end, what it was. It was a genuine practice match, where each team could use

15 players so all your bowlers and batsmen got a run. Predictably, the intensity of the game wasn't really there in the end. Saying that, I knew how important it was for us before the 2007 World Cup to beat England in the first practice match—that really got things going at the time.

You could argue that the collapse of the England one-day team in Australia had given us a false sense of our potential and created an illusion that we were in better shape than we were. I knew that around the team there was a view though, that even though we had won against England, we still weren't playing a perfect game of one-day cricket. In that series, we had occasionally let them in and, in the end, only just scraped over the line a number of times. I knew we were a fair way away from being at our best and I'm sure most of the other guys felt that as well. But don't forget that, most importantly, we had Ricky coming back into our team, returning from his finger injury, and he would strengthen the batting line-up. Shaun Tait, who had been out injured during the England ODI series, was also back.

The match against Zimbabwe was a fairly routine 91-run victory—a nice way to start a competitive tournament—but I couldn't believe the accusations flying around afterwards that we had somehow been involved in 'spot-fixing' by scoring too slowly. The story had been floated in a small local paper, but we ignored it. It was just a little local rag, after all. But then, just before the quarter-final, the *Times of India* ran the story on its front page, so suddenly it had a bit of bogus credibility.

It was very annoying more than anything, and frustrating. In fact, I felt a lot of pressure going into that first game, because there was no doubt we should win against Zimbabwe. The wicket we played on was pretty slow and a bit two-paced, so I found it hard to get my timing initially. Also, you didn't want to take any big risks because it was the first game in the World Cup and you want to create a solid platform for the rest of the tournament. I was trying to score—trying to take the bowlers on—without taking too many risks and Brad was the same, but in the end we were pretty slow to get going.

We had Chris Mpofu at one end; he's a fast bowler I hadn't seen before so it took me a while to line him up. And Ray Price is a pretty cagey left-arm orthodox bowler who bowled well. In the end I got 79 and we got 262 and won fairly easily. But to hear that report was the craziest thing. How in the world do people make this stuff up? I just don't understand it, or how they can get away with it, because in the end it's personal slander to say someone's cheating.

After the Pakistan scandal, that's how the cricket world is now. Unfortunately there's a lot more suspicion about events in sport. It's ironic, because part of the whole pleasure of watching sport is seeing the unexpected, the unusual, the heroic and the downright weird. Things happen out of nowhere and unexpected events occur, but now, because of what happened with the Pakistan team, everyone's suspicious. It's a very sad reflection on the state of world cricket at the moment. It wasn't until the *Times of India* article came out that the ICC took a stand; they said that what the paper had written was a disgrace, and they publicly defended us. In any case, none of this would ever change the way I play. In the end the journalists aren't out there; they don't know the full details of what's going on and they just see things from exactly the same vantage point as an ordinary fan. And the press on the sub-continent do get behind their teams in a big way, so you can't take any of it too seriously.

Of course, before the 'spot-fixing' fiasco blew up, we had to deal with the story that Ricky had wrecked a TV in the dressing room after he got run out against Zimbabwe. It was an amazing direct hit by Mpofu from the deep when Ricky and Michael Clarke were going for a second run.

I was in the back of the change room when Ricky got out, so I didn't see what happened; but when I heard the story about him hitting the TV with his box and damaging it, I thought it sounded a bit far-fetched, to be honest. Then I remembered that Ricky's protector had split—in Perth, I think it was—and that he'd had to get a new one immediately. So someone was sent out to a sports shop and presumably got the top of the range—this was the Australian cricket captain, after all—and it was made out of titanium. So it's true that he threw his box, but it wasn't just a typical plastic one—the titanium protector is quite heavy and, obviously, a lot stronger, and unfortunately it did hit the TV, which turned out not to be quite as robustly constructed.

Normally, you wouldn't even hear about a minor dressing-room incident like that, but a dressing-room attendant leaked it. It was a cheap LCD screen; Ricky, who would never have meant to damage anything, immediately apologised and said he would pay for any damages incurred. Unfortunately, once it was leaked to the media, it took on a life of its own and suddenly the story was that he had trashed an expensive TV with his bat. It was a huge controversy over nothing.

Our next game, against New Zealand in Nagpur, could have been a potential problem; after all, the Kiwis have been up and down with their form in recent years. It might not have been the best gauge of how we were going, but we did play a pretty complete game against them. Everybody got a few runs; I got their opener Martin Guptill's wicket, Mitch Johnson and Shaun Tait got most of the rest of them and we won by seven wickets with 16 overs to spare.

The next game, against Sri Lanka in Colombo, was washed out—called off in the thirty-third over of their innings. The worst thing for us was that we missed out on a really competitive chase against high-quality spin bowlers on a turning wicket.

Even if we'd lost, it would have given us terrific experience and prepared us for the later games in India.

The conditions in India were always going to be much more suited to the Indian team than they were to us, just like that wicket against Sri Lanka was. In all the games leading up to the Sri Lanka match in Colombo, the wickets had had pace and bounce in them. In fact, the balls were often bouncing a lot more than they really should have. Then, as soon as we played Sri Lanka, they prepared it totally differently—it had no grass on it. It was a very dusty wicket, totally unlike the wickets that had been played on previously. So it was always going to be a big challenge for us to chase down anything over 200.

When the match was called off we shared the points but it was disappointing not to get the chance to give ourselves a confidence boost from a win.

The next two games, against Kenya and Canada, pretty much went according to the script. And then it was our first real test—Pakistan in Colombo. They bowled very well, but I thought if we'd been able to get another 30 or 40 runs we'd have been okay. We didn't need a huge total against them, because their batting is so volatile and in fact we had them 6 for 142. But they were only chasing 176 so there was no real pressure. If the target had been 216, say, we would have won that game, I've got no doubt.

But once again the biggest issue was our batting collapse. Unfortunately I didn't get many runs so I can't really talk, but we collapsed in a big way: Brad Haddin top scored and Michael Clarke did okay, but neither of them broke 50, and then we lost our last six wickets for less than 60 runs. As I said, Pakistan did bowl unbelievably well and the wicket was doing a little—seaming and inconsistent bounce—but we should have been able to stick it out for a bit longer and get another 40 runs.

That defeat illustrated a failure typical of our team at the moment—batting collapses. We lose one wicket and then we can't stop the rot; we end up getting bowled out for nowhere near as many runs as we should get. If we'd won that game, we'd have played the West Indies in the quarter-final. And then, who knows?

But there's one aspect that was positive in my view. I've always believed that you don't want to paper over cracks—you want to get to the root of any problem and you don't need anything hiding what's going wrong. That's how I am; how I've always been. Something's got to happen to really make everyone stand up and go, 'Okay, what are we going to do about this?' This can't be allowed to continue, because we're not getting the results that we want.

In the quarter-final against India in Ahmedabad, I felt we probably had enough runs on that wicket to be able to win the game. When I got out (for 25) I thought if we could get between 240 and 260 that would be a defendable total, because the ball was turning a lot and we could hopefully get it to reverse as well.

I thought we might actually do it when I got Sehwag for 15; even when Tendulkar went for 53, we were a definite chance. We dragged them back to needing at least a run a ball until a three-over period, when they got 39 runs and that signalled the end of the game. If we'd been able to hold those three overs together a bit better than we did, it would have been a significantly different game, because they were starting to really feel the pressure.

And the pressure on them was huge. If India had been knocked out in the quarter-finals on home soil, the players wouldn't have been able to get back to their homes. That's what happened in 2007, when they got knocked out in the first round. Indian fans love their cricket and they worship their team, but they won't tolerate failure. As it was, they went on to win the tournament—deservedly so.

The plus side from that match was seeing Ricky's return

to top form. His 104 was phenomenal and he hadn't played an innings of that calibre for a little while. Considering the pressure that he was under for a number of different reasons made it all the more impressive. The ball was turning a lot, especially from Harbhajan Singh, who's had a lot of success against Ricky. I think that innings alone is going to give his international cricket a boost for a couple of years.

The World Cup was a disappointment. But, here in Australia, the final matches were overshadowed by the announcement everyone was waiting for: what was Ricky going to do about the captaincy? And would he even have a say in the matter?

CHAPTER 30 **THE CAPTAIN'S KNOCK**

The morning it was officially announced that Ricky Ponting had decided to step down from the captaincy of the Australian Test and one-day teams, I got a text from him telling me that he had made up his mind to go. I was relieved for him and glad to know he was going to keep playing. He still has an awful lot to give Australian cricket, as he had shown in our last match in the World Cup.

I was talking to Justin Langer about this on our way back from the World Cup. He had asked me what I thought Ricky should do, and I said I thought he should step down. Not for any other reason than that the terribly harsh and cruel smashing he'd been taking from the Australian media was diverting attention away from what an amazing batsman he is; not *was*—IS.

And the negative reporting was taking away from all the incredible things he'd done as a captain: the Ashes wins; the games they won from nowhere; the times he'd held the team together—it was as if these triumphs had never happened. I felt it was very unfair on a guy whose stature in the game is so high. I didn't think he needed to deal with all this anymore, and that's why I thought he should hand over the captaincy and concentrate on being one of the best batsmen the world has ever seen.

But the reality is that the captain in cricket is the one who, like the coach in football, decides what happens on the field. He picks the batting order and has a lot of influence on selection and on support staff. The captain is the front man and, when things start to go wrong, he's the first one to cop criticism. That's just how it is; but in Ricky's case, the negatives were starting to overwhelm the positives in what has been and continues to be a truly outstanding career.

Of course, as soon as he made the announcement, everybody turned around and said how great he'd been as a batsman, but people forgot what a good captain he'd been too. His influence in getting Andrew Symonds into the team for the 2003 World Cup in South Africa was an outstanding piece of captaincy. That was all down to Ricky.

He insisted that Roy should be the fifteenth man, saying he was convinced he would come good. Roy had done nothing special with either bat or ball in ODIs up to that point, but Ricky could see he had a rare talent and was convinced he would bring something special to the team. He played his first game against Pakistan and scored 143 not out, and went on to be picked in the Australian one-day team of the century.

Roy's not the only player who's benefited from Ricky's faith and support. There's me, for a start. Not many captains would have stuck by a player who kept getting injured and, for a while, needed to be used cautiously in big tournaments. More than that, Ricky was one of the prime movers in me opening the batting for Australia. I have no doubt Ricky told the selectors I had the game, the temperament and the technique to open the batting; and I think I've proved him right.

If Ricky hadn't been captain, I don't think I would have been given the opportunities that I've had, especially with all my injuries. Most other people would have said—and some *have* said—'He just keeps getting injured, let's find someone else.'

I owe Ricky a huge debt of gratitude, which is why I was relieved and pleased when he gave up the captaincy but chose to stay with the team. Without the burden of the captaincy he is free to concentrate on his batting and not be responsible for everything that goes on within the team. I think he's going to have a lot of success in the next few years.

Obviously Ricky's departure didn't come as a complete shock to us. There had been rumours circulating for a while and they just got more intense. We were aware of them during the World Cup, but I can't say they bothered us much in the dressing room. I can't tell you how all that stuff affected Ricky, because he's such a strong guy and doesn't show his emotions much.

Being captain and going through a lot of issues over the years, he's had to keep his emotions in check. There was a lot of crap going around that he was dealing with, that he didn't want the players to know about, and he was happy to be the buffer between us and stuff we didn't need to worry about. One thing I do know—throughout the last three or four months, you could tell that it was starting to get to him.

It's worth comparing Ricky's experience with Sachin Tendulkar's. Tendulkar, unlike Ricky, wasn't a particularly successful captain and only had the Indian captaincy for two short spells in his career, but he let it go to concentrate on his batting. Now he's a normal, albeit senior, member of their team and he's contributing when he can. But at least he doesn't have to face all the criticism if they lose a game or a Test match.

It's a shame that Ricky copped so much towards the end. One of the final straws, I think, was how much fuss the media made of his so-called dummy spit after his collision with Steve Smith in the World Cup match with Canada. It was no big deal but I have to admit, when I saw it I thought, 'Ooh, that doesn't look good, Ricky.'

In his defence, when you have called for the catch and you're concentrating on the ball, and somebody just charges into you from nowhere, you get a real shock. It's happened to me before: you're focused totally on the ball, and then all of a sudden you get the fright of your life because someone's just jumped in your way to catch it. It definitely annoys you: firstly, because you get a genuine shock and, secondly, you could have dropped the ball. And either of them could have been injured, because their bodies weren't braced for the impact.

We've all seen footage of that terrible collision between Steve Waugh and Jason Gillespie going for the same ball in the Test match in Sri Lanka in 1999. Steve broke his nose, Jason broke his leg, and that put him out of cricket for a year. So I reckon Ricky's reaction was shock at the collision, and then irritation about how it could have gone horribly wrong. I don't know exactly what he was thinking when he walked away from the other players there; but that whole business was just another little indication that he needed to free up his mind.

The way the media turned on Ricky was reminiscent of how they treated Matthew Hayden. He was getting smashed for two months—then, the second he retired, it was 'Oh, what a legend! What an amazing player!'

Many people think Ricky is the best Australian batsman since Don Bradman, and his stats would certainly back up that claim—nearly 13,000 Test runs, 39 centuries and 56 50s... and probably more to come. His one-day record is just as remarkable: more than 13,400 runs, 30 centuries and 79 half-centuries at a strike rate of over 80. Of course, the moment he stepped down as captain, it was amazing how quickly they went from 'We've had enough of you' to 'Wow, what a cricketer!' I suppose it takes a player's retirement from the team or the captaincy for people to appreciate what they've been able to do. But even when it's time to go, why not show some respect for the player and what they've been able to achieve beforehand?

Looking to the immediate future (now the recent past, as you read this), our new leadership team is about to be well and truly tested. With Tests and ODIs in Sri Lanka, followed by Tests and ODIs in South Africa, the only upside for our new captain is that at least it's away from home and a little further from the relentless scrutiny of the media, not that that matters so much in these days of instant communication.

But it's a totally different pressure being away from home. The scrutiny is less and you don't see much of what's written in the press unless you go looking for it. So, from the point of view of scrutiny, the pressure is a lot less intense. The downside is, of course, that you are away from home. You don't know exactly where you are or where you're going half the time, you don't have your favourite places to eat and you miss your usual routine. But, in terms of trying to build the team and change a few things, being away from home should make the transition a bit easier.

My part in this, I believe, is firstly to support Michael and then to do what I can to help the team. The best advice I could give Michael is to not go down the road Ricky followed of being across everything all the time. It wasn't because he was power hungry, but because he wanted to make sure everything was done right. Even though it was a fantastic thing for the team—to know he was looking after our best interests constantly—it took an inevitable toll on him. The answer is not just to delegate, but to choose the right people around you to delegate responsibilities to. You can only ask people to do stuff if you are sure they will do it as well as you would have, to the finest degree, otherwise you are just creating more headaches for yourself.

Little things like travel arrangements, which may seem trivial, become very important when you are away from home so much. Botched travel arrangements can upset a whole team in one hit. That's the kind of thing Michael doesn't need to be doing himself . . . but he needs to make sure that whoever is doing it has it properly covered.

The same applies to tactics and training. Whoever is looking after that side of things—and that could be one of my roles—Michael needs to know they are doing it right without having to supervise them every minute of every day.

Another priority is to help individual players to play to the best of their abilities, because there's no doubt that the best teams are the ones that can produce two or three outstanding individual performances in every game. A perfect example of that was the England team in the Ashes series. Their batsmen were at their best and their bowlers were at their peak. Whatever they were doing to prepare, the results speak for themselves. I think there are Australian players over the past couple of years who haven't done as well as they might have, so we need to get the infrastructure around the group and the environment within the group to a place where players can perform to the peak of their abilities.

As far as names go, I would have had Usman Khawaja in the team from the start of the Ashes series. He is the most impressive young bloke I have seen in years. He is really switched on and very intelligent, as well as being phenomenally skilled. The first time I saw him was at the Gabba a couple of years ago, when he was playing for New South Wales. I've hardly scored a run at the Gabba, apart from a Shield final when the wicket was super flat, but this guy batted superbly and scored 140.

He handled himself really well when he was picked in the team and he's very switched on to what professional sport is right now. And that's another issue. You have to have the right people around the group for the team to function properly, and he has already slotted right in.

Tim Paine, the wicket-keeper batsman—and possibly as a

batsman alone—is another very impressive young guy who I expect we'll start to see coming into the Test side. There are others, but what you are looking for is supremely talented players who are good team men—tough and accountable for what they do.

But the critical relationship in the team will be between me and Michael. How well we can work together will determine how well the team plays, so I see my most important task in the immediate future as doing whatever it takes to support him. In a period of change, the players need to know the guys steering the ship are working as a team so they can too.

CHAPTER 31
HEALING AUSTRALIAN CRICKET

After the Ashes disaster, Australian team management and cricket fans were understandably looking for answers. How could we fall from grace so quickly? How could the most feared and successful cricket team in the world suddenly become also-rans? This is a big worry, not just from the point of view of the cricketers but for the hundreds of thousands of ordinary Australians who love to watch us winning.

Like it or not, we are part of the entertainment industry and sometimes in the change rooms we will talk about going out and putting on a show. In my second innings at the SCG against England, I decided to go out and entertain the fans if I could. We were never going to win the match, but we could show off our skills. I was going okay . . . until another run-out put paid to that plan.

Entertaining the crowd may not sound like a purist's idea of cricket, but it's a fact of life—lose too often and the fans will disappear really quickly. Let that go on for too long and the TV-rights payments will go down, because people won't want to watch us if we are rubbish. That said, the one-dayers here and in Bangladesh showed that we are on the right track. We have a new captain and the future of our batting looks exciting.

For instance, as I've said, Usman Khawaja is an absolute gun and, for my money, should have been the Test side's number six batsman from the start of the Ashes. Along with players who are already emerging in the team, like Steve Smith, and old hands like Ricky Ponting, Michael Clarke and Mike Hussey, our batting looks to be spoiled for choice.

But what happened to our once-feared bowling attack? Where are the bright young talents to replace McGrath and Warne? We are going through a period of profound change in Australian cricket and nowhere is it more obvious than in our bowling. What is becoming apparent is that we may have reached the limit of what we can expect our young bowlers to do.

Quite simply, there is more top-class high-stakes cricket being played now than there ever has been. And there's no question that the most physically demanding aspect of the game is bowling.

Based on my own experiences, it's worth rethinking our attitudes to the way bowlers train and have their injuries treated. When we started the one-day series against England, Shaun Tait and Dougie Bollinger were just back from injury. Ryan Harris got injured in the Tests and, as I write, many of the best of the next generation of fast bowlers have been out injured too.

James Pattinson is only bowling one-dayers and Twenty20s because he's had problems with his back. The best young bowler by a long shot in my opinion, Josh Hazlewood, missed out on the India tour with a back injury and his replacement, Mitchell Starc, went down with a side strain.

In the past, too many people in cricket looked at injuries to bowlers and said: 'Everyone goes through it.' But that was such bullshit—these injuries weren't inevitable and the traditional way of dealing with them wasn't always the best way.

Traditionalists in cricket are often suspicious of of 'trendy' new ideas about injuries, their treatment and, especially, their prevention. Take Pilates, for instance—a joke to some, but the regime, which involves stretching and building your core strength, probably saved my career as an all-rounder.

Looking to the future, we have a whole new format of the game to contend with and that means even more pressure on the top-class players and greater demands on their bodies—especially the bowlers.

I think now would be a very good time for Australian cricket to build a team of specialist doctors and physios, even some from other sports who've had some experience with AFL players, for instance, and with different athletes in general. And that's what you need everywhere, across the board. People with a different vision from the traditional view of our sport. They need to see you as an athlete, how your body works and what you have to do to stay fit.

Sports medicine is a highly developed science these days and we can't have players' careers hanging on whether their trainers are old school or open to new thinking and proven methods from other sports.

Young players shouldn't have to go through the heartache of being injured all the time and having to put up with not knowing if and when they're going to play again. I've been there and done that, and it's horrendous.

And there needs to be a structure so that wherever they are, players can be sent to the right person with the right knowledge for their specific injuries—or, even better, people who can tell them how to prevent injuries happening in the first place.

Don't get me wrong—Cricket Australia's doctor, Trefor James, was excellent with some of the things that I went through, like my stress fractures and shoulder. But then, with all the other soft tissue things, it was a different kind of specialist I needed. And Alex Kountouris was brilliant with me, embracing Victor's concepts, and working with me when Victor couldn't be with me overseas. But it was through Victor's guidance that I went to see specialist doctors about getting an epidural to free up the nerve tension in my legs. That's the level of care and treatment that every professional cricketer needs and deserves.

I don't think you can have one person who's expected to be an expert in everything. You need specialists and you need to spread the knowledge around the states, making sure you've got the right people in place in every team set-up. That's going to cost money; but weigh that against the cost of having so many Australian bowlers injured at any given time. My problem was I was over-training and doing the opposite of what I needed to do to help my body withstand the rigours of bowling. And if I hadn't bumped into Victor, a physio in a different sport entirely, I would never have achieved the things that I have now as an all-rounder.

Look, anyone can get injured in any sport at any given time, for the simple reason that athletes regularly push their bodies to the limit. But you've got more chance of getting injured and of that injury being worse and taking longer to heal if the prevailing attitude is that it's 'just one of those things that always happens'.

The physical pressures on the modern cricketer are increasing every year. We can't leave their training and treatment to chance, dependent on who's in charge where they happen to spend their formative years. I, for one, would take a wage cut if it meant more money was spent getting the best people in the right places.

CHAPTER 32 **STUMPS**

10 July 2011

As I write this I am in a training camp in Brisbane as we build up our preparation for our tours to Sri Lanka and then South Africa. It feels like we are at the end of one era and on the threshold of another.

I recently returned from playing in the IPL in India and at the end of that tournament Shane Warne, our captain for the Rajasthan Royals, announced his retirement as a player from all forms of cricket.

Prior to that, the Australian team gave Michael Clarke a great start to his career as Australian captain with a 3–0 whitewash against Bangladesh. In the last two of the three ODIs, I found myself racking up the runs with a rejuvenated Ricky Ponting at the other end. Ricky scored the winning runs in the second match—the one where I got 185—and then he opened with me in the third and final match, in which Mike Hussey scored his first one-day century in four years.

Change is definitely in the air. Sadly, when we got back, Cricket Australia didn't offer my long-standing opening partner Simon Katich a contract. On a personal level, at least, I'm going to miss him.

It's going to be interesting to see what Michael and the selectors and coaches want to do with Ricky in the Test batting order. Obviously he's been a great number three, but he could clearly bat at four or five and would also be the perfect candidate to add some much-needed steel to our middle order. That's where Steve Waugh had so much success, because he was able to hold it together whenever it looked shaky. Ricky is definitely of that mould. By the time you read this, we'll have played our first Test series in Sri Lanka and then South Africa under the new regime, so all will have been revealed.

Cricket is a performance-based game—if you're not performing, you can't expect to get picked. Ricky has bought an extension to his career with his century in the World Cup and his performances in Bangladesh and I'm glad he's been given the chance to prove himself. Players who've had an amazing career like his obviously get a bit more leeway during slumps because everyone knows there's a very good chance they will turn the corner and start scoring runs again. As a top-class batsman going through a lean spell, one dropped catch or one edge that goes in the gap rather than a fielder's hands can be the defining moment that turns your batting around and you're away again.

But everyone comes to a point in their career where they have to choose between persisting and hoping it will turn around or retiring on their own terms. One player who seemed to go way too soon was Warnie, my captain in the IPL. When he retired from international cricket in 2007, he was still bowling almost as well as he had throughout the Ashes series in England 18 months earlier.

In his final series in Australia, Warnie got five wickets at the MCG, broke the world record and took 23 wickets all up; he scored 196 runs and was still bowling beautifully. He could have kept going, I'm sure. He even got a Man of the Match this year in the second round in the IPL. But he retired close to his peak and that's why people say maybe he could have kept playing. And although I would have loved him to do so, that's the perfect time to go—when people are saying 'Why is he going?' rather than 'Why doesn't he go?'

Another star who probably went a bit too soon was Damien Martyn. That was an interesting one that came out of nowhere. He's a lovely, lovely guy, he's got a really good heart, and he's been very good to me. But for him to leave as dramatically as he did, in between the second and third Ashes Tests in 2006, caught people off guard. He didn't tell anyone, not even Ricky, who was best man at his wedding. He just said 'I've had enough' and he was gone.

That strained a few friendships for a while but Damien has never been one for the media and the pressure that goes with it, so he felt that was the only way he could get out cleanly. His mates were always going to try to talk him out of it and he didn't want to go through that. He was a phenomenal player and a major reason why Australia was so good.

Justin Langer was another player who retired fairly early—his farewell was the same match as Warnie's—and I've heard that he might have regretted going quite so soon. He played two more years of county cricket in England, but he certainly left with his reputation intact.

When my time comes—and I'm hoping that's a long way off—I'll do my best to get the timing as right as I possibly can. You can never know how it feels until you go through it, but I never want to be in the position where I've hung on too long. I'd retire too soon rather than go through that and leave it too late.

But that's the furthest thing from my mind right now. I got some big scores in Bangladesh, and my bowling for the Royals in the IPL was good with consistently low figures. But mostly I'm just happy to be playing cricket and I have a lot of time to make up after all those injuries held me back for so long.

That said, I've done okay. I'm vice-captain of Australia; I open the batting; I can still take wickets without leaking too many runs; and I field at first slip. It's the kind of fantasy a little boy in Ipswich used to act out in his backyard.

And, yeah, I'd like to have kids some day with my gorgeous wife. But it will be at a time when cricket doesn't get in the way of me being a father (rather than the other way round) because, like everything else in my life, I want to do it right.

And I have my music, which helped me through the worst times and has given me something to look forward to in the future, beyond cricket.

So, if I met that cheeky kid from Ipswich right now, what advice would I give him? Believe in your dreams? Never give up? Don't spend too much time in the gym?

I suppose the best advice would be to believe in yourself and back that up with 100 per cent effort in everything you do. You won't succeed every time, and people might misunderstand you and what you are trying to do. But if you are honest with yourself and those around you, you'll never go far wrong. And you'll always know, whatever the outcome, you gave it your best shot.

ACKNOWLEDGEMENTS

I'd like to thank my mum and dad and sister Nicole, who were so important in getting me to where I am today. I want to thank my gorgeous wife Lee, who's been with me through the best and worst of times, and her fantastic family too.

I also want to acknowledge the friends, coaches, teammates and medics who have been there for me all the way... you know who you are!

I am grateful to Richard Walsh for making this happen and everyone at Allen & Unwin for making it work.

And finally, thanks to Jimmy Thomson whose skill as an interviewer and author allowed me to tell my story in my own voice.